Commercials Are Hot—
But So Is the Competition

Working in commercials is one of the most exciting careers in showbiz, and the hunt for performers with special magic never ends. The market for talent is huge, and so are the rewards—and now two of the top names in the business have written the most complete and practical guide to breaking into commercials and making the most of the many professional opportunities it provides. The wealth of expert advice answers such questions as:

- What should you wear when you have a head shot taken—and how do you pick the best ones?
- How do you pursue a career in regional markets outside the major cosmopolitan areas?
- Who are the key players in the commercial industry—and what part do they play in your career?
- What seven qualities give you the winning edge in an audition?
- How does a parent both promote and protect a child in the fast commercial track?
- And how can you win in the high-stakes game of—

BREAKING INTO COMMERCIALS

WITHDRAWN

TERRY BERLAND, formerly the head of casting for the third largest agency in the world, BBDO in New York, now heads her own casting company and teaches a workshop, "Acting in Television Commercials," around the nation. **DEBORAH OUELLETTE** is an award-winning photographer and writer in the industry who serves as a judge and guest speaker at regional and national modeling and talent competitions.

"If you're looking for the bible on getting into commercials, this is it! This book will teach you how to successfully break into this very lucrative field. It logically and thoroughly covers all the basics—from head shots through bookings. If you follow these tips, you're halfway there." —Daisy Sinclair, Head of Casting, Ogilvy & Mather advertising agency, New York City

"In an industry changing as rapidly as ours, actors need to read as much as possible. I learned from this book. You will too." —Jerre Hookey, former National Director of Organizing and Southwest Regional Chief, Screen Actors Guild

"This book is filled with insight, information, and inspiration for all aspiring actors."—Professor Ellen Faith Brodie, Director of Theatre, Eastern Connecticut State University

"The wisdom of a veteran casting director and the viewpoint of a photographer-writer mix well to give newcomers to commercial acting all the how-tos, tips, and references to break in. ... On the basis of their collective experience and interviews with more than 75 industry pros, Berland and Ouellette completely debunk some of the myths surrounding success: that talent is the only quality that matters; that you can pay to get on camera; and that all you need for voice-overs is a great demo tape. ... A good reality check about acting for both kids and adults." —Barbara Jacobs, *Booklist*

"The most comprehensive book on the how-tos of doing commercials, this book is the bible for all actors. It gives them all the tools they need to help them help themselves." — Liz Lewis Casting Director, Liz Lewis Casting Partners, New York City

"You can't get the part unless you get the audition. *Breaking Into Commercials* tells you how to get them and book them." —Nancy Vines, commercial television and radio producer, New York City

"The book will teach you about getting your commercial headshots, how to put together an acting resume, and what training you will need. There is also a valuable chapter on avoiding scams. If you want to know what to expect on a commercial audition and how the casting of commercials is done - this book is for you. A very useful resource for any commercial actor." —**Donna Grayson, Actress, Los Angeles**

"This book is dead on." —**Cynthia St. John, Actress, Aspen, CO**

"What a wonderful book for newcomers ... The sections for regional actors, models moving into talent careers, and children in the business make for a well-rounded look at the industry and how it works." —**Tom Persing, Actor, Detroit, MI**

"My agent had Terry Berland on a list of recommended acting coaches, so I bought her book. It's great! What's unique about the book is the in-depth advice on space work and beats... Great advice!" —**Susan Lee-Bustamante, Actress**

"This book is fabulous! ... After reading it, I found myself recommending it to every new actor that came into the agency. ... Simple, concise language. Helpful photographs and illustrations. A MUST for the beginning actor!" —**Lisa Staton, Russell Langley Model Talent Agency, Tulsa, OK**

"I used the section that suggested playing to things that don't exist off-camera, left and right, incorporating the whole room. Thanks to that, I booked my very next audition as a principal in a commercial." —**Peter Louis, actor, Los Angeles**

BREAKING INTO COMMERCIALS

The Complete Guide to MARKETING YOURSELF, AUDITIONING TO WIN, and GETTING THE JOB

2nd Edition, Revised and Updated

Terry Berland and Deborah Ouellette

SILMAN-JAMES PRESS   LOS ANGELES

First Edition
10 9 8 7 6 5 4 3 2 1

Library of Congress Cataloging-in-Publication Data

Berland, Terry.
Breaking into commercials : the complete guide to marketing yourself, auditioning to win, and getting the job / by Terry Berland & Deborah Ouellette ; with a foreword by Jason Alexander.-- 2nd ed., rev. and updated.
p. cm.
Includes bibliographical references and index.
ISBN 1-879505-83-5 (alk. paper)
1. Television acting--Vocational guidance. 2. Television advertising--Vocational guidance. I. Ouellette, Deborah. II. Title.

PN1992.8.A3B47 2006
791.4502'8023--dc22

2006005087

Cover design by Wade Lageose for Lageose Design

Printed and bound in the United States of America

Silman-James Press

1181 Angelo Drive
Beverly Hills, CA 90210

Contents

9. THE AUDITIONING PROCESS   *84*

Getting Auditions. Finding Out About Calls. Internet
Submissions. How an Actor Is Selected to Audition. What
to Do When You Get the Call. The Day of the Audition.
What to Wear. What to Expect When You Get There.
What to Do After You Are Called into the Audition Room.
Direction Lingo. The Actual Audition. The Call Back.
When You Can Expect To Be Informed if You Got the Job.
Seven Elements That Give You the Competitive Edge.

10. THE TECHNIQUE   *99*

Getting Started. Entering the Audition Room. Commercial
Space. Exercises. Body Language. In the Audition Room.
Taking Your Mark. Working with Cue Cards. Memorizing
Copy. Relating to the Camera. How You Are "Framed" (How
You Look in the Camera). Rehearsing and Taking Direction.
Analyzing the Script. Leaving the Audition Room.

11. THE SELECTION PROCESS   *116*

The Creative Team. How the Talent Are Selected. Who
Sees the Auditions During the Selection Process. The
Callbacks. Presenting the Callbacks to the Client. Time
Between the Final Selection of Talent and the Shoot.
Understanding the History of a Commercial.

12. THE CALLBACK, THE BOOKING, THE SHOOT   *123*

The Callback. Information You Should Be Given When
You Get the Callback. Who Will Be at the Callback. How
You Should Conduct Yourself at the Callback. What the
Creatives Are Looking For. The Booking. How Much Time
Elapses Between the Callback and the Shoot. Information
You Should Be Given When You Are Booked. Wardrobe.
The Shoot. What Is Expected of Actors on the Set. What
Goes Into the Preparation for a Commercial Shoot. What
Is the Usual Location of the Shoot. What Happens the
Day of the Shoot. What Happens When the Actors First
Get on the Set. What Is Expected of Actors in Terms of

the Contract. At What Point the Product Is Introduced to the Actors. Things Actors Should Avoid While on the Set. How Long a Commercial Takes to Shoot. Is the Commercial Shot in Segments? How Many Takes Can an Actor Expect? Who Directs Actors? Do the Actors Have Any Input?

to Cross Over. Training. Opportunities in Foreign Markets. Compensation: What a Model Can Make in Print and Commercials in the United States. How a Typical Audition in Europe Differs from One in the United States. How Models Are Paid for Commercial Work. Interviews with Elle Macpherson, Carmen, Tim Saunders, and Patrick Johnson.

SECTION III. Wrapping It All Up   *219*

Acknowledgments

Our deepest appreciation goes to everyone who helped us bring this book to life. We couldn't have done it without you.

Jason Alexander, Elle Macpherson, Halle Berry, Carmen, Tim Saunders, Patrick Johnson, Judy Savage, Helen Rogers, Alan Simon, David Vando, Vincent Cirrincione, Carol Ingber, Al Onorato, Barbara Mullins, Tom Jourden, Barbara Goldman, Charlie Adler, Sue Schacter, Lori Wyman, Karmen Kruschke, Gregory Bouldin, Laura Fogelman, Kathy Hartigree, Heather Laird, Steve Garrin, Nick Omana, Karen Apicella, Nancy Mancuso, Liz Lewis, Jeff Danis, Bob Lasky, Michael D'Ambrosia, Andrew Bilgore, John Jennens, Karmen Leech, Kristine Wallis, Sharon Chatten, Gloria Gutierrez-Anderson, Bob Bergen, Jennifer Arens, Kimberlee Lukas, Karen Tank, Debbie Boyd, David Reivers, Peter Trencher, Forbes Reiley, Steve Guilmette, Carey Arben, Bill Arben, Michaelene Thrush, Susan Maizner, Robin Carus, Craig Lockner, Ron Sorenson, Ray Bengston, Jack Turnbull, Traci Danielli, Robert Schroeder, Nancy Johnson, Lynn Clark, Joan Lauren, Kelsey Edwards, Garry Tice, Rich Hogan, Jerome Butler, Conrad Bachmann, Craig T. Mathew, Michael Helms, Nancy Jo Gilchrist, Corbin Bleu, Robert Kazandjian, Al Clardy, Chanel Kong, Morgan Thrash, Jenna Boyd, Cody Arens, Hayden Tank, Jack "Bean" Lucas.

Foreword
By Jason Alexander

When asked how I got started as an actor, I tell people I "fell" into the business . . .

I can't remember a time when I wasn't performing. I don't know where my interest came from, but it was entrenched by the time I was six. When I was twelve or thirteen, I was taking it seriously enough to do everything I could do locally—in New Jersey, where I grew up.

I was doing school plays, community theater, and children's theater. One of the children's shows we were doing was seen by a television producer who thought it would be a neat idea to film it as a children's special for television.

In order to do it, we all had to join the union. The show aired in New York, New Jersey, and Connecticut. The day after it aired, a manager (Neiderlitz & Steele) called me up and asked if I would like to be a client. I stayed with them for the next nine years, and they guided me into the business.

Throughout college, all I did was commercial work, which was great. I always thought of commercials as thirty-second movies. I was working with people who really knew what they were doing. It had all the excitement of doing film work with none of the tedium because it moved so fast.

Fortunately, my career was always progressive. The work I did always begat other work, and I was lucky that it stayed of a certain quality. Even though some things flopped, the people I got to work with were spectacular.

There was my Broadway debut, *Merrily We Roll Along*, written by Stephen Sondheim and George Furth and directed by Hal Prince. The show was not a success for them but it sure was for me.

My next show, *The Rink*, was only a moderate success, but with stars like Chita Rivera and Liza Minnelli, the composer John Kander and lyricist Fred Ebb, and the playwright Terrence McNally, I was surrounded by brilliant people.

Then I worked with Neil Simon, which was a tremendous opportunity. Some years later, I won a Tony for *Jerome Robbins' Broadway*, which, ironically, was a show I never wanted to do. I thought it was going to be a humongous dance review, and I could move but not dance . . . certainly not like that. I finally got dragged into that show, which turned out to be a great experience.

I also started doing little teeny roles in film, and every now and then, I'd be out in L.A. doing a series.

I was never one to sit back and let things happen. It's very important for actors to take charge of their careers and always work at fine-tuning their craft.

When asked what advice I would give to actors who have taken one weekend workshop and feel they have mastered some technique, I always say that in my experience, the craft of acting is something that comes with age, maturity, and insight. People without training think that all you have to do is learn your lines and show up; professionals know that it takes a long time to learn the tools, techniques, and skills that are as important to an actor as color is to a visual artist or theory is to musicians.

Some of these tools are very technical. Others are instinctual. The technical skills came very easily to me, which is not necessarily the norm for most people. Most people struggle with the technical skills.

What I had trouble with was what we call the emotional life of the character. For some actors it comes naturally, and, in fact, that's all they can do. They're emotional as hell, but they don't know how to craft it or shape it.

So, no matter which end of the fence you come down on, I think it takes a lifetime of work to bring the other half up to snuff.

There are very successful, well-known actors who have never taken a class in their lives. They don't believe in it. They don't do any homework. They just show up on the set and do what comes naturally. And they do it very, very well. But my feeling is that without a technique or craft, there's no way to prepare. You can only cross your fingers and hope for the best.

I don't think you can study enough. The trick is to find someone who speaks your language and uses techniques you understand. It's a very delicate situation, being in class, because you're using your own ego and your own imagination as tools. And your tools are often criticized.

How do you find a good coach? Word of mouth. By observing. The best way is to talk to someone whose work you admire. Find out if they're studying and where. Go check them out. It's really trial and error. You'll know if someone is speaking your language and if it's an atmosphere you think you'd like to work in.

If you don't know any actors, call a local university that has an acting program and see if any of the teachers or professors teach outside the school, or call the local unions to see if they have any recommendations.

Anyone who reads my story is going to think that this is the easiest business in the world. Unfortunately, nothing could be further from the truth. *The first thing you're going to find when you get into the business is the biggest Catch-22 in the world:* Do you want to work as a professional or as an amateur? If you want to work as a professional, you have to get into the unions, and you can't get into the unions without a professional job. One way to get into the union is to audition for a union job and to get booked.

Challenge number two is, how do you market yourself? Nobody knows how to market him/herself. Actors have a very unrealistic idea of what they are about. Homely people think they are leading men and leading ladies. I've seen very funny people try to be dramatic actors. I've seen people who have no sense of humor try to do comedy. Old people try to play young, young people try to play old.

Certainly you have to believe that you can do anything. You should believe that, but on a realistic, commercial level, you have to know what it is that you present.

Are you going to New York, L.A., or Chicago? Are you going to London? Are you going to go to good regional theater? Are you going to focus on theater? On television? On commercials?

Challenge number three is learning to control your career. Actors have to try and do career planning. Many actors tend not to do this, and nobody seems to tell them that they have to.

Actors have to go and read, and when they find material that's right for them that can be developed, they should develop it. Buy it. Get into improvisational theater groups and get up on stage with people. If you sing, develop a sort of cabaret act. Form theater groups within your community. See what kind of theater thrives in your area and have something special ready that will get you noticed. This way, you're not always going to them and begging for a job. They will come to you at work and say they like what you do.

You have to own your career. It's the hardest thing to do, but if you don't do it, you are just waiting . . . and waiting *kills* talent. Waiting kills careers.

What it takes to make it in this business is a certain level of *desperation*. I always tell people, particularly young acting students, "If there's anything else you could do and be happy—not even exquisitely happy but just happy—pursue it, because, in my observation, this business is only for people who have no other option." If it is not your end-all, be-all, something you really must have or you'll jump off a bridge, then don't get on the bridge. It's not for you.

However, if you decide it *is* for you, you need a sense of bravura. You need a thick hide that's only thick on the outside. It has to be very thin on the inside or your vulnerability, your compassion, will die. And no actor can survive without them.

I don't know how to tell you to develop that hide. I don't think anyone does, but it is an absolute job requirement. You're going to hear "No!" a hell of a lot more than you'll hear "Yes!"

What's the best way to deal with the inevitable frustration and rejection that goes along with a career in this business? Have a life beyond the business.

Find other things you love to do. Have people outside the profession in your life. Don't get stuck with acting as your only realm.

Stay involved with your community. Stay involved with current events. Learn other things. Learn a skill. I once spent months learning to roller-skate, then got a job because I knew how to roller-skate.

Learn a language. Learn a new business. Go someplace you've never been before, even if it's only ten miles away. Observe people. Talk to people in other professions so if you ever play a stockbroker, for instance, you've done your research already. Just don't get stuck. You have to stay in motion.

It's a real didactic profession because it comes down to "I got it" or "I didn't get it." It's that hot and cold.

Actors always crack me up because they'll do an audition and they'll ask the agent to call and get feedback. What good is the feedback? It's only one person's opinion. "Did I get the job?" "Yes or no." If I did, then I did good. If I didn't get it, for whatever reason, it didn't happen.

The only reason you need feedback is if somebody says, "He comes in with a real chip on his shoulder," or "He comes in and his hygiene is not good." This is the only kind of feedback you want to get. Other than that, you took your shot and it did or didn't happen.

I think, in the business, there's an illusion that everything has to happen very quickly. There are a lot of young stars. The movies in particular right now are youth-oriented and there's a feeling that if you haven't participated in this business by the time you are twenty-five or thirty, it's too late.

My feeling is that anyone who is supposed to be doing this and who has real ability, real commitment, will find success. And success is defined very individually.

There are some people who will feel successful playing the classics at the Seattle Repertory. There are other people who will feel extraordinarily successful making six figures a year doing commercials, even if they've never performed elsewhere. Others will not be happy until they are box-office stars.

Success comes in many forms and you have to decide as an actor, "What do I want?" "Where will I be happy?"

Success is not always about making money. It's not always about being in a big theater. It's not about being in front of a camera. And it doesn't have to happen fast.

You may not get a particular job. You may not do well at an audition, but you are working on your craft. The craft gets better. You perform the craft and you do it over and over and over again . . . and you *love* it.

You enjoy doing it. You love studying it. You like displaying it.

Actors get better every year they're living. It's a craft about maturity. So live. And grow. And stop knocking your brains out trying to succeed on somebody else's terms.

Succeed on your own terms and in your own time.

Good luck!

Introduction

Our goal in creating this book is to help you break into commercials with a clear, concise sense of how the industry works. People all around the country from every walk of life are exposed to commercials. Many people who watch commercials, hear them on the radio, and see them in print aspire to do commercials as a full- or part-time career.

Commercials seem more accessible than parts in film or TV shows—and they *are*. More people have been able to break into the business and join the Screen Actors Guild (SAG)[1] through commercial work than through any other medium in the industry. Roles in commercials are cast for performers of all ages, types, and ethnicities. According to union figures, over a five-year period, SAG members averaged approximately $600 million per year for commercial work. All over the country, advertising agencies, producers, directors, and casting people wade through hundreds of head shots and résumés daily, searching for new faces to use in the next ad campaign.

Commercials have changed lives. With the earnings from commercial work, actors have financed college educations, underwritten family businesses, and supported themselves while making the transition into film and television.

---

[1] SAG is the union governing actors in film, motion pictures, television and television commercials (see Chapter 8: What You Need to Know About Agents, Managers, and Unions).

Commercial work is big business, but it is not easy. Everyone can think about being in a commercial, but not everyone knows how to go about entering the field. Competition is fierce. To make it in this industry, you have to be better prepared than the person sitting next to you at the audition. Talent alone won't do it. It takes a combination of talent, business savvy, training, the ability to audition effectively, and a lot of hard work. To get to the point where you have the competitive edge, you must invest the time and energy necessary to fine-tune your skills to razor-sharp precision.

Our travels around the country and involvement in the educational development of talent have given us firsthand information on the wants, needs, dreams, aspirations, and misconceptions of today's performers. Our combined professional experience of forty-three years (Terry has been a casting director and industry coach for more than twenty-five years, and Deborah has been an industry photographer and writer for more than twenty years) gives us an everyday, hands-on perspective on what it takes to make it in the business.

This is the first book of its kind to acknowledge that most actors who make it to the "ivory tower" (major markets) start out in secondary, regional areas. We have interviewed professionals in every state who either represent, cast, or book talent—individuals who enjoy developing actors, care about their talent, and are interested in maintaining a high level of professionalism.

This book will provide clear guidance from a collaboration of professional insights all over the country to those of you who are just breaking into the business, as well as to seasoned professionals. We want you to find the highest degree of professionalism in your own market.

You must be aware that there will be trials and tribulations, frustration, and rejection. And then there are the scams—rip-offs by unsavory individuals or groups who make their living preying on unsuspecting people who desperately want to break into the business. A virtual gauntlet of obstacles and disappointments awaits you if you tread unknowingly into a world where both magical and tragic events can occur. The more you know and understand about the business beforehand, the more likely you are to avoid the pitfalls, *and* the better your chances of launching a successful career.

Your commitment to reading *Breaking Into Commercials* and applying its concepts are major steps toward developing a career in commercials. You'll learn to create a winning promotional package, write a strong résumé and cover letter, set goals, and network effectively. You'll discover how to meet the right people in the industry. You'll develop the competitive edge needed to become the next "new face," and you'll learn how to give a winning audition so that you will be considered for the job regularly.

By collaborating with some of the most respected names in the industry, we have been able to create a complete framework for making a serious move into commercial work. *Breaking Into Commercials* takes you step-by-step through the entire process of becoming a commercial actor. We'll take you into the audition room, teach you how to read a commercial script, and show you what to expect on the set after you book a job. Special summary pages and commercial exercises will help keep you on track and focused on your goals.

By the time you get to the final chapter of *Breaking Into Commercials*, you will have a strong base from which to expand your career. To reinforce some of the most important concepts necessary to create a successful commercial career, we conclude the book with invaluable advice from industry professionals from markets across the country. You'll learn the common misconceptions fledgling actors have about the business, industry "pet peeves," and what it takes to really make it as a performer. You'll close the book feeling prepared, well-informed about the industry and how it works, and confident that you know enough to get out there and go for it.

To get the most from this book, read each chapter thoroughly (and keep the book handy as a quick reference), then act on any exercises or activities suggested. Doing so will help keep you on track and ready for the next step. This book was meant to be an "active" reference. By doing each exercise and reviewing the special summary pages at the end of the chapters, you'll be well on your way to getting your commercial act together.

Our best wishes go with you as you make your way through what we hope will be an exciting, fulfilling, lucrative career.

Terry Berland
& Deborah Ouellette

SECTION 1

PUTTING TOGETHER A WINNING PROMOTIONAL PACKAGE

1.

Getting Head Shots

The Makings of a Good Commercial Head Shot

In this business, to really go out and sell yourself, you need a calling card, and that calling card is your commercial head shot.

The commercial head shot is your most important marketing tool. Getting the right shot is essential to finding work in the industry and represents an initial opportunity to (a) introduce yourself, (b) show a dimension of your personality, (c) arouse the interest of the viewers, and (d) make them want to meet you. A great head shot can literally make or break your chances of getting called in for work.

It helps to know something about commercial technique *before* having a commercial photo session. Take a workshop from a professional to explore commercial technique and discover who you are. Also, watch commercials on TV. This will begin to give you a point of reference—a point of view as to attitude and an understanding of the energy required for commercial shoots.

You should have a realistic idea of what type you are commercially (age range, physical look, and personality traits). Examples of physical "looks" include:

- *Character:* This is someone with extreme features (large nose, bushy eyebrows, puffy cheeks, heavy, etc.), likeable, or even funny-looking. If you fit into the character category, a chipped tooth or a space between the teeth could add to or be natural for the character.

- *P&G* (Proctor & Gamble look): A generic, middle-American look with well-proportioned, middle-of-the-road, attractive features. Extremely beautiful people or character types do not fit this category.

- *Pretty or handsome* (but not a model, not glamorous): This is someone who is natural and approachable.

- *Model type:* Some with above-average looks, extremely good-looking, or striking. Model types generally have high cheekbones, strong jaw line, perfect teeth, excellent skin, and a well-proportioned, toned body. Prototypes: Hally Berry and Mark Wahlberg.

- *Slightly offbeat/slightly quirky:* Individuals who are specifically different from the average, middle-American look. Prototype: Ben Stiller and Drew Barrymore.

- *Quirky/good-looking and funny:* Prototypes: Rosanna Arquette, Kate Hudson, Cameron Diaz, Hugh Grant, and Luke Wilson.

- *Urban/city type:* Someone with a stylish edge, with an intense, trendy look.

- *Suburban type:* Plainer, casual, relaxed, sporty, rugged, outdoorsy looking.

- *Ethnic:* Caucasian, African-American, Asian, Latino/Hispanic, Indian, Native American, Jewish, European, etc.

- *Slacker:* Age about 16-25, lazy, laid-back, unruffled by anything.

- *Scruffy:* Male-unkempt, couple-of-days' beard growth, ripped jeans.

- *Alternative types:* Actors with tattoos, piercings, and/or extreme hair styles.

When viewing commercials, study the actors. Make note of the types of people and which products they are used for. What are their energies? What are they wearing? What hairstyles do they have? Which products use humor? Where might you fit in? Could you be the "mom" or "dad"? A seasoned executive? A student? A construction worker? Don't box yourself into one type. Notice all the opportunities available to you. The more you know about commercials, the more comfortable you will be at your photo shoot.

Commercials are generally energetic and upbeat. People in commercials are friendly and approachable. No one is evil-looking, scary, or really angry. Instead, they are frustrated in a manner that invokes humor and is approachable.

Your commercial head shot should show the depths and layers of your personality. You should have a spark of attitude. Most of the time it has a degree of playfulness to it. There should be a spark of energy in your eyes. A smile is always good. It allows the viewer to see your clean, white teeth.[1] A good head shot is generally taken straight on (so the camera can capture all your features and the viewer can look straight into your eyes). If you are the alternative type, show it. Do not homogenize yourself. Anything goes.

Your head shot exists in a casting director's hands or is viewed on a computer screen for about five seconds. You'll either be chosen or not. The eyes have to speak to the casting director, producer, or director. And very important: Your picture needs to look like you. A great head shot is not about perfect makeup or hair; it's about communication and openness that invites the viewer into the photograph.

Differences Between a Commercial Head Shot, a Theatrical Head Shot, and a Commercial Composite

An actor might have three different photographs with three different looks that he or she uses to get work.

Your *commercial head shot* (figs. 1, 3 & 5) is used to get work in commercials. Head shots are usually in color as a result of the Internet system of casting (between casting directors and agents). This trend started in Los Angeles and spread to other major markets. (See more on Internet casting in Chapter 9: Getting Auditions.) Redheads can benefit from a color shot to show off their hair color. If a redhead uses a black-and-white shot, it is a good idea to put a label on the front of the photo that says, "redhead."

When you use a color photo, be sure you don't rely on the color to pop and make you stand out instead of showing the depths and layers of your personality. In Los Angeles, where all commercial head shot sub-

---

[1] Advertisers are looking for good teeth—not discolored, stained, or chipped ones. If you are about to have your teeth fixed (or lose weight or have your hair styled), do so before your photo shoot. Your photo must be the best possible representation of what you currently look like.

missions given by the agents to casting directors are submitted over an industry Internet service, the most up-to-date head shots are submitted in color. Color gives the photo dimension.

Regardless of whether you go with a black and white or color photo, your head shot should be well-illuminated and have an overall bright appearance, showing depth and layers of your personality, and letting the happy, upbeat side of your personality or a distinctive, playful edge shine through; you should look very warm and approachable—generally "pleased to be here."

Head shots should either be head-and-shoulder type (figs. 1, 2, 3, 4, 7, & 8), three-quarter length shots (fig. 5), or horizontal (fig. 2). Borders can vary: clean (figs. 1, 2 & 5), with sloppy borders (figs. 3, 4 & 7), or borderless (fig. 8). Head shots can be creative as long as the photographer makes sure the focus stays on you and not on his work.

The finish should be semi-matte, not glossy. There are excellent labs available for making lithographic copies (lithos). Most important is for the casting director, when viewing your photograph, to see the subtle attitudes, depth, and layers of your personality in your face and eyes.

Simple, clean-looking makeup and hairstyling as well as careful attention to wardrobe selection are important for these photos. Open-necked collars and medium tones set the right ambiance for a successful commercial photograph. Clothing and jewelry should not distract the viewer's eyes from moving directly to the face and eyes of the photo.

Theatrical head shots (figs. 2 & 4) are more serious, showing strong eye contact and dramatic attitudes. Hair, makeup, and wardrobe choices may be more dramatic. Deeper-toned backdrops may be used along with subtle-to-rich variations in lighting. Actors use these shots to get parts in theatre, television, film, and soap operas. For work in industrial films[2] or corporate videos, actors may use either their commercial or theatrical head shot.

Commercial composites (fig. 6) are in color and generally consist of three to four photographic prints, each of which shows a unique facet of one's personality, a different energy, or a different character type. They are used for commercial printwork, which consists of magazine ads, brochures, and catalogues.

---

[2] Industrials are promotional films used either to educate or to promote companies. They can be produced strictly for in-house use or to be shown at promotional events such as trade shows.

How to Get the Best Head Shot

FIND A GOOD PHOTOGRAPHER

Locating a good photographer can involve a considerable amount of research, but the results will be well worth the effort. Word of mouth is always the best referral. Talk to agents, casting directors, coaches, and other actors to secure leads.

If you have none of these resources, the next step is to look in local and regional trade publications. If you live in or around Los Angeles, pick up a copy of *Back Stage West*. It carries photography ads. In New York, see *Back Stage*. In Chicago, refer to *Audition News*. Photographers also post ads at local drama clubs and in bookstores. In major markets like New York, Los Angeles, and Chicago, there are plenty of professional resources. In smaller, regional areas, however, you may have to turn to the Yellow Pages to help find someone to shoot your head shots, but make sure the photographers listed specialize in industry head shots.

QUESTONS TO ASK

- Does the photographer prefer to shoot in the studio or "on location" (somewhere other than the studio)?
- Does the photographer prefer to shoot standard head-and-shoulder shots or three-quarter body shots (fig. 5)? Is she comfortable doing both?
- Does the photographer shoot film or digital images?
- How does the photographer present her proofs (paper proofs, contact sheets, in studio on a monitor or CD, online)?
- How far in advance is the photographer booked?
- Is a deposit required to hold the booking?
- What happens if you have to cancel? How much notice is required to cancel, and is there a cancellation fee?
- How much will the photo session cost?
- How many rolls of film (or digital images) are included in the shooting fee?
- Are there any enlargements (prints) included?
- Who owns the negatives (or digital images, if applicable)?
- Is there a hairstylist and/or makeup person available? If so, is there an extra charge for this service?

- How many changes of clothing are allowed?
- How much time should you put aside for the shoot?
- How long after the shoot does it take to see your proofs?
- How long does it take to get enlargements made?
- How much does it cost for extra prints?
- Is retouching[3] included in the print fees? If not, how much will it cost and does the photographer provide for this service?
- Can the photographer recommend a printer to make larger quantities of your photographs?
- What happens if you are not happy with the results of your shoot (or the enlargements)?

VIEW THE PHOTOGRAPHER'S WORK BEFORE YOU MAKE A CHOICE

After hearing what each photographer has to say concerning these issues, decide which ones you still want to pursue and make an appointment to see their work. Look carefully at each professional's portfolio (sample photographs), then ask yourself:

- *Do the head shots all look the same, or can you see each actor's individual personality shining through?* You should not be able to identify the photographer by any one specific image. The photograph needs to be about the subject, not about the photographer.

- *Are the photographs well lit and printed correctly?* A good commercial head shot should display all the characteristics of a well-developed print. This means if our photo is in black and white, you should see a rich black tone (check the iris of the eye) and a clean white tone (see the "catch-lights"[4] in the eyes) somewhere in the print, as well as a nice range of gray tones throughout the image. The image should be sharp, crisp, and in focus. The lighting should clearly separate the subject from the background and, if the setting is outside, the background should be out of focus. Nothing in the picture should distract from the subject. There should be no obvious, unflattering shadows. The photographs should not show excessive grain[5] and should be printed on high-quality, matte-finished photographic paper.

---

[3] On commercial prints, a photo artist (retoucher) tries to minimize minor flaws in the image, touching up temporary blemishes, stray hairs, and scratches or dust spots (white spots caused by dust on the negative or image).

[4] Catch lights are the reflections in the eyes caused by the photographer's light(s).

[5] Grain is generally caused by overexposure or overdevelopment of the film (high-speed films are naturally grainy). This exaggerates the tiny dots that make up the image, producing an unacceptable print. NOTE: In digital photography, this effect is referred to as digital "noise."

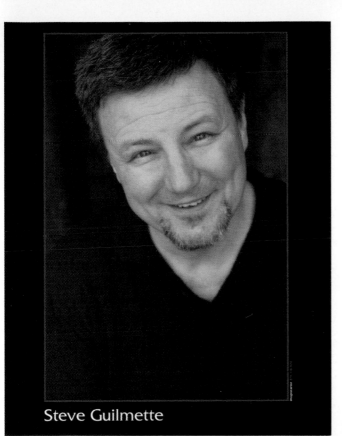

Steve Guilmette

FIG. 1: Commercial head shot

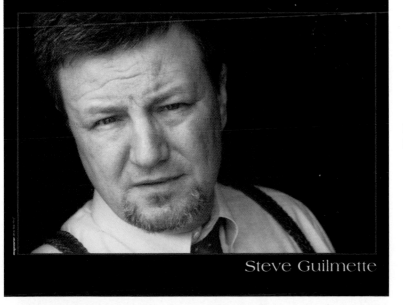

Steve Guilmette

FIG. 2: Theatrical head shot

FIGS. 1 AND 2: Two shots illustrating the difference between commercial and theatrical shots.
PHOTO CREDIT: Michael D'Ambrosia Photography.

FIG. 3: Commercial shot

PETER TRENCHER

FIG. 4: Theatrical shot

FIGS. 3 AND 4: Another example illustrating the difference between commercial and theatrical shots. **PHOTO CREDIT:** Robert Kazandjian.

PETER TRENCHER

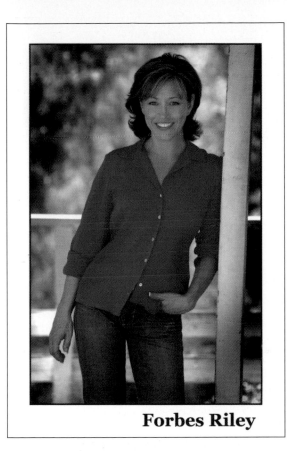

Forbes Riley

Fɪɢ. 5: Female commercial three-quarter body shot (Forbes Riley). Pʜᴏᴛᴏ ᴄʀᴇᴅɪᴛ: michaelhelms.com

Fɪɢ. 6: Commercial composite. Printed with permission of Lazarus Jackson.

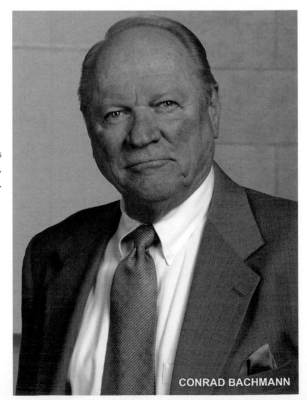

SET YOUR TIVO!!!
for my
Guest Starring Role on

SHE SPIES
"MANHUNT"

Sunday, October 6th,
Midnight on NBC
★ Check local listings ★

check out my recent appearance on

MONK
"Mr. Monk Goes to the Theatre"
★ In Re-runs ★

Victoria's people are:

AAA - Mark Measures: 310- 859-1417
WMA Animation & Voiceover: 310-859-4085

Victoria Hoffman

FIG. 7: Head shot postcards are an excellent way to keep in touch with people in the industry and to show some individualism and personality. PHOTO CREDIT: Karmen Kruschke.

FIG. 8: Borderless
commercial or theatrical shot.
PHOTO CREDIT: Craig T. Mathew.

CONRAD BACHMANN

After viewing each photographer's work, take time to go over your notes (you should have a lot to work with by now), decide which photographer you're most comfortable with, and call to make an appointment.

NOTE: Although it's important to take price into consideration, don't let that be the key factor in selecting a photographer. Your commercial head shot can open (or shut) doors for you, so it pays (literally) to work with the best photographer within your budget.

Prepare for the Shoot

Once you decide on a photographer, it's time to get together everything you will need at the shoot. Most photographers will discuss wardrobe, hair, and makeup do's and don'ts either at the initial consultation or when you call to book your shoot.

Clothing should direct all attention to your face. V-necks do that naturally and are great choices for photo shoots. Solid colors work best—avoid busy patterns or polka dots. Textures are wonderful—sweaters and jackets work well. Bring lots of casual stuff. If you have a doubt about it, bring it; the photographer can help you decide which things to wear once she sees it.

Bring in as many changes of clothing as possible. You won't use them all, but it is much better to go through everything with the photographer and decide what would be best to wear.

Bring your favorite clothes. Textures are good; perhaps a sweater with nooks and crannies. Fabrics like wool, cotton, and demim work well. Avoid logos, turtle-necks, and busy patterns. Stick with medium tones, simple styles, and open necklines.

WARDROBE CHECKLIST
- Make sure your clothing is clean, fitted, in good condition, and well-pressed.
- Choose simple styles with open necklines.
- If you want to wear glasses in the shoot, make sure they have "no glare" lenses or purchase a set of frames in your favorite style without the glass. This will prevent glare from the photographer's lights and reflectors.

- Leave your hat at home. Agents and casting people want to see your hair. If you are bald, they need to see that too.

- Don't wear distracting ruffles, bows, patterns, or jewelry. No gold chains or earrings on men, please. Guys, if you do decide to wear your earring, know that it puts you in a very definite character category. Be sure that is what you want. If so, don't expect to get a call to audition for the wholesome dad, boyfriend, or guy-next-door based on this particular photo.

- Do not turn the collar up on your jackets and shirts. Doing so may imply an attitude that is not consistent with the energy required in commercial work.

- Avoid wearing white. When viewing a photograph, the eye naturally goes to the lightest area of the print first. Your goal is to have the viewer focus immediately on your face and, more specifically, your eyes (some photographers whiten the whites of the subject's eyes to draw the viewer's attention to them). If you wear white, the viewer's eye will go to your clothing first, then travel to the face and eyes. Stay with medium-toned clothing (something that will produce a rich gray tone in black and white), which, with a medium-gray background, will wrap around the subject and draw the viewer's eye to the most important part of the print—*you!*

Your hair should be clean, healthy, and styled in an attractive manner (no "big" hair). Stay away from overly trendy hairstyles. If your hair reflects a specific fad, you will limit your opportunities to audition. Most advertisers go with current styles. In smaller regional areas, advertisers tend to prefer a more generic look—a neutral, classic, all-American image. Make a choice as to how you want to market yourself.

Younger guys should decide on the image they want to market. If you are young and trendy, your photo should reflect that. If you are portraying a more conservative look, come to the photo shoot freshly shaved. If you grow a beard as fast as you can cut it, bring your razor with you (watch the new blades—opening an artery can create serious complications at the shoot). An option might be to come in with a beard or partial growth, then shave part way through the shoot, giving you two different looks. Discuss this choice with the photographer before the shoot. There is less work for bearded fellows, but if you can grow a beard fairly quickly, it might turn out to be an asset.

NOTE: Commercially, there is usually not enough time between the call and the shoot to grow a beard. Know that the way you present yourself at the audition is how you would be cast.

Females should not look like you are wearing makeup in your commercial head shot. The look for commercials is clean, fresh, and energetic. Women often have a tough time getting a good commercial shot because the photographer (or the women themselves) wants to capture their pretty side instead of bringing out the depths and layers of their personality. Commercial shots are not glamorous. Make sure you end up with a "personality" shot, *not* a beauty shot.

Los Angeles makeup artist Karman Kruschke notes, "The stylist's goal is to make people look as they will look when they go into the audition, so I try to get some history on their experience in putting on their own makeup. If someone doesn't wear a lot of makeup, it's important not to put a lot on them—at least, the look is not very made-up. The skin should look nice and smooth. No heavy lip or eyeliner. This is not a fashion shoot. It's not about how beautiful you can be for a day. It's about looking and being who you are."

The makeup artist may do some corrective work to minimize heavy circles under the eyes. There may be a need to highlight or darken specific areas of the face to bring out cheekbones or play down other features. That's why you'll hear, "Oh, God. I would *never* wear this [makeup] out in public." And you never would—except for a photo shoot.

Men generally require only a bit of powder to tone down overly shiny skin. They may also need a little corrective work. Trust the stylist to do whatever is necessary to make you look good in front of the camera.

Aside from the obvious benefits of having a hair/makeup person available at the shoot, having a stylist there also means you don't have to worry about anything (like whether your makeup is shiny or if your hair is out of place, or whether your clothing needs adjusting). This goes for the photographer, too, so both of you are free to do what you do best—you to act and the photographer to take pictures.

Below are a few more suggestions for preparing for your photo shoot:

- Get a good night's sleep before the shoot. It is important to arrive at the session well rested, in a positive frame of mind, and ready to give your best.

- Have everything you need for the shoot laid out the night before to avoid rushing to get it all done the next morning. This will save a *lot* of unnecessary stress.

- Bring some of your favorite music to the shoot—something lively and upbeat to help set the mood for a pleasant, comfortable session.

- Do not schedule anything important directly after the shoot. It will be hard to keep your mind on the task at hand if you are thinking about whatever you've scheduled next.

- If for any reason you feel that you cannot give one-hundred percent to the shoot, call and try to reschedule. The camera doesn't lie. If you have a headache or are in a negative mood, you *will* see it in the pictures.

Giving careful consideration to the planning and preparation of your photo session will help guarantee successful results.

What to Expect the Day of the Shoot

Plan to arrive at the photographer's studio approximately fifteen to twenty minutes prior to your scheduled appointment (allow yourself plenty of time to shower and dress). When you arrive you'll be told where to stand (and change) your clothes. The photographer will go through your wardrobe, helping you select the best pieces for the shoot.

At some point during the process, you'll be expected to pay the photographer. You may be asked to sign a release or agreements of some form, outlining the specific conditions of the shoot—price, services rendered, plus any specific considerations. *Be sure you read the document before signing it.* Pay special attention to any part of the agreement that deals with the photographer's claims concerning copyright. By law, it is illegal to make a copy of a photographer's work without explicit permission. This means that you may not take your original photographs to a lab and have a duplicate negative made from it. This is a direct violation of copyright law, for which both you and the lab can be sued. Likewise, it is illegal to make unauthorized copies using self-serve print machines, or to use home or other computer equipment to scan, print, or burn

CDs of copyrighted images on home computer equipment. Unless your contract states otherwise, your photographer has the exclusive right to make copies of your photographs for you.

Some controversy arises here. Many people argue that when an actor pays the photographer to create a head shot, this becomes "work for hire" and therefore does not come under the same provisions of copyright law. But, if you sign an agreement giving the photographer total control over use of the pictures (and most photographers will not shoot unless you sign, agreeing to respect their copyright), you may find yourself in a pickle when you try to get mass reproductions of your pictures without getting explicit permission from him or her.

When you take your original photographs to get reproductions from a printer, the printer will require a release from the photographer before expediting your order. Technically, mass production of head shots involves an entirely different photographic process. A photographer who offers this service generally sends the original pictures out to a printer who specializes in mass reproduction of industry head shots, then marks up the price anywhere from twenty-five to one hundred percent or more. To do this is neither illegal nor unethical; however, keep in mind that if you are able to take your head shots directly to the printer yourself, you avoid paying the markup. If you sign an agreement without making a specific provision that allows you to use the printer of your choice, you may have no choice but to order all reproductions through the photographer.

The law clearly protects photographers against copyright infringement. One way to avoid misunderstandings later is to read carefully any agreement put before you and negotiate an arrangement that serves your best interests. Many actors refuse to sign any kind of agreement. Very few photographers are willing to turn down an attractive fee just to stand on principle. If you do decide to work with a photographer who insists you sign an agreement, be aware that, as with any other contract, *both* parties have the right to negotiate the terms. This doesn't have to be complicated. Simply have the photographer cross out (and initial on all copies) the parts you don't agree with. There is usually space on any agreement for additions and amendments. That is where you'll put any special considerations the two of you have worked out.

When you negotiate your contract, keep in mind that you want to:

■ Deal with the printer of your choice, without going through the photographer.

■ Use your originals for publicity without paying an extra fee to the photographer. Most agreements give the photographer the right to use your likeness in their advertisements and other publicity—you paid for the shoot, it's only fair that you be free to do the same.

NOTE: Make sure you request that the photographer not stamp any part of the enlargements you purchase with a copyright notice. Photographers do this to give public notice of their claim to copyright. Without it, they are still protected by law. With it, you will have one heck of a time getting a printer to make reproductions from your original prints.

Negotiating a fair agreement allows both you and the person who creates your commercial head shot to utilize the results in a manner that enhances both parties' career interests.

After you've paid the photographer and agreed to the terms of the shoot, it's time to let the hair/makeup person (if available) work his magic. Then you'll get into your first outfit and you're ready to shoot.

What happens during the actual shoot is as individual as each photographer's style. Some photographers suggest specific scenarios to help draw out the subject's personality. Others are naturally comedic and charming, using their own personality to entice you to reveal yours. Any successful shoot is a collaborative effort in which photographer and actor work together to create an image that will attract the eye of casting directors.

Selecting the Right Shot

After the shoot, film photographers either send the film out to a professional lab to be developed or do the developing themselves. Next, the negatives are laid out on a single sheet of photographic paper and exposed to light in the darkroom, creating a contact sheet—a mini set of proofs exactly the same size as the negatives from which you will select the images to enlarge.

Digital photographers may be set up to show proofs immediately after the session (talk about instant gratification). Others prefer to go over the results first, then make or show proofs later. Digital proofs may be shown on paper, on a computer monitor, or online.[6]

If you're not accustomed to looking at contact sheets, a magnifying glass (or photographer's loupe) can be very helpful. Generally, photographers indicate which images they prefer. It's a good idea to take the contact sheets home, look them over carefully, and then put them aside for a while before making a final selection. If you have access to other industry professionals (agents, casting directors, acting coaches, other actors), you may want to ask which ones they think represent you best. Select a couple of shots that best capture your personality. After choosing the best shots, take a critical look at each image. Check for expressive eyes, that you look relaxed, and are portraying positive body language. Many times, your agent will want to decide which shot they want you to use.

NOTE: If your photographer used digital equipment to create your headshots, she may be willing to "burn" (copy) the images to a "read-only" CD.[7] If the proofs are being displayed online, all you have to do is give your agent, etc., the website address where the proofs are "posted" (displayed) along with the access code[8] (if applicable) and they will be able to view the proofs for as long as they are available online. Same goes for viewing online proofs created by film photographers.

After deciding which images to enlarge, consider anything you may want retouched. Have your selections enlarged and take a last look to see that all the qualities you want for your final shot (which seemed to be there when you looked at the proofs or contact sheets) are indeed there.

Retouching

Before you run off to the printer with your eight-by-ten, discuss with your photographer any touch-up work that needs to be done. For example:

- Are there any temporary blemishes or dark areas under the eyes?
- Are there any distracting features in the photograph such as stray hairs or unwanted reflections in the eyes (or glasses)?

---

[6] Many photographers, retouchers, and printers display proofs online (on the Internet) via a special link on their business website.

[7] A read-only CD means you can view the contents of the CD but you cannot make copies.

[8] When viewing proofs online, the photographer will generally give you an access code—a series of numbers, letters, and/or symbols that, when typed into the correct link on photographer's website, will give you access to your proofs online. NOTE: Expect the proofing site to be protected against unauthorized copy-making of the photographer's images.

- Are there minor scratches or spots on the print?
- Would the image be enhanced by lightening the white areas of the eyes?

If the answer to any of these questions is yes, then the photo retoucher is your next stop before going to the printer. There are two types of retouch artists:

- A *traditional retoucher* is an artist who specializes in working with pho-tographs (and/or negatives). Realize that, with traditional retouching, some problems may not be completely eliminated, but can be improved upon. With skillful retouching, only the trained eye can tell that the work has been done.

- A *digital retoucher* specializes in using computer technology to enhance both digital and film-based images. Images are either scanned (film) or uploaded (digital) into the computer, then retouched or enhanced using a special program—such as Adobe Photoshop—designed specifically for that purpose. Many digital photographers prefer to do their own retouching and enhancements. Others use outside artists.

NOTE: Depending on the skill level of the digital retouch artist, almost anything you can imagine (and are willing to pay for) can be done. There is literally no end to what can be done to an image when a gifted digital artist is at the helm. You can swap out body parts, lose weight without dieting (finally!), grow taller, even get a digital nose job. At the hands of the right artist, reality can be created from scratch or completely altered—it's sheer magic, the digital darkroom.

However tempting it may be to go overboard, remember that when you walk into the audition room, you must look like your photo. For your commercial head shot, resist overworking a print. A light touch goes a long way in retouching commercial head shots.

Unless the photographer has indicated otherwise, the cost of retouching is generally not included in the price of the print. If the pho-tographer does not do her own retouching and/or does not farm this part of the job out, ask for a referral to a good photo artist. Most photogra-phers prefer to maintain control over the work being done to their images, so they will either do the touch-ups themselves or hire the work out.

The cost of retouching varies, depending on the job being done and the caliber of the artist doing the work. Always get a quote before having the work done and be very specific when communicating about what to do and how much is enough. Most retouchers charge by the amount of time it takes to do the job. Complex retouching jobs cost more than those with simple, basic enhancements. Assuming you have a head shot you're happy with, the extra investment to fine-tune your presentation makes good business sense.

Retouching a print is a one-time investment. As long as nothing happens to the original image—or the version of the original that was retouched—any enhancements should last a lifetime. Handle your prints by the edges only and keep them out of direct sunlight or they may begin to fade or discolor.

One last reminder about retouching—*don't over do it!* The purpose of retouching is to enhance the print, not to change the way you look. Remember, when you walk through the door, the casting director expects you to look like your pictures. If, for instance, you have the artist straighten your teeth in the picture, and then come to an audition with crooked teeth, you have misrepresented yourself. You do not look like your picture. What happens if the call is for a toothpaste commercial, which requires you to have perfect teeth? Do you think a casting director would ever call you again after you deliberately misrepresented yourself? Probably not.

Trust your photographer and the retoucher when it comes to deciding whether or not to touch up a print (and how much). Don't try to make everything look perfect. Just have the artist minimize anything that takes away from your personality.

Working with Printers

In many cases, the enlargement process has been eliminated. Digital technology has made it possible to show proofs on a computer monitor, retouch them, and send a press-ready image directly from a digital file. Many photographers are set up to deliver the entire job from shoot to finished mass-reproductions.

Film-based photographers may opt to convert your images to digital files or use the traditional film-to-print method for creating a master copy of your head shot. In that case, once you have a "finished" eight-by-ten (printed well and retouched, if necessary), it's time to take the master copy to a printer who specializes in mass-producing photographs for actors. It pays to shop around. It is not unusual to use a printer from another state. Get referrals from other actors and agents. Printers across the country vary in price and in what you get for the money. Call and request a price list and samples from several printers. (If you're really on top of things, you took care of this while waiting for your final images to come back from the retoucher.)

Again, while price is a consideration with most people, make your final decision based on quality of service. If two or more companies produce work of equal quality, but one gives significantly more reproductions for the money, it's easier to narrow your selections.

An order form is usually included with each printer's information packet. Be sure to indicate exactly how you want your copies produced. The preferred format is eight-by-ten reproductions on matte (non-glossy) double-weight stock. Have your name printed on the front (see sample headshots included in this chapter). Avoid fancy type styles and oversized or undersized letters. Also, expect to pay in full at the time you place your order.

Picture Postcards as a Marketing Tool

Picture postcards (see fig. 7) are a great way to keep in touch with the industry. You can send postcards to announce something you're currently appearing in, just to say hello, or to remind casting directors that you're still out there. Some actors even use them for thank-you notes.

Some people have their postcards printed horizontally, placing two head shots side by side, showing two different aspects of their personality. Others take a humorous approach, creating a comedic photograph, appropriately captioned to amuse the recipient.

The same printer who mass-produced your head shots can create a mini version printed vertically on postcard-sized paper with your name on it. Picture postcards are a wonderful, cost-effective tool for marketing yourself as a commercial actor.

How Much Will It Cost and How Long Will It Take?

COSTS

Photographers: These vary in price depending on what part of the country they work in, their level of experience, and the amount of prestige they have built up in their market. Rates can range from $200 in regional areas to $650 in larger markets. As with anything else, higher price does not necessarily guarantee higher quality.

Stylists: Expect to spend approximately $100 to $150 for a makeup person/hairstylist. The same person should be able to do both.

Film/processing/contact sheets/online proofing (any or all as applicable): These costs are usually included in the photographer's shooting fee. Whether shooting digital or film-based images, there is usually an extra charge to present your session on paper proofs (4x5 or 4x6 proofs on photo paper). Photographers who create paper proofs may require a deposit against the value of the proofs before allowing you to take them from the studio.

Digital photographers may also give the option of burning your proofs to a "read only" CD, which you may then take home or show other industry professionals, who can then help you decide which images to enlarge. There may or may not be an extra charge for creating the CD.

Enlargements: If not included in the shooting fee, eight-by-ten enlargements can run on average $35 to $40.

Retouching: Budget approximately $25 to $50 for a basic retouch (more for complicated jobs).

Printers: Lithos can run from $120 per 500 black-and-white eight-by-tens to $150 for color. Mass-produced photographs run approximately $285 for 500 black-and-white or color. Picture postcards run approximately $100 for 500 black-and-white, $125 to $200 for color.

All things considered, expect to spend approximately $700 to $1,200 by the time you've gotten through the process of shooting, enlarging, retouching, and printing your photos.

TIME FRAME

There are many variables to consider here. The amount of time it takes to get through the process may change due to individual schedules or unforeseen problems (your original CD or prints get damaged or lost, for instance). Basically, these are the time frames you may reasonably expect:

- *Researching photographers* (including calls, interviews, portfolio review, and making appointment): Approximate time frame: 2 weeks.

- *Getting proofs back from the shoot*: Approximately 2-7 days. A film photographer may give you the option of getting your shots on a CD (most reproduction houses prefer digital format). Digital photographers may have images available to view immediately after capture, at the end of the session, or within a few hours or days (if posting online or making paper proofs). Getting input on proofs, making your selections, and getting order to photographer: 1 week. Expect to add up to 2 weeks' turnover time for smaller, regional markets that have fewer professional photographers.

- *Getting enlargements back from the photographer*: With the most up-to-date methods, the enlargement phase is eliminated. With digital technology, the photographer can view your proofs on her computer screen, retouch the image(s), and print mass reproductions for you. If the photographer is not set up for mass reproductions, she can either burn the image to a CD or send an online image directly to a printer to create your mass reproductions. This can take approximately two days to one week, depending on if she sends the work out to a professional lab.

- *Retouching by a lab or a photographer*: Allow approximately one day to one week. In regional areas where there are fewer professional photographers, this process can take approximately one to three weeks. Turnover times for mass-produced head shots and picture postcards are approximately two to three business days for lithos and four to five business days for photographic copies.

Total amount of time to get through the process: Approximately 4-8 weeks.

Eight weeks! You can see why it is important to get moving right away. Use the tip sheets that follow to help yourself move smoothly through each step as you create the most important part of your marketing package. Your ability to get through the step of getting your pictures done could very well be the first indication of whether you have the wherewithal to continue in this business.

SUMMARY

TO-DO LIST:

- Research photographers
- Call for appointments
- Choose photographer
- Make appointment for photo session
- Prepare for shoot
- Order enlargements
- Arrange for retouching (if needed)
- Order mass reproductions from printer

Congratulations! You've just completed one of the most important tasks in compiling your presentation package. You have your commercial head shot. You're ready to move on to the next step.

2.

Résumés
and Cover Letters

What Is a Résumé and What Is Its Purpose?

WHAT GOES ON A RÉSUMÉ AND IN WHAT ORDER?

Do include:

- *Your name* (centered at the top of the page).

- *Union affiliation* (if applicable), or note that you are "SAG eligible" if that's the case.

- *Agency representation* (if applicable). In regional areas, your agent generally will provide you with stickers or labels to put on your résumé to show that they represent you.

- *Statistics*[1]

- *A phone number* (other than a personal number) as a contact. If you have an agent, only the agent's name and number should appear as the contact.

- *Experience* (credits in theater, film/TV, commercials, etc.).

- *Training* (classes, workshops, college degrees, etc.).

- *Special skills* (dialects, American Sign Language, sky-diving, horseback riding—anything you do *well*).

---

[1] Statistics (stats) include your name, union affiliation and agent (if applicable), height, weight, eye and hair color, and a contact number. NOTE: If you have an agent, only the agent's contact info would be included. If you have no agent, include a cell phone, machine, or pager number where you can be reached. Do not list personal contact information like home phone or address.

Don't include:

- *Your social security number, your address, or your personal phone number* (for security reasons).

- *Your age or an "age range."* Let casting directors look at your photo and decide for themselves if you are what they are looking for.

Presenting the Information on Your Résumé

How you list industry-related experience on your résumé depends on which market you will be working in. In Los Angeles, film and television credits are usually listed first (fig. 9). In New York, theater credits are mentioned first. If you live in smaller, regional areas, start with your strongest credits. When in doubt, list theater credits first. Theater provides a strong foundation for actors and is the purest form of acting experience.

If you're just starting out, you'll probably be relying primarily on your look, training credits, and special skills to open doors for you. After you have a well-developed résumé, your experience (credits) will be your best PR tool. Don't worry if, at first, you don't seem to have much to put on your résumé; there are ways to present your humble beginnings (without lying) that will give your presentation a professional appearance while you're building your credits.

In a beginner's résumé, for instance, present community theater experience. Mention the name of the production, the role you played, and the theater or theater group. Figs. 10 and 11 demonstrate how a regional beginner's résumé can be cleaned up to look more professional without exaggerating or fabricating credits.

When listing *commercial* experience on a résumé geared toward the Los Angeles, New York, or Chicago market, it's best to simply put "List Upon Request" next to that category. Listing a commercial could imply that you have a conflict, which would eliminate you from any related casting opportunities. If you are pursuing work in a region where there are no union commercial opportunities (or if you don't plan to pursue these opportunities), it is the trend to list commercials you have already done to show that you have experience, or to list ad agencies and production companies you have worked with.

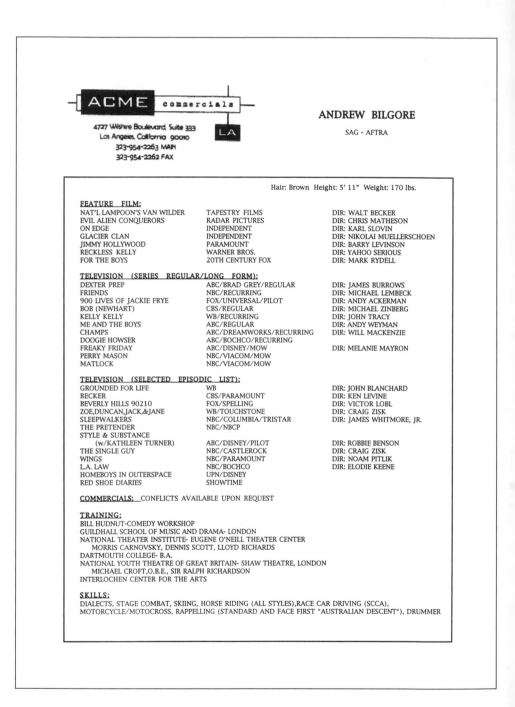

ACME commercials

4727 Wilshire Boulevard, Suite 333
Los Angeles, California 90010
323-954-2263 MAIN
323-954-2262 FAX

LA

ANDREW BILGORE

SAG - AFTRA

Hair: Brown Height: 5' 11" Weight: 170 lbs.

FEATURE FILM:

NAT'L LAMPOON'S VAN WILDER	TAPESTRY FILMS	DIR: WALT BECKER
EVIL ALIEN CONQUERORS	RADAR PICTURES	DIR: CHRIS MATHESON
ON EDGE	INDEPENDENT	DIR: KARL SLOVIN
GLACIER CLAN	INDEPENDENT	DIR: NIKOLAI MUELLERSCHOEN
JIMMY HOLLYWOOD	PARAMOUNT	DIR: BARRY LEVINSON
RECKLESS KELLY	WARNER BROS.	DIR: YAHOO SERIOUS
FOR THE BOYS	20TH CENTURY FOX	DIR: MARK RYDELL

TELEVISION (SERIES REGULAR/LONG FORM):

DEXTER PREP	ABC/BRAD GREY/REGULAR	DIR: JAMES BURROWS
FRIENDS	NBC/RECURRING	DIR: MICHAEL LEMBECK
900 LIVES OF JACKIE FRYE	FOX/UNIVERSAL/PILOT	DIR: ANDY ACKERMAN
BOB (NEWHART)	CBS/REGULAR	DIR: MICHAEL ZINBERG
KELLY KELLY	WB/RECURRING	DIR: JOHN TRACY
ME AND THE BOYS	ABC/REGULAR	DIR: ANDY WEYMAN
CHAMPS	ABC/DREAMWORKS/RECURRING	DIR: WILL MACKENZIE
DOOGIE HOWSER	ABC/BOCHCO/RECURRING	
FREAKY FRIDAY	ABC/DISNEY/MOW	DIR: MELANIE MAYRON
PERRY MASON	NBC/VIACOM/MOW	
MATLOCK	NBC/VIACOM/MOW	

TELEVISION (SELECTED EPISODIC LIST):

GROUNDED FOR LIFE	WB	DIR: JOHN BLANCHARD
BECKER	CBS/PARAMOUNT	DIR: KEN LEVINE
BEVERLY HILLS 90210	FOX/SPELLING	DIR: VICTOR LOBL
ZOE,DUNCAN,JACK,&JANE	WB/TOUCHSTONE	DIR: CRAIG ZISK
SLEEPWALKERS	NBC/COLUMBIA/TRISTAR	DIR: JAMES WHITMORE, JR.
THE PRETENDER	NBC/NBCP	
STYLE & SUBSTANCE		
(w/KATHLEEN TURNER)	ABC/DISNEY/PILOT	DIR: ROBBIE BENSON
THE SINGLE GUY	NBC/CASTLEROCK	DIR: CRAIG ZISK
WINGS	NBC/PARAMOUNT	DIR: NOAM PITLIK
L.A. LAW	NBC/BOCHCO	DIR: ELODIE KEENE
HOMEBOYS IN OUTERSPACE	UPN/DISNEY	
RED SHOE DIARIES	SHOWTIME	

COMMERCIALS: CONFLICTS AVAILABLE UPON REQUEST

TRAINING:
BILL HUDNUT-COMEDY WORKSHOP
GUILDHALL SCHOOL OF MUSIC AND DRAMA- LONDON
NATIONAL THEATER INSTITUTE- EUGENE O'NEILL THEATER CENTER
    MORRIS CARNOVSKY, DENNIS SCOTT, LLOYD RICHARDS
DARTMOUTH COLLEGE- B.A.
NATIONAL YOUTH THEATRE OF GREAT BRITAIN- SHAW THEATRE, LONDON
    MICHAEL CROFT,O.B.E., SIR RALPH RICHARDSON
INTERLOCHEN CENTER FOR THE ARTS

SKILLS:
DIALECTS, STAGE COMBAT, SKIING, HORSE RIDING (ALL STYLES),RACE CAR DRIVING (SCCA),
MOTORCYCLE/MOTOCROSS, RAPPELLING (STANDARD AND FACE FIRST "AUSTRALIAN DESCENT"), DRUMMER

FIG. 9: Professional résumé (Andrew Bilgore).

John Jennens
419-535-7722

Height: 6'2"   Weight: 190 lbs.
Eyes: Brown   Hair: Brown
Suit: 44L   Shirt: 16 ½ / 34-35
Pants: 34/36   Shoe: 10 ½

TV COMMERCIALS/INDUSTRIAL FILMS
List available upon request

TRAINING
Acting: Manchester College, North Manchester, Indiana

Commercial: Bowling Green State University, TV Commercial course
             Terry Berland – TV Commercial Workshop

EDUCATION
Bachelor of Arts, Communication-Radio/TV/Film
Bowling Green State University, Bowling Green, Ohio

THEATER
High School and College

SPECIAL SKILLS & INTERESTS
Motorcycling, Automobile (standard and automatic), Truck Driver, Auto
Restoration, Bicycling, Carpentry, Construction, Piano, Harpsichord, Trombone,
Voice, Volleyball, Basketball, Hockey, Ice Skating, Tennis, Swimming, Radio &
TV Announcing, Voice Overs.

CURRENT OCCUPATION
Video Production

PREVIOUS EMPLOYMENT
WKBN TV (CBS), Youngstown, Ohio – Sports reporter and Anchor
WVBKC AM, Chardon, Ohio – News reporter and News Director

FIG. 10: Undeveloped résumé
(John Jennens)

JOHN JENNENS
(419) 535-9722

Height: 6'2"   Weight: 190lbs.
Eyes: Brown   Hair: Brown
Suit: 44L   Shirt: 16 ½ / 34-35
Pants: 34/36   Shoe: 10 ½

THEATER
"The Thirteen Clocks"   The Prince
"The Imaginary Invalid"   Father
"Night of January 16th"   Defense Attorney Stevens
"Cheaper By The Dozen"   Frank
"The Valiant"   James Dyke

TELEVISION-RADIO
WKBN – TV (CBS), Youngstown, Ohio – Sports reporter and Anchor
WBKC – AM, Chardon, Ohio – News reporter and News anchor

TV COMMERCIALS/INDUSTRIAL FILMS
List available upon request

TRAINING
Acting: Manchester College, North University, TV Commercial course
Commercial: Bowling Green State University, TV Commercial course
             Terry Berland, Los Angeles – TV Commercial workshop

EDUCATION
Bachelor of Arts, Communication – Radio/TV/Film
Bowling Green State University, Bowling Green, Ohio

SPECIAL SKILLS
Video Production (Videography, Editing), Voice Overs, Motorcycling,
Automobile (standard and automatic), Truck Driver, Auto Restoration, Bicycling,
Carpentry, Construction, Piano, Harpsichord, Trombone, Voice, Volleyball,
Bowling, Baseball, Basketball, Hockey, Ice Skating, Tennis, Swimming.

FIG. 11: John Jennens' developed fledgling résumé

Be sure to include TV credits including:

- *Series Regular:* A series regular is one of the main characters that the series revolves around.
- *Guest-Star or Co-Star:* Co-Star is a small part that is more than five lines. Usually a one-scene Guest-Star is a large part with a lot of dialogue. It is the billing right under the Series Regular. The billing of Co-Star or Guest-Star is determined by the show itself.
- *Recurring Role:* Can be used in any category where you are reappearing on the show.
- *Under Five:* A part where you are speaking under five lines.

After you've outlined your experience in the industry, it's time to list any industry-related *training* you've had. Begin with classes you've taken—scene study, improvisation, or cold-reading, for instance—and workshops. Specifically list the training and the name of the person you trained with. If you are working in a small regional area and the person you trained with is a well-known coach from a large market, include the market the coach comes from. If you have a degree in theater arts, put it in your résumé (M.F.A. in Acting, Yale School of Drama, for example). Certainly include any voice and dance training.

In the beginning of your career, casting directors will be considering the extent and focus of your training as well as where and with whom you trained. Especially at the early stages of your career, it's important to demonstrate your devotion to the craft by developing the training portion of your résumé. Take ongoing classes, take part in community theater, and take every opportunity to audition (there's no better experience than on-the-job training). Before you know it, your fledgling résumé will become a focused, professional promotional tool.

Last on your résumé is a section listing *special skills.* Any special talents you have that might be useful in the business would be listed here. Start with your strongest special skill first. Things like dialects and mime, or any musical instruments you play well. Athletic abilities are extremely important, such as skydiving, horseback riding, tennis, volleyball, and skiing. Be specific when mentioning special skills. For example, don't list vague categories such as "martial arts." Instead, specify "Karate (black belt)."

If you drive a car (automatic and/or stick-shift), motorcycle, and/or truck (pickup to eighteen-wheeler), mention it. Almost anything else you do well—like electronics, photography, American Sign Language, foreign languages, and CPR, for example, can be noted in the special skills section of your résumé. If you enjoy working with animals and/or children and babies, this is a great place to mention it.

NOTE: If you say you can do something on your résumé, you had better be able to do it—and do it *well*. Limit the list to activities you can perform at an advanced or professional level.

Printing Your Résumé

Agents and casting directors go through literally hundreds of head shots and résumés weekly. The last thing they want to do is spend a lot of time looking through a poorly organized list of credentials. It is in your best interest to see to it that your résumé is attractively laid out, is easy to read, and draws immediate attention to your strengths as a talent.

Use the sample résumés in this chapter to help you lay out your own material. You can use your home computer or have your résumés professionally typeset. Keep in mind the following do's and don'ts when setting up your résumé:

- Take care to line everything up neatly on the page.
- Try using all caps to help distinguish headings from the rest of the material. Use bold typeface for headings. It is easy to read 12-point type. Try a slightly larger type for headings (14-16-point), with 24-point type for your name. Experiment a bit before committing to print.
- Attach your résumés to your head shots in all four corners with a stapler (or an adhesive that won't damage or show through on the picture or the résumé). Make sure the paper is trimmed to the exact size of your eight-by-ten head shots. Attach your résumés to your head shots as you need them (a small quantity at a time). *Never* give an agent or casting director a head shot and résumé unattached. Doing so looks lazy and unorganized. The résumé can easily get separated from the photograph, in which case you are left with no way to be identified or contacted.
- You may use your home computer to print your résumé on the back of your head shots, but don't print up too many at once. You will be updating your résumé constantly. And you will want to hand in the most current version of your résumé every time you audition.

Don't clutter your résumé with full sentences and non-industry information. Think in terms of an outline of your experiences and abilities.

Use a letter-quality or laser printer to make copies of your résumé as you need them. If you make Xerox copies of your résumé, make sure the machine delivers good, clean copies (no streaks or spots, please). Clean the glass before each use and take care to line up the paper in the machine properly.

If you have your résumés professionally typeset, the printer will give you a range of prices based on the number of copies you order. When ordering, keep in mind that you will be updating your résumé often. Try to negotiate a quantity that includes occasional updates as needed. Don't forget to ask the printer to print your résumés on eight-by-ten (not eight-and-a-half-by-eleven) paper. When using a computer, you will have to trim the résumés to fit your headshots yourself, using a paper cutter—not scissors—for a clean, professional look.

Updating Résumés

Your résumé should be updated regularly to include new credits, training, and special skills. Using your home computer, simply insert the new information and delete less-impressive credits, reformatting as necessary. If your résumé was professionally typeset, your printer will help you reformat your material.

Consider leaving a bit of white space (unused area) on your résumé in each category. That way, you could easily insert new information by neatly hand-printing a line or two until you create a new document. Be sure to use a black pen to match the type.

NOTE: When creating their original résumés, some actors leave a section at the bottom of the page to add updates. This allows them to continue (temporarily) using the résumés they have on hand.

What Is a Cover Letter and What Is Its Purpose?

A cover letter is a letter of introduction (fig. 12). Sent along with a head shot and résumé, a cover letter is a polite way to introduce yourself and to ask for what you want. If, for instance, you are looking for representation, you would send your head shot out to agents, requesting an appointment. Keep your cover letter brief and to the point. Using a contact name as a referral (mentioning the name of a colleague or mutual acquaintance) can be helpful in catching the attention of agents and casting persons. They will naturally gravitate toward someone who has been referred by a person they are familiar with and trust.

Some sample statements you might make in your cover letter include:

- I've just graduated from . . .
- I've taken a commercial workshop from . . .
- I'm ready for work.
- I'm in such-and-such play.
- I'm looking forward to meeting you.
- I'd like an appointment.

Once you have created a good cover letter, you're ready to start sending out your head shots and résumés.

Targeting Your Head Shot/Résumé Mailings to the Right People

The first group of people you'll want to target your mailings to is agents and/or managers. You can get a list of SAG-franchised agents for any market by calling the nearest SAG (Screen Actors Guild) office to your area.[2] Be aware that in small regional areas that are "right-to-work"[3] states, most—if not all—agencies will not be SAG-franchised. If that is the case, check your local phone directory for talent agents in your regional area. Be sure to do some research to make sure they are legitimate businesses (see Chapter 8: What You Need to Know About Agents, Managers, and Unions).

Casting directors can be found in directories for both major and secondary markets.[4] For example, the *Ross Reports* in New York and Los Angeles lists casting directors. Other resources are the *Biz Directory* in the Dallas/Austin area and *Performink* in Chicago. *The Screen & Stage Directory:*

---

[2] Refer to the Appendix at the back of the book for SAG listings.

[3] In a right-to-work state, companies cannot refuse to hire someone because he does not belong to the union or does not want to join the union.

[4] For more on secondary markets, refer to Chapter 14, Working in Regional Markets.

(date)

Alisa Harris
324 East Beaumont
New York, NY 10036
(212) 555-1234

Betsy Berg
Betsy Berg Talent Agency
5 East 60th Street
New York, NY 10036

Dear Betsy,

I recently graduated from Yale School of Drama. Comedy is
my strong point. I am a member of Gotham Improv Theater
Group. Terry Berland saw me perform in a recent showcase
and suggested I get in touch with you.

I am looking for representation and would love to make an
appointment to meet you. Thank-you for your time and
consideration.

Looking forward to hearing back from you.

Alisa Harris

Alisa Harris

FIG. 12: Sample cover letter.

The National Casting Guide is a national directory with more than 5,000 listings, including all casting directors; film commissions; regional, summer, dinner, and children's theaters; plus model and talent agencies nationwide. You can purchase the book from www.pgdirect.com.

There are Internet sites in every part of the country where actors can resource information. Be wary of sites that are based on gossip. The way to find out about legitimate-information sites is to connect with actors in your area. Participate in community theater, contact local agencies, and check out the drama section of your neighborhood bookstore. Consider attending talent seminars, workshops, and/or conventions in your area. Be sure to check out the credentials of the casting directors or agents advertised as attending the event. Most casting directors can be found on the Internet.

Once you have prepared your promotional tools, compile a list of the people you want to direct your mailings to. Send a single head shot, résumé, and cover letter in an eight-and-a-half-by-eleven envelope to each person on your list. Keep track of whom you send mailings to, when you sent them, and any responses you get.

Follow up on Your Mailings

Usually, agents will call you if they are interested in meeting you. If you have not heard anything approximately two weeks after you do a mailing, follow up with a phone call to make sure the person received your package.

Most likely, you will be talking to an assistant. Ask for an appointment. If the answer is no, thank them for their time, hang up, and make the next call. If the answer is that the agent is too busy to give appointments at this time, the best way to follow up is by sending your picture postcard mentioning any updates regarding your acting career. If the answer is yes, thank the assistant or agent for her time, get your appointment time and date, tell them you are looking forward to meeting them, hang up, and make your next call to try to secure another appointment with another agent. Usually your appointment time will be a week or two away. Just because you get an appointment for a meeting does not mean the agency will necessarily represent you. Setting up several appointments could shorten the process of finding representation.

It could take several months for an agent who is interested in you to call you in for an interview. You'll be making a lot of calls and appointments in this industry, so it's important to have on hand the proper tools to (a) keep in touch with the industry, and (b) keep track of your activities, appointments, earnings, and expenses.

The next chapter will help you get yourself organized, motivated, and focused.

SUMMARY

RÉSUMÉS

- Prepare an attractive, easy-to-read, one-page résumé of personal/ professional information, including:
- *Name*
- *Union affiliation* (if applicable)
- *Agency representation* (if applicable)
- *Phone number where you can be reached* (cell phone or agent)
- *Statistics* (height, weight, hair and eye coloring)
- *Experience* (credits in theater, film/TV, commercials, etc.)
- *Training* (classes, workshops, college degrees, etc.)
- *Special skills* (dialects, sign language, skydiving, etc.)
- Get your résumé printed. Remember to print small quantities at a time, upgrading information as needed. Have your résumé printed on paper the exact size as your professional head shot, or trim it.
- Attach your résumés to your head shots in all four corners (using staples or glue).
- Create a cover letter to accompany your head shot/résumé submissions. Try to include the following:
- *The name of a colleague or mutual acquaintance* (if possible)
- *A class or workshop you've taken* (or degree recently earned)
- *A production you're currently in* (or have recently completed)
- Compile a list of people (agents, managers, casting people, etc.) you want to target your head shot/résumé mailings to. Keep records of whom you mailed to, the date of each submission, and any follow-up notes.

- Follow up on each submission (to make sure your head shot arrived and to request an appointment).
- Have picture postcards on hand for any kind of follow-up communication to agents, managers, casting people, or producers.

3.

Other Tools
You'll Want to Consider

Now it's time to consider a variety of tools that actors use to stay on top of opportunities in the industry. Agents and casting directors are not willing to chase you down to give you a job. It is your responsibility to make yourself accessible to them at all times, or they will simply call someone else. Being unavailable to receive calls and messages can result in lost wages, lost contracts, and lost opportunities.

Equipment for Keeping in Touch

CELL PHONES
A cell phone is your number one tool. You want to be able to be reached immediately. Your agent may be calling regarding an audition taking place within the hour, a booking, or a change in appointment time. When the agent picks up the phone to reach you, it is a good idea to be available to take the call. If you try to return the call later, the agent may not be able to speak to you at that moment, and a game of phone-tag begins. How many times do you think an agent will go back and forth before deciding it's easier to simply call someone else? Whenever possible, make a point of being available to receive important calls.

There are, however, legitimate reasons why you may not be able to receive calls. For example, if your phone is in an area with no reception.

Or you may have turned your cell phone off while in a studio auditioning or at a booking. (Make sure your cell phone is off during those times.) Check your messages often and make a point of returning calls promptly. Numerous companies offer cell phone products and services at reasonable rates, so there is no excuse to be without one.

ANSWERING MACHINES

An invaluable communication aid, the answering machine takes calls for you when you're not available to do so yourself, allowing the caller to leave a message that you can retrieve later. Costs range from well under a hundred dollars to several hundred dollars. A good, dependable machine doesn't have to cost a lot and more than pays for itself in service rendered. If possible, consider the following options when purchasing an answering machine:

- *Call screening* allows you to decide whether or not you want to take the call when you are home. Most basic machines have this option, but check to make sure. It can come in handy when you're studying or rehearsing material and don't want to be disturbed.

- *Two-way recording* allows you to record both sides of the conversation. This is useful when you're given an appointment and don't want to hold up the agent or casting person while you write down all the information. Make sure the other party knows you are recording the call—it's the law.

- A *built-in message-retrieval system* lets you call your number from wherever you are to take your messages off the machine.

- *Caller ID*—If for some reason you can't understand a message left on your service, the caller ID displays the caller's phone number so you can return the call.

ANSWERING SERVICES

Some people still prefer answering services. An answering service will take calls for you. Just know that you still must be accessible when your service tries to reach you. If they are available, you can find such services in the Yellow Pages or in industry directories. Your local phone service may offer voice-mail services, which will take calls for you when you're not available to answer the phone.

A monthly (sometimes weekly) service fee is charged, whereas an answering machine involves a one-time cost. All things considered, the purchase of an answering machine should prove to be more cost-effective and convenient than voice-mail and answering services. A little research should help you determine which option will work best for you.

Agents must be able to get information to you quickly. If you are unavailable to receive a call, you must get back to them as soon as possible. Cell phones, answering machines, and/or services are indispensable communication aids to make sure you keep in constant touch with important people in the industry.

Record-Keeping Supplies

Since making commercials is a business, it is important to keep accurate records. Keeping track of expenses, income, appointments, and audition information is crucial to your success as an actor. You'll also need to write thank-you notes and keep a journal of your goals and networking efforts. (Chapter 6, Networking and Goal-Setting, explains these essential tasks.) The minimum requirements for keeping track of all of these things include:

- *Daily planner/appointment book or Palm Pilot*—to keep track of auditions, callbacks, jobs, and other appointments. A section for notes, important calls, and new contacts is helpful.

- *Record-keeping materials*—including a journal for keeping track of income and business expenses for tax purposes and a travel log to record mileage and other travel-related expenses.

- *Networking/goal-setting journal.* This can be any notebook or hardcover journal converted to detail your day-to-day, weekly, monthly, yearly, and long-term (five to ten years or more) goals, as well as whom you need to network with in order to accomplish them.

- *Thank-you notes.* The local office-supply store should be able to provide you with a variety of stationery, record-keeping journals, and convenient-size travel logs, as well as standard tables on allowable business deductions. If not, try the business section of a good bookstore.

4.

Training

How Classes in Commercial Technique, Improvisation, Scene Study, and Cold-Reading Prepare You to Do Commercials

Commercials have one thing in common with all other acting media—you (the performer) have to come off as real. The only difference in commercials is that the work is done in a shorter time and in a smaller space. Studying improvisation, cold-reading, and scene and monologue study provides a solid foundation for—and adds ease and excellence to—acting in commercials.

Classes in *commercial technique* teach you how to act out a situation in a fifteen-, thirty-, or sixty-second format. They should do the following:

- Teach you how to analyze a script.
- Teach you to make the most of the physical space you're given to work with.
- Show you how to let out your personality.
- Eliminate self-consciousness in front of the camera.

The result of your commercial training should enable you to step up on the mark that you are given to work on, and in that small amount of space, immediately give dimension to your performance and the space.

In *improvisation classes*, you are given the framework of a scene, scenario, or sketch—the gist of an idea. You make up your own lines, create your own relationships, and bring out your own personality. Improv classes help you:

- Learn to loosen up, become less inhibited.

- Learn to think fast (and in this business, this is a definite plus).

- Exercise the creative muscles in your brain. Improv training will help you learn to take direction and make decisions quickly and seamlessly.

In *scene/monologue study*, you spend weeks or months working on the same material. Each time you approach it, you bring new levels to your performance. You learn to do in-depth research, script analysis, and background and relationship histories, which are really the core of an actor's work—creating "real" relationships. An actor can be brilliant in an acting class yet not be able to audition well at all.

The greater your knowledge of acting, the easier it is to do television commercials, because a TV commercial is actually a mini-scene.

Cold-reading classes teach you how to audition with little or no preparation. Cold reading teaches actors to assess the material quickly, pick out the clues given in the text, and then let their individual personalities come through in a committed manner. Every commercial audition is essentially a cold reading. You do not receive any material (script) ahead of time. You arrive at your audition, pick up the script, and prepare right then and there.

Finding a Good Coach

In larger markets like Los Angeles, New York, and Chicago, it is fairly easy to find a good coach. In smaller, regional areas, it can be tough. Word of mouth is always a great way to find out whom the better actors are training with. Ask for referrals from local agents, managers, casting people, and other actors.

If possible, audit the classes you're considering to see if you like the way the coach relates to the class and if you would fit in. Do not be surprised if many coaches feel that auditors are a disturbance. Especially in the more dramatic scene-study classes where the work is deep and layered, auditing may be considered a breech of privacy. In larger markets, where the names and reputations of prominent coaches are well-known, it is easy to check the credibility of any coach or class. And you should do so.

Try to train with the best coaches you can afford, and know that if you come from a smaller market, you may need to go to a larger market periodically to get professional training.

Good actors never stop training. Expect to invest a considerable amount of time and money in ongoing classes and workshops. You must also be willing to honestly assess your strengths and weaknesses as an actor if you are to succeed in your career.

It is important to find coaches you really "click" with. Each coach has her own teaching and communication style. Sometimes you may have to try two or three (or more) coaches before you find one who teaches in a manner that facilitates the way you process and apply the information being offered. It doesn't mean that any of the others were bad coaches. Success in classes and workshops has a lot to do with how you process and utilize information—and how willing you are to do so. When you are ready to receive the information and find a coach you can really relate to, you'll get much more from your classes.

Cost of Training

How much should you expect to pay for classes? This varies, depending on the location and size of the class and the credentials of the teacher. In major markets for a theatrical ongoing class with a top-notch, well-known coach, expect to pay approximately $150-$200 for a five-hour class once a week for four consecutive weeks. These programs vary from four to twelve weekly classes to a two-year program. Private coaching can run you anywhere from $75 to $150 per hour.

A commercial class, once a week for six weeks, for three hours each week, can run you $350-$400. A two-to-three-day on-camera workshop with a well-known teacher may run $200-$300. If you are in a regional area, these well-known coaches may be willing to come to your area to give a workshop. Keep an eye out for opportunities to train with these coaches.

A few well-directed calls to several schools and coaches should give you a nice range to consider. Again, study with the best coaches you can afford.

FINAL NOTE: Be wary of schools that want to sell you a package where photographers are included. You should make your own decision as to which photographer you want to use (see Chapter 1 on photographers and Chapter 5 on scams).

How Often You Should Train

In this industry, training is a way of life. Any time they're not actually working, successful actors are working out in class. To do well in any career, you must take the relevant courses and then take refresher courses to stay current and to fine-tune your professional skills.

Newcomers to the business will spend the bulk of their time in class. You can expect to spend several years developing basic auditioning and performing techniques until you are consistently able to book work in the industry.

At some point, bookings will begin to take priority, with study taking place in between jobs. Just know that in some form or another, be it on-the-job training or formal classes, sharpening your skills must become a way of life if you are to become successful and stay on top in this business.

Creativity is an ongoing process. The university level is just a taste of what performing is about. After that, if you have decided you want a career in acting, you will want to go to a market like Chicago, Los Angeles, or New York and get into a school where you can really develop. Class is the place where one gets nourished and grounded—the place where creativity soars.

Finding a good acting coach involves looking for someone who is current—someone who does not try to make actors into something they are not. The coach should use each person's uniqueness and raw ability to help develop him into a marketable commodity.

Interview with Sharon Chatten

Sharon Chatten, acting coach to many celebrities, says:

> Most beginning actors think if they learn how to "say the words right," they will get acting work. They don't realize that an actor, for many roles, is required simply to be themselves. Thus, the actor needs to be able to bring who they are in their own life to the script. They must access their own way of speaking, use of their body, personality, intelligence, sense of humor, and feelings to the given dialogue.
>
> Very often, I hear directors complain that a particular actor "sounds like an actor" and not a real person. Often these actors have to be told from the director to "stop acting. Just talk to me." To be truthful as an actor, you need to be able to go into the deepest, honest layers of a performance. This takes a lot of practice and the willingness to get to the deepest layers of yourself.
>
> As an actor continues to study and grow, he can then of course approach the roles that are different from himself. But this character work must be carefully crafted to be done well. Most casting directors for film and television bring in actors who seem very close to the type of role they are trying out for and do not require character work.

When you first come to a larger market (no matter how much work you were doing in your smaller, regional area), know that you are coming in at square one. You will have to swallow your ego and be willing to learn how things are done in the larger market. Your goal at first is simply to learn what it takes to do well in the new market. Know that you may have to get new head shots and/or rework your résumé. You may have to fine-tune your cover-letter writing skills. It may take a while to acclimate. Use that time in class, learning and/or fine-tuning your craft with the best coaches you can afford. Concentrate on learning to audition effectively—and to create and/or take advantage of opportunities to perform.

It's important to start networking and taking advantage of the vast opportunities that come with being in a major city. Go to union functions, attend readings and lectures, and don't be afraid to ask questions. Find out who the agents, casting directors, and directors are.

A quick caveat: Exercise caution when meeting people. Make sure they are who they say they are. A bit of research and a few well-directed phone calls should help you determine if the person you are dealing with is legitimate or not (see Chapter 5 for information about identifying and reporting scams).

People who take their careers seriously work continuously to fine-tune their skills, whether they are doctors, lawyers, teachers, or performers. Those in the top of their fields engage in ongoing study and take courses. It's a way of life. Top athletes spend countless hours in the gym, working out regularly so that they maintain a high level of fitness and performance. Likewise, actors must flex their creative muscles regularly to stay on top of their game. And the place actors go to work out is in class.

5.

Scams

Unfortunately, there is a rather unsavory element invading the industry—one that feeds on the hopes and dreams of unsuspecting thespians—promising fame and fortune, separating you from your money, and then delivering little or nothing. These charlatans of show business are called scam artist. They're slick. They're smooth. And they're ruthless in the pursuit of a quick buck.

Why Scam Artists Are So Successful

Frankly, scam artists are very good at what they do. They often make an impressive presentation, citing the names of well-known agents, managers, production companies, and "stars," all of whom they claim are their close industry contacts. Scam artists prey primarily on young aspiring actors and parents who, in their excitement and enthusiasm at the prospect of getting involved in the business, forget to take the necessary steps to ensure that the people they are dealing with are who they *say* they are and can do what they say they can do.

People who normally exhibit amazing common sense have been known to throw caution to the winds when it comes to making decisions concerning their (or their child's) potential career in show business. As scam artists become more creative and elusive, aspiring talent and their parents must become more scrupulous in discovering which industry-related activities are legitimate and which are not.

How to See a Scam Coming a Mile Away

By applying some common-sense rules, you should be able to avoid being taken by a scam artist. Before getting involved with anyone who claims to be able to help you build your career, consider the following:

- You should never have to pay someone up front to get work in the industry. Think about it: If you were going to get a job at Burger King, you would never consider paying them for the privilege of working for them. You would never consider paying up front for an employment agency to get work for you. They would get a commission or fee *after* getting you a job. It's the same with agents and managers in the business. They make money when *you* make money, by taking a percentage of your income (SAG-franchised agencies, for example, take ten percent of your earnings) as commission for getting you the job.

- If anyone tells you that, for a certain amount of money, they will get you an audition, guarantee you work, or "make you a star," turn tail and run. There are no guarantees in this business. As in other industries, talent people must invest a considerable amount of time and effort before they can hope for ongoing success. Anyone who tells you otherwise is full of beans.

- There is no reason you should have to disrobe to interview or audition for a job. Both the unions and the networks in commercials that audition and air in the United States prohibit nudity. For auditions, you could be asked to wear a two-piece swimsuit (females) or a bathing suit (males). Other common requests would be for you to wear a halter-top or an outfit that shows off your figure. When the commercial is filmed, there are ways to close in with the camera to imply nudity. This might be done in a shower or bathtub shot in an ad for a soap product, for example.

- Steer clear of interviews and auditions to be held in personal hotel rooms at unseemly hours. Never put yourself in a position where you could be taken advantage of. Newspapers and magazines are full of frightening stories about young, inexperienced people meeting so-called agents, managers, casting people, or photographers who turn out to be kidnappers, child-molesters, rapists, and murderers. In some cases, failing to use common sense can result in personal disaster.

Even in a legitimate work situation, sexual harassment can be a problem. For example, one young model/actress was hired to do a print advertisement in which only her head and shoulders would show. During the photo session, the photographer asked her several times to open her blouse. This young lady handled herself appropriately, refusing to open her top (why would that be necessary in an ad showing only her face?) and reporting the incident immediately to her agent. The agent then called the client, who fired the photographer.

Individuals who harass and defraud talent can leave a bad taste in the mouths of those who have been taken. Such behavior demeans the efforts of legitimate industry professionals and reflects poorly on what is otherwise a terrific working environment. As aspiring talent become more scam-conscious—making wiser, sensible choices—the negative publicity surrounding the industry will begin to dissipate. Use your head when deciding whom to work with, whom to trust. The payoff will be a career unmarred by frauds and tragedies.

Remember: If it seems too good to be true, it probably is.

Common Industry Scams

Here are four things to avoid:

- Ads in newspapers and magazines seeking talent of all kinds, no experience necessary. You go to these interviews and voila! You are the most amazing talent and/or look these people have ever seen. *You* are going to be a star! Chances are, these folks are going to do one of the following:

- Ask you to pay to be interviewed by them for the opportunity of being represented by them *or* ask you to pay for the privilege of being seen by them.

- Ask you to pay to be in a special publication or website that goes out to all the agents, managers, and casting houses (no one hires from these publications or websites).

■ Say how much work they could get you if only you would pay them to supply the required pictures of you—no matter how wonderful your existing pictures are, they will not be suitable for whatever they are doing—and they just happen to have a photographer with them to take those pictures.

■ Tell you they think you're just wonderful, but you need a little coaching—and they just happen to have a seminar that will teach you everything you need to know.

All of this is usually a one-time-only opportunity. Only so many people will be accepted, and *you* (you lucky dog) are one of them. But you have to act fast. It's now or never.

Time to go. Leave the room. *NOW!*

■ Agents or managers who offer to represent you as a talent without asking you to read something or, in some cases, without even having *seen* you. All you have to do is send in a small fee . . . This should send up an immediate red flag. Reputable talent agents simply don't sign up actors without having them come in for a formal interview to see if they have the right look, talent, and experience to be marketable to their clients. (And remember, you never should be required to pay fees up front.)

■ Ads in newspapers for a talent agency looking to sign people. They then ask you for money to sign you as a talent.

■ Impressive websites for acting schools who charge you money before you get there. You arrive and the school has misrepresented itself. Call other people in the industry and check around before you sign up with a school.

■ Websites that claim you can be cast from your picture appearing on the site.

■ Photographers who come into town (often on the pretense of being a "big name" in some major market) and books sessions based on the premise that they are scouting for some big agency or are otherwise able to guarantee a connection resulting in paid work. Again, there are no guarantees. Although there are good test photographers who are brought in to smaller, regional areas to photograph talent (by reputable local agencies and schools), they do not promise you work—they are simply there to help you develop your book (models) or to take talent head shots.

Be suspicious of so-called "famous" magazine photographers. Chances are, if they really shoot covers and tears[1] for major magazines, they wouldn't have the time or interest to come to a regional area to test models and shoot head shots.

In a common scam, a photographer comes into smaller, regional areas with slick ads and a lot of hype about whom he knows and what he's done. The local talent lines up and signs up for a series of pictures, paying (of course) in full, in advance. If all goes well, the actors have a lot of fun and can't *wait* to see the results. They're happy. The photographer's happy. And why shouldn't he be? He's just made several thousand dollars, he's on his way out of town, and he's not coming back. The pictures? Well, if there ever was film in the camera (or a memory card if shooting digitally), it was put there for show. The actors will grow beards before they ever see any prints.

Make sure you know whom you're working with if you use an out-of-town photographer. If someone says she shoots or scouts for a well-known agency or magazine, get specific information (name of agency or publication and a contact who can vouch for her).

- A "major production house" coming to your town, auditioning talent for parts in a feature film. You're fabulous, an amazing talent—but not a member of the union. This creates a problem, but if you give them a few hundred to several hundred dollars, they will cut through the red tape, get you into the union, and you're ready for work. No. No. NO! There are very specific conditions for joining the unions. A simple call to the local SAG office (see the Appendix) will tell you how to qualify to become a member of the union.

Reporting and Investigating Scams

If you suspect that a person or group in the industry is misrepresenting themselves, don't hesitate to make some phone calls to check out their claims. Start with the Better Business Bureau to see if there are any complaints. Ask your local Chamber of Commerce if the suspicious person or group is registered with them.

---

[1] Tears (tearsheets) are pages from commercial print advertisements, editorials (fashion pages or covers), and catalogs that models tear out to place in their modeling book (portfolio).

Generally, anyone involved in businesses that exchange goods or services for money must have a business license. He should be able to produce a copy of that license, and you should be able to verify its validity with the government agency that issued it. (Look on the license itself to find out whom to contact.)

Scam artists are usually eager to get rid of someone who is too smart to be taken, focusing instead on those more likely to fall victim to their deceptive games. Those who are on the up and up will not object to you checking out their credentials, their contacts, and their prior business activities. So unless you know you are dealing with a well-known, reputable person or company, check things out before jumping into anything that seems even remotely suspicious.

If, in spite of everything, you find you've been "had" by a con artist, don't be embarrassed to admit it. Call the Better Business Bureau and the press about what happened. Doing so protects others from being scammed and will help make sure the offenders either make restitution or are prosecuted for their crimes.

If you are scammed, try to learn from the experience. Become a wiser, more conscientious consumer so that no one can take advantage of you again.

Interview with David Vando

David Vando, an industry consultant, gives valuable advice on how to avoid becoming a victim of modern industry scams. The owner of Model's Mart in New York City (www.models-mart.com), which supplies educational material to actors and models, David is an expert on the demands of working in the industry. He travels extensively around the country speaking at international model/talent conventions.

> Young aspiring models and actors from all over North America are being victimized by a variety of different scams geared at both performers and at very ambitious, anxious parents who hope to get their children into the business.
>
> In New York, there are ongoing problems with people trying to take advantage of young talent. Recently, I did some research while helping a number of government agencies in New York City

and in Washington D.C., to prosecute people who were running scams or operating illegal, improperly licensed agencies.

This is a significant breakthrough because up until now, this issue was sort of kept in the closet; no active government action was ever taken against these people. In New York, both talent and modeling agencies must be licensed—posting a $10,000 bond that serves as a legal safeguard in the event someone brings a complaint against a licensed agency. This way, you would get paid for an illegitimate nonpayment.

Phony agencies create a major problem for the industry. They have no license and are not bonded, so if you do business with them, you do so at your own peril. One of the first things newcomers to New York should do is to make sure that any agency they interview with is properly licensed with the city and state of New York. That's very easy to find out. Just call the Better Business Bureau of *any* state to find out if an agency is duly registered and/ or licensed as required by state laws.

Agencies do not necessarily *have* to be franchised by the unions. However, if an agency is not SAG or AFTRA franchised, check whether it's a registered business and bonded [see "All About Agents" in Chapter 8].

Many scams play on your vanity. You are told that for a certain amount of money, you can have a big career. There is no such thing as instant success. Most people who are thought of as overnight successes have actually worked very hard at it for a very long time.

We are all guilty of letting our emotions and our excitement and our visions blind us, keeping us from using our own common sense. If someone asks you to pay to be "discovered," you should thoroughly investigate him. Legitimate agencies make money by finding work for you. Any other attempts to get money from you are very dubious. This includes Internet websites hosting pictures of models and actors, which are a waste of money that would be better spent developing your career.

An agency that is representing you and feels you need a better head shot can certainly give out the names of good photographers to consider, but you should be free to interview them yourself, making your own negotiations as to cost and the type of materials you need. Your agency may guide you, but it should not be part of a photographic studio or any other merry-go-round collecting fees from you.

You should be able to compare prices and talk to other performers to see whom they've worked with. Speak to experienced actors about who the local scam artists are. Word of mouth is most helpful. Don't be afraid to ask questions. Be suspicious of anyone who doesn't want to answer questions about his business activities.

Check out people's credentials. It's one thing if you are allowed to participate in a talent search or a convention where only schools that are licensees participate. The purpose of those conventions is to educate new talent and, in some cases, allow reputable agents and managers to select talent for possible future professional development.

Any school that says, "Come to my classes and I'll make you a star" is doing the student a disservice in the same sense as a fly-by-night scam coming through your city and having a one-night stand at some hotel. Good schools do not make promises they cannot keep. They can only give you the best training they can.

I went to Columbia University, and they never made any promises to me. They made things *available*. Reputable corporations have sent people to interview students, but no promises were made. Be wary of anyone who says, "Give me some money and I'll make contacts for you." "I'll get you interviews." "I'll get you an audition." You are headed for a disappointment if you do business with these people.

The development of a show-business career is a long process. People usually have to work very hard to get an agent. Agents usually have to work very hard to get them their first interview. How do I know? Because I experienced it for myself. It's never an easy process.

6.

Networking
& Goal-Setting

Who you know, how well you stay focused on your goals, and whether or not you follow through have a tremendous effect on your career and its progression. It's important to surround yourself with a strong network of industry friends. You must also learn to set clear, attainable goals and take consistent, continuous steps to turn your dreams into reality.

Networking

It is not secret that successful people tend to surround themselves with a select group of industry friends and colleagues. Networking with the right people can move your career along at an accelerated rate. Who are the "right" people?

Fellow Performers

Associate with fellow performers who are motivated and active in the pursuit of their goals and who have a positive, outgoing nature. Hanging out with unmotivated people with negative attitudes will drain you emotionally and creatively.

Make it a point to spend time with people who are excited about their lives, who take advantage of the opportunities available in the industry, and who know how to make the best of a situation, no matter how crazy things get. Remember, the people you surround yourself with are a mirror of yourself and the way you relate to the world around you. Like attracts like. Take care to spend your time only with people who support you and whose efforts you admire.

Industry Professionals

Make yourself visible to the movers and shakers of the industry—agents, managers, casting directors, directors, producers, etc. Attend workshops and conventions where there are opportunities to meet and talk with people who may be in a position to help you build your career. Read trade magazines in your area for a list of classes and other networking opportunities (see Appendix at the back of this book for major market listings).

Make it a point to get to know everyone worth knowing in your market (and always have copies of your head shot/résumé with you). Be courteous to and appreciative of every contact. Even though the person you just met may not be able to make a direct impact on your career, he or she may be able to steer you toward someone who can.

Show sincere appreciation for anyone who does something nice for you. Sending thank-you notes to the agent who gave you an appointment, the casting person who called you in, the receptionist who was so helpful at the audition, or the coach who took a special interest in your career, for instance, not only brightens that person's day but also can help advance your career. Everyone wants to feel appreciated. Unfortunately (or fortunately for you), many people fail to properly thank those who have gone to bat for them. Thank-you notes are memorable. If you send one, the recipient will remember your thoughtfulness the next time your name comes up, and perhaps will be eager to do something nice for you again.

You'll never succeed if you spend your time at home on the sofa dreaming about your first Academy Award. Get out there and meet people, whenever the opportunity arises.

Networking Websites

Keep an eye out for networking websites in your area. The Internet is a great way to find out about classes and casting opportunities in smaller, regional areas. Remember, you should not pay for any networking opportunity. Watch out for scams (see Chapter 5 for more information on industry scams).

Mentors

Nothing helps young, aspiring talent catapult to success (talent and training aside) more than having a strong, successful mentor. A good mentor believes in you, sometimes (at first) more than you believe in yourself.

Mentors serve as role models, teachers, confidants, and friends. They shoulder the tears when you take a fall and give you a swift kick in the pants if you start to slack off. Having a mentor who is well-known and respected can not only raise your self-esteem considerably, but also elevate your standing in the industry. People can't help but notice that this influential person has faith in your ability to do well in the industry. You'll find that with the right mentor, doors previously closed to you suddenly begin to open.

How do you *find* a mentor? Generally, a mentor finds you. He or she may notice how hard you've been working, how much promise you seem to have. Mentors are often at a point in their lives when they have had a certain degree of success and now want to give something back. And, lucky you, they decide to take you under their wing and guide your career. That is one way it happens.

Another option is for *you* to spend some time deciding whom you would like to be your mentor. Look for someone you admire who has the personal and professional traits you desire and who, over time, seems interested in helping you develop your career.

Often, talent managers take on the role of mentor, grooming an actor into a well-rounded, marketable commodity. You may have a mentor who focuses primarily on one or two aspects of your career. A mentor may come into your life suddenly, bestowing his or her special gifts (lessons) upon you, and then move on to someone else who needs help more. Some mentors become lifelong comrades. In either case, if you're lucky enough to find a mentor, count your blessings and take care to make the most of the opportunities your "guardian angel" has to offer you.

Goal-Setting

There is no question of the direct correlation between success and the simple act of setting one's goals down on paper. Goal-setting helps you to stay focused as you work on the day-to-day activities necessary to do well in the industry. Remember:

If you are failing to plan, you are planning to fail. There are numerous books and tapes on the subject of goal-setting, all which cite the following tips for setting solid, achievable goals:

■ Make a habit of regularly writing down your goals.

Studies show that the simple act of writing down your goals sets the wheels of success in motion. The process puts your dreams in clear focus so that you can prioritize them and begin taking action to bring each goal to fruition.

■ Break your goals down into the following categories:

■ *Yearly goals*–Write a broad overview of the things you would like to accomplish over the next year.

■ *Monthly goals*–At the beginning of each month, prioritize those things you want to get done over the next thirty or thirty-one days. Be more specific as you break down your yearly goals over the next twelve months.

■ *Weekly goals*–Begin each week by writing down your goals for the next seven days. Be realistic about what you can accomplish in this amount of time and make sure that you spend time working toward the accomplishment of your most important achievements. (It's easy to get wrapped up in the day-to-day stuff, neglecting the tasks that would really make a difference in your career.)

■ *Daily goals*–Little by little, you've been breaking your most important goals into smaller and smaller pieces (yearly, monthly, and weekly). Now divide your goals into even smaller "bites," planning something to do each and every day to move your career forward. As you complete each step on your daily "to do" list, you'll begin to notice that you are making strides in the major, annual goals you set for yourself.

Deciding what *specifically* you want, then consistently taking *action* to do the things that make you more marketable will provide the strong foundation necessary to create an ongoing experience of achievement.

As you write out your goals, it's important to know that you can't have it all, certainly not all at once. It's very hard to succeed if you are scattered, pursuing too many major goals at one time. For instance, it would be very hard to become a doctor and an actor at the same time. Becoming a doctor involves many years of study and practice. Becoming an actor requires equal dedication in time and effort to stand a chance of succeeding. Over time, you could certainly become both a doctor and an actor (the late Graham Chapman of *Monty Python* fame did just that), but it would be very difficult to pursue both careers at the same time.

You must prioritize your list of goals and be reasonable about what can be accomplished in a given block of time. Go over your list and as you attempt to decide which goals you are going to pursue (at this time), ask yourself:

- Do I *really* want to accomplish this goal? Am I willing to make this goal a priority in my life, working every day in some way to make this dream a reality? Am I willing to pay the price of achieving my goal—to devote the time and effort necessary to make things happen? What am I willing to sacrifice in the pursuit of this goal (TV time, nights out socializing)?

- *Why* do I want to achieve this goal? Be honest with yourself. Make sure the goal you set is chosen for the right reasons, that you are doing this for yourself, that it's something you *need* to do—not because someone else wants it for you. You will have to work very hard to achieve your goals. Do some soul-searching to make sure that what you are trying for is something you really want.

- What are all the wonderful things that will happen if I am able to achieve my goal? For instance, "If I lose weight, all my favorite clothes will fit, I'll look better on-camera, etc." Visualizing all the fabulous results of achieving your goals will inspire you to follow through.

- What are the not-so-wonderful things that will happen if I *don't* achieve my goal? Spend some time contemplating the results of *not* taking consistent action to see your plans through to completion.

"I didn't follow through on a connection I made at the casting. As a result, the part went to someone else." "I never did sign up for that cold-reading class. As a result, I was visibly inexperienced at the audition." Just thinking about what you felt like when you didn't achieve a goal, then comparing that to the way you felt when you did, should motivate you to take action today to complete one of the vital tasks you've listed on your goal sheet.

When you get right down to the root of the meaning of the word succeed,
you find it simply means to follow through. —F.W. Nichols

As you work your way through your list of goals, you may over time find that certain goals no longer seem important to you. Your priorities can (and do) change. Be flexible when this happens. Review your goal sheet periodically and update it as needed.

Also pay attention to which efforts are producing positive results for you—and which ones aren't. Revise your strategy when necessary. Keep doing whatever is working; stop doing whatever isn't. Be willing to try new things (no guts, no glory), and be willing to make mistakes along the way. Realize that behind every setback is the opportunity to learn and grow.

Be willing to do whatever it takes to accomplish your goals (providing it is neither illegal nor immoral). Take classes, get out and meet people, work on your public image, eliminate the "negatives" from your life. Make time to plan out your life—and no excuses. There is always time to do the things that are really important to you.

If you're not doing something on a regular basis to make your dream a reality, it could be that you don't *really* want this goal at all. Only you can decide how badly you want to change your present circumstances. A bit of soul-searching as you review your progress should provide you with the answers you need. Remember:

If you do not take the time to write down specific goals and consistently
act on them, you will wind up working for someone else who did.

There are no shortcuts to greatness. Greatness comes with consistent effort and begins with the little things you do each day as you build your career. Stay focused and determined to succeed, and before you know it, your wildest dreams will begin to become reality.

SUMMARY: SUPER SUCCESS STRATEGIES

STRATEGIES FOR CONSISTENT GOAL-ATTAINMENT

- Write your goals on paper and refer to them regularly. Doing so keeps your goals in clear focus. Studies show that people who write their goals out on paper tend to achieve much more than those who do not.

- Be specific about what you want to achieve. For instance, "I want to be called in for more auditions a year by casting directors, so I will have the chance to make more money," then determine the amount of auditions you want to be called in on.

- The more specific and detailed your plan of action, the better the chance you will reach your goal when you plan to reach it. For instance, if you are currently being sent out on five auditions a year, an attainable goal could be, "Next year I want to be sent out on twenty auditions a year from the starting date of this exercise."

Once you've decided how many auditions you want and the time frame you want to do it in, be very specific about what you're going to do in the next year that will generate more interest in you. Make a list of things to do that will help you achieve your goal to the level you've aspired to. For instance "I want to build up my résumé with classes to reflect my comic ability. I want to take an improv class, a comedy class, and I want to do more comedic theater pieces." Make a list of things to do that will help you achieve your goal: "I am going to look up and call three acting classes today. I am going to look for theater audition opportunities in the trades." Refer to the list at least once daily (preferably first thing in the morning and again in the evening), and try to do something every day that will bring you closer to reaching your goal.

- Review and revise your goals regularly, as needed. Keep your goals in plain sight and review them often to see what's working, what's not, and whether or not the goal needs to be revised before it is truly attainable. Maybe your goal was not realistic. Maybe you need more time to attain it. Sometimes the desire for the goal diminishes and another goal takes priority. Goal-setting should be an ongoing process.

- Associate with achievers. Watch the company you keep. Surround yourself with supportive, positive people. Find people who are doing what you would like to be doing, who inspire you to achieve and maintain a level of excellence. Avoid those who find a million excuses for not achieving their goals. IF you are surrounded by people who don't support your desire for growth, find a new group of friends and colleagues who do. Your success depends upon it.

■ Take consistent action in attaining your goals. *NO MORE EXCUSES!* Whatever you want to do, get off your butt and get to it. No matter where you are now—no matter what your financial state, your educational level, or where you live—start with whatever resources are available to you and *get going.* There will never be a "perfect time" or a "perfect" set of circumstances. The best time to begin is now. Even a small effort, when consistently applied, will create phenomenal change. In fact, the simple decision to write and act on clear, precise goals produces a certain positive momentum. All things are possible. You *can* create the kind of life you want if you invest regularly in these simple, highly effective goal-setting techniques.

I know of no more encouraging fact than the unquestionable ability to elevate his life by conscious effort. —Henry David Thoreau

Goal-Planning Sheet

TO-DO LIST	NOTES
	NEW CONTACTS
IMPORTANT CALLS	**THANK-YOU NOTES**

FIG. 13: Sample goal-planning sheet.

SECTION 2

TAKING YOUR ACT ON THE ROAD

7.

The Key Players
in the Industry

Now it's time to meet some of the key movers and shakers in the commercial industry. They are instrumental in the advancement of your career, so it's important to know who these people are and how they fit into your life as a performer.

Agents

The agent is the person who represents you, who secures auditions for you. He or she accepts bookings for you, negotiates money and the terms of employment, receives the payments you get from the booking, and distributes the money (minus his or her commission) to you. The agent protects you according to the guidelines of the unions.

If you have any questions or complaints, your agent is the one to straighten them out for you. Some problems or issues that could potentially arise include:

- While on a shoot, the contract you are signing states that the commercial is running (airing) in a different way from what you were told when you booked it.
- You were booked as an extra and you are now recognized in the commercial. You feel you should be upgraded to a principal.

■ You are no longer under contract for a commercial and a friend of yours calls and says that the commercial is running again.

It's your agent's responsibility to keep records of your bookings and product conflicts (products you are under contract for). However, ultimately you are your own business manager and must keep your own records.

Managers

It is the manager's job to help you shape your overall career. You might, for instance, be doing a lot of commercials, then decide it's time to move more into film. Your manager should be able to tell you if your timing is right and, if it is, introduce you to film opportunities.

With your manager's help, all aspects of your career (theater, film, commercials, etc.) should be considered and a plan of action put into effect. Your manager is someone else on your side, taking your hand and offering personalized attention and guidance as you develop your career. Managers have fewer clients than agents, so they can take time to develop talent. However, managers technically cannot directly secure bookings and negotiate monies for you.

Casting Directors

The casting director is the one who calls the actor in to audition, either directly or through an agent. He or she is responsible for the initial selection of actors from all available talent. The casting director also directs the actor during the audition, then presents this audition CD to the creative team.

A casting director may be the first person of importance to see your work. If she believes in you and likes your work, she will call you in on any audition she feels you are right for, even if you don't have an agent. In this case, the casting director could be instrumental in introducing you to an agent. Although you can obtain auditions directly from the casting director, ultimately, you have more exposure to auditions when you have agency representation. Many casting directors will call your agent with different character descriptions, referred to as "breakdowns," which results in expanded opportunities to audition for actors who have agents. A casting director gets no payment or commissions from an actor.

Producers

The producer is the person who puts together all the elements of the commercial's production and is one of the members of the creative team who has a say in who gets booked for the job.

Directors

The director is the one who actually directs the spot. Often, the director's opinion as to which talent will work best for the spot holds great weight. (For more on producers and directors, see Chapter 11: The Selection Process).

8.

What You Need to Know
About Agents, Managers, and Unions

All About Agents

Agents are always looking for talented individuals who have the potential to book jobs and make money for them. As a talent, you are most marketable when you are properly trained and prepared to go out on auditions. Being prepared means having your marketing tools in order, especially your professional head shot and résumé.

You must supply your agents with a quantity of head shots. The agent acts as a go-between with the casting directors, producers, and ad agencies, making sure the actor gets paid the appropriate amount of money. This eliminates the talent being put in the middle of the uncomfortable position of bickering about money when a problematic situation occurs. The agent can step in and be the bad guy, always looking out for the talent's best interests.

A SAG-franchised agency is required by both SAG and AFTRA to obtain a license from Consumer Affairs. The talent agency is bonded so that it is able to handle the talent's money. If an agency doesn't follow the rules and regulations of the union, the union can take away its franchise. The actor is thereby protected by the rules and ethics set down by the union.

Many small regions do not have SAG agents because there is not enough, if any, SAG work available. Regions that have a fairly equal amount of union and nonunion work have both union and nonunion agents.

Most actors in most regions are registered with and may be sent out by more than one agent within a given market. In Chicago, this is called being *multi-listed*. In New York and other areas, it's called *freelancing*. The other way of being represented is to sign an exclusive agreement, meaning that a single agent represents you. Los Angeles is a *signed* town. An actor there is represented exclusively by one agent for commercial and one agent—which could be different from his commercial agent—for film and television. You could also have different agents exclusively for voice-over, sports, dance, and industrials.

How to Find a Good Agent

There are several methods by which talented people find good, reputable agency representation. The major union markets are New York, Los Angeles, and Chicago (see the chart in the Appendix indicating opportunities for all other regions). Each market has directories of talent agents published by knowledgeable people in the industry. Ask other actors about agents they have dealt with. Call the nearest SAG branch office (see the Appendix) for listings of licensed agencies in or near your area. The last resort would be to go to the Yellow Pages.

Check out any agency that is not SAG-franchised. Call the Better Business Bureau and make sure it has a business license. Call production companies, ad agencies, theaters, acting schools, and other actors to see what they know about the agency.

Do You Want a Manager?

With a manager, you have another person working on your behalf, and this can be beneficial. A manager is often more willing to work with newcomers in the industry, taking a more personal interest in developing budding careers. Agents need people who are ready to work. They are generally too busy booking people for jobs to spend time developing talent. A manager, on the other hand, might advise newcomers on all aspects of their career. A good manager acts as a business consultant, a middleman between agents and talent, a mentor, a confidant, and a "shrink."

If you are working in secondary markets such as Florida, Atlanta, or Texas and are looking to make the move to New York or Los Angeles, it might be a good time to consider finding a good manager. A good manager would be one who has agent contacts to introduce you to and get you signed with in New York or Los Angeles. Be sure your manager is well connected, which would mean more potential opportunities for you. Competition is fierce in this industry, so the more people you can get behind you, the better.

The New York and Los Angeles markets are more manager-oriented because the industry is much larger there, which makes it easier to get lost in the shuffle there than in smaller areas. A good manager in the major markets can be a real asset.

The downside of having a manager is that you have to pay them fifteen percent when you get booked in addition to the agency commission. So experiment a little when you first start out. Go out there without a manager and see how it goes. If you are not getting the results you want after a while, try getting a manager and see if things improve.

If working with a manager means you are working more, then the extra commission is well worth paying.

Conducting a Dynamite Interview

So, you've done your homework, you've researched the available agents in your area, you've done your mailings, and you've followed up with a call to each a week later. Congratulations! You've gotten your first request to come in for an interview. Go to your interview clean and casual, looking like yourself. Dress to suite your type (see Chapter 1 for a list of looks and types booked for commercials).

Questions to Ask Before Taking on an Agent or Manager

When meeting with agents and managers, keep in mind that ultimately you are interviewing them as much as they are interviewing you. Make sure you are comfortable with the person you are dealing with and that you are satisfied with their answers to the following questions:

- Are you a SAG-franchised agent (or a member of the National Conference of Personal Managers)?
- Who do you represent (clients and/or talent)?
- What can I expect from you as an agent/manager?
- What do you expect from me?
- What kind of contract (if any) would I be signing?

You should discuss with an agent (and especially a manager) what, at this point, you want out of your career. He should be aligned and attuned to you and your needs. If the agent or manager doesn't have the same aspirations for you that you have for yourself, he should tell you what direction he sees for you. If you do not like what he suggests, he is not the right person to represent you.

Usually, you have one meeting with the agent who has shown initial interest in you, and a second meeting with all other agents in the office. They then decide if it would be mutually beneficial for them to represent you.

Here are a few tips from industry pros on attitude and presentation at that all-important meeting.

LAURA FOGELMAN, AGENT, LOS ANGELES: "You have about five minutes to win people over and knock them out during the interview. You have to be positive, upbeat, and keep the conversation going. If you are boring, you are dead in the water. That's it. I have people who come in to my office and sit in a chair, wait for me to ask questions, and give me one-word answers. It takes two people to have a conversation. One-word answers give me nowhere to go. Find things to talk about. It's easier for us if someone comes in and is very conversational and chatty. It makes us want to talk more.

"Also, actors have to look interesting when they walk in the door. They have to dress the part. I don't mean upscale. They just have to have themselves put together. They should have a sense of style. The girl should be unique and interesting, in a way that makes people want to look at her. I have seen girls come in in coveralls and look fabulous because they have a whole 'look' down pat. Have a sense of style and look confident when you walk in the room."

KATHY HARTIGREE, AGENT, ATLANTA: "Personality is very important. If a person doesn't have a flexible, pleasant personality, the indication is that they're going to be hard to work with. It is also important that actors understand the industry. If they say things in their interview that make me aware that they don't understand how the industry works, I am concerned because we're dealing with professionals here."

TRACI DANIELLI, AGENT, FLORIDA: I expect talent to show up and be on time. Also, it's important for actors to just be themselves. Don't try to be something you are not. Don't try to impress me by throwing around important names or bragging about the work you've done. Don't be negative or make excuses. I have heard every excuse in the book. I know it's hard, but don't be nervous. Just relax and be yourself.

ROBERT SCHROEDER, AGENT, CHICAGO: "I like actors but I like people even more! I am always looking to meet talent that have something new to say. I want to sit down and speak to a person, not an actor. I can read your résumé to find out what you have done. Speak to me about what you want to do or what you like to do on the weekend. Things you are interested in outside of acting. Don't worry about what we are looking for. Be comfortable with who you are. Let us know what you have to offer. You are the person who can play you best."

NANCY JOHNSON, AGENT, DALLAS: "Attitude and presentation at the 'all important meeting.' You must have a PhD:

P = Purpose (not ego). Presentation. Positive mental attitude.

H = Hopeful, happy, honorable, and hustle!

D = Dedication, determination, durability.

"Going to an acting interview is different from going to a job interview. You should look comfortable and casual. You should wear clothes that reflect your personality and look. If you are a funky-type person, you would dress funky. If you are a conservative, you would dress conservatively. If you are an upscal- type person, you would dress upscale."

LYNN CLARK, AGENT, DETROIT: "Don't get dressed up. Clothes should be casual, clean, and fit well. You should be articulate, polite, and outgoing."

Keeping in Touch with Your Agent

Once you have found an agent, ask him how often and when you should be in touch. Some agents want you to call in every so often. Others prefer you not call them unless you have some specific business to discuss. Calling every five minutes to see if they have anything for you is generally regarded as a nuisance—don't be pesky. Unnecessary calls tie up the phone lines and frustrate the agent.

Your agent's function is to be on the phone all day working with casting directors to secure appointments for you with production companies and ad agencies, negotiating contracts, and straightening out any problems or issues that come up. Consider a typical day in the life of an agent. The agent is communicating with the casting director, preparing a breakdown consisting of either lists of actors or photo submissions (either hard copy or Internet submissions), getting appointment times from casting directors, calling appointment times out to actors, getting confirmations from actors, and giving confirmations or cancellations back to casting directors. The agent also receives or puts out calls for callbacks and bookings.

Understanding what agents do can help you realize that, although it is important to stay in touch with them, you must do so in a manner that is productive for both you and your agent. For example, send your agent picture postcards when you're appearing in something, when something important is happening in your career, or just to say hello. This way, you are keeping your face in front of the agent without taking up valuable time that could be spent arranging auditions and bookings.

Don't automatically assume that your agent is not working hard for you just because you are not auditioning or working enough.

Handling Contracts and Agreements

SAG-franchised agents use a standard union contract to sign their talent. Always read it over and don't be afraid to discuss changes you desire. The answer will be yes or no. You sign a one-year contract, which is renewable for three years after the first year. Nonunion agency contracts should be gone over carefully before signing. Be sure to ask questions about any points that seem vague or unreasonable. You do not have the protection of the union with a non-franchised agency, so be especially cautious.

The two main points to check for in a nonunion contract are commission and the "out clause." Beware if the commission is more than twenty percent. The standard nonunion commission is ten to twenty percent. Pay particular attention to the out clause, which indicates the conditions for getting out of the contract. The contract should indicate either how many auditions the agents needs to get you out on or bookings you need to secure within a specified amount of time for the contract to remain binding. If the out clause is not satisfactory to you, have a lawyer examine the contract before you sign it. After you and your lawyer discuss areas that should be amended, take the document back to the agent, who may or may not be willing to renegotiate the terms of the agreement. Just know that ultimately, only you can decide whether signing the final version of the document is in your best interests.

Why Actors Might Want to Drop Their Agents

The number one reason actors want to drop their agents is that they are not being sent out on enough auditions. They think if they were with someone else, they would have more opportunities. Sometimes, it's simply a case of the-grass-is-always-greener mentality.

The people who jump around tend to be the ones who are having a difficult time booking jobs. The agent could very well be submitting the actor for auditions, but the casting director or whoever decides who gets to audition is not choosing that actor. Here is where your picture is very important. You might not be getting chosen because your picture is not capturing the eye of the casting director. If you suspect that you are losing opportunities because your head shot isn't strong enough, ask your agent if she thinks you need a new one.

If you're getting called for auditions but not getting called back and/or booked, it could be that your auditioning skills are not honed well enough to have the competitive edge. Consider taking more classes in on-camera auditioning technique; ask your agent for referrals to good coaches in or near your area.

An actor may choose to leave his agent if he disagrees with the agent as to what types of castings he is being sent out for. Most people want to leave their agency because they are not getting enough work. Actors must remember that "getting work" is not what an agent does. An agent's job is to get actors auditions and interviews. The actor must then "win" the job.

If you are not happy with your agent, arrange a meeting to discuss the issues. If you cannot come to a satisfactory conclusion, it may be time for you to leave. Remember, however, that the agent still gets residual payment for any jobs secured for you while you were represented by them. Other than that, most agents agree that if you are not happy with them, it is better for all concerned for you to move on.

Why an Agent Might Want to Drop an Actor

The number one reason agents want to drop an actor is repeated unprofessional conduct. For example, if you do not show up on time, do not show up at all, try to bypass the agency by giving your phone number to a producer or ad agency, or are difficult to work with.

You must trust the agent you are working with and be able to take constructive criticism. Agents generally do not drop actors because they are not booking. They expect it could take a year or more to book something. As long as you are selected to come in and audition, you are enthusiastically auditioning, your craft is honed, and you have a positive attitude, your agent will stick with you.

The Unions and Their Jurisdictions

The unions—SAG, AFTRA, and Equity—represent the industry; each union has its own contract. You may call each union and request a contract. Each union governs specific areas of the business:

- *The Screen Actors Guild* (SAG) governs actors appearing on film, television commercials, industrials, and television voice-overs.
- *The American Federation of Television and Radio Artists* (AFTRA) has jurisdiction over live and taped television shows and commercials, soap operas, disc jockeys, and radio performers.
- *Actor's Equity Association* (Equity) governs performers and stage managers in live theater.

WHY JOIN THE UNION?

In regions where the work is split fairly equally between union and non-union work, actors will be faced with the choice of either joining the union or not. It may be wise for an actor to choose not to join for the first couple of years. After you build up a lot of credits and are booking frequently, you may reconsider joining the union.

If you are seeking work in a region where most of the jobs are union commercials, you'll want to become a member of SAG and AFTRA as soon as possible. Membership in either of these unions is an indication that you are not "green." It means you have already done the work it takes to become a member. Agents will feel they are taking less of a chance on you because you have already proven yourself.

Benefits of joining the union include:

- *Protection*—Union contracts establish minimum (scale) payments for talent performing in all industry-related media under their jurisdiction. They also make sure that performers on union jobs are employed under reasonable working conditions. The unions determine work standards and establish guidelines for the education of children in the business. SAG-franchised agencies must follow the rules set down by the union. If there are problems with franchised agents or on union jobs, the union is there to make sure the talent's interests are protected.

- *Health insurance, pension coverage, and cost-of-living adjustments* (COLAs).

HOW TO JOIN THE UNION

The easiest union to join is AFTRA. All you have to do is fill out the application, pay the membership, and—voila—you're a member.

There are basically three methods by which performers become eligible for membership in Equity:

- If you are hired to appear in an Equity production, all you have to do is bring your contract to the nearest Equity office and pay your membership initiation fee.

- If you are a member of another union, SAG or AFTRA, for instance, and have fulfilled certain work criteria (one principal role, one "under five"[1] AFTRA job, or three days of extra work), you can join

---

[1] An "under five" is a speaking role of less than five lines.

Equity by (1) bringing in your contracts or written verification from the parent union[2] and (2) paying the appropriate fees. NOTE: Your parent union dues must be paid up before you can join Equity.

- *The Equity Membership Candidate Program* (EMC) involves working your way into Equity by finding a job with a participating theater as a production person or an understudy, depending on the specific theater. To become eligible, you must accumulate about fifty weeks of this kind of work.[3] Notify the union when you become eligible to join.

There are several ways to join SAG. The most common:

- Getting a job on a union project. After you do one union job, you become "Taft-Hartleyed," meaning you can do as many union jobs as you want for the next thirty days, after which you must join the union and pay your dues before you can do another union job. If you don't, the ad agency who employed you will be fined.

- Getting hired as an extra on three union jobs. Check with your local SAG office. Rules and regulations regarding extra work vary from state to state.

- Entering SAG through your parent union. Check with SAG for current requirements. Again, your dues for the parent organization must be paid in full before you can join a sister union.

In a right-to-work state, companies cannot refuse to hire actors because they do not belong to the union or because they do not *want* to join the union. The biggest misconception union actors have about working in a right-to-work state is that they can do both union and non-union work. Union actors who work on nonunion projects are violating Rule One of the agreement they signed when they joined the union. Right-to-work states are Alabama, Arizona, Arkansas, Florida, Georgia, Indiana, Iowa, Kansas, Louisiana, Mississippi, Nebraska, Nevada, North Carolina, North Dakota, South Carolina, Tennessee, Texas, Utah, Virginia, and Wyoming.

---

[2] The first union you join is your parent union.

[3] The fifty weeks do not have to be consecutive. Sometimes you can test out after forty hours. Check with Equity's current requirements for the EMC program.

Interviews with an Agent and a Talent Manager

Now that you have become familiar with the roles of agents, managers, and unions in the business of making commercials, you may want to read the following interviews, which explore the nuts and bolts of these jobs. Carol Ingber, of Ingber and Associates in New York, and Al Onorato, who works as a talent manager in Los Angeles, offer these insights:

CAROL INGBER, AGENT:

What does it mean for an actor to sign with an agent? What is freelancing?

To *sign* with an agent means the talent signs a SAG and AFTRA agency contract to be represented exclusively by that particular agent for one year. This means the actor cannot go out on commercial auditions for any other agency. After the initial contract, the actor has the option to sign for either one, two, or three years.

The reason people feel they need to be signed is so that they have a business relationship with someone who will groom them and take care of them. My first responsibility as an agent is to my signed clients. If a casting director calls and gives me a time slot for an actor, I'm going to give the time to my signed clients first.

Freelancing means an actor can work with multiple agents. In New York, actors can freelance. In Los Angeles, however, actors must sign exclusive contracts with one agent.

What do you look for when deciding whether or not to represent an actor?

I look for someone who has a good attitude, someone who treats people with respect regardless of their position in the business. If one of my assistants says to me, "I just got off the phone with so and so who sent in a picture. She really sounds nice on the phone," I'll make a point of remembering that person. In an industry where today's assistant can become tomorrow's agent, it pays to be respectful to anyone you work with in the industry.

I treat talent in a professional manner and I expect the same in return. I'm not interested in people who either show up late or not at all. If I leave a message for them, they should not wait twenty-four hours to return my call. I expect actors to tell me when they're going out of town or "booking out."[4] It's important for agent and talent to work as a team. Our work together involves a fifty-fifty partnership.

---

[4] When talent "book out," they give the agent or manager dates when they are not available for work.

If you sign a talent who doesn't book right away, how long will you continue to represent him?

When I believe in someone, I'll continue to work with him as long as it takes. I have a client who has been with me six years and she just booked her first network spot. I have had clients who have booked right away, but I also know that it can take a solid year before a good streak starts.

There is no longer a statistical rule as to how many times it takes to audition to book something. This is because of the competition factor. Now there are fewer auditions to go out on and more people in the field, so the competition is stiffer.

What is the actor's job in developing his career?

To be professional. To take classes. This is his part in the teamwork with the agency. When talent are not up to par, they have to listen to their agent. If their agent says they have to do something, they must *do it!*

What do you look for in a head shot/résumé?

I like to see that an actor has done some theater work. I look for a picture that sort of hits me. I may be attracted to something in the cover letter. It's hard to define specifically what makes me want to call someone in. Something in the presentation grabs my attention and makes me want to meet the person.

Any thoughts about what should be in the cover letter?

Don't write a two-page letter. Every agent knows why you're writing us. Make it short and sweet. I get more than thirty pictures a day. I want to be able to read the note fast.

Do you expect actors to have a demo tape/CD?

No. I don't look at them. I would rather get an idea of the actor's potential from observing the person in front of me.

What do you look for in a general interview?

Actors come across best when they are just being themselves, but if I ask an actor where he comes from, I don't want a fifteen-minute dissertation. Let the agent guide you. There are certain things we need to get out of that first meeting. What you think is important may not be. Say what you need to say and allow your personality to come out. Don't respond to the agent's questions with one-word answers, but don't go on for a long time, either. Try not to come across as desperate or overanxious.

Are there pet peeves actors should avoid?

Actors who don't want to accept early audition calls are high on my "peeve" list. I have to be in my office at 9:30 A.M., after going out to the theater and returning home at 1:00 A.M. If I have a client in the show, we may go out afterwards, yet I still have to be in the office at 9:30 A.M. If I am not, you will have a problem with that. And if I can do it, *you* can do it too.

Actors with bad attitudes don't go over very well with agents. You see this in actors who don't return phone calls, don't tell their agent when they'll be out of town, and blow off auditions. Some actors treat commercials lightly, as a secondary interest, yet commercials can be a powerful venue for actors to showcase their talent. I have seen a lot of clients who have gone on to TV and film because they were good in a commercial and were noticed by someone. Actors have been written up in *Newsweek* because of a sensational commercial they've appeared in. I have gotten calls from Spielberg's office and Neil Simon's office, asking about actors they've seen in commercials. Commercials can definitely lead to better things.

Will you work with someone who isn't in the union yet?

Of course. It's very exciting when an actor gets his first booking and is waivered[5] into the union. Commercials are the way for many people to get into the union. I am interested in talented people with an acting background. This includes people who have studied in small colleges in the Midwest as well as students from Yale or Julliard.

How much can someone earn from a single commercial?

An actor can make anywhere from $535 to $100,000 or more from one commercial. I have a client who has made six figures from a spot that has been running for six years. In fact, I have known many actors who have appeared in commercials that have run for years and have easily made six figures.

What is the most important piece of advice you can give to actors?

Believe in who and what you are. Hang in there and don't give up. Always be honest with the people you are working with. You'll get a

---

[5] Being waivered, or Taft-Hartleyed, is basically an entry into the union. The waiver allows you to work on as many union jobs as you want within a thirty-day period, after which you become a "must join." This means that you must be prepared to join the union for the next job you get after the waiver.

lot further if you make a habit of being honest with yourself and with others in the business.

AL ONORATO, MANAGER:

What is the difference between an agent and a manager?

The basic difference is that SAG-franchised agents are licensed and managers are not.

Agents are interested in finding jobs for their clients. Managers are interested in shaping their client's careers for the long term. Also, agents generally handle a lot of people, while a manager has to be selective. For instance, an agent may handle a hundred people. A manager would have perhaps twenty-five.

A manager puts a lot of time and effort into nurturing and building the career, whereas an agent doesn't have time for that kind of personal attention. If, for example, someone is going to an audition, a manager would work with that person on the material, doing as much preparation and getting as much information on the audition as possible and following up on the results. It is also up to the manager to try to get feedback as to how an audition or a meeting went and how the talent is doing in one-on-one situations.

How does someone find a good manager?

Get out and talk to people. It's like finding a doctor, a minister, or a dentist. Many times, you just have to go on instinct. Ask managers for their ideas on building a career. Ask what types of people they handle. You might inquire about other people in the business they network with. The word *clout* comes in here: If they need to get someone on the phone—be it the casting director, the head of a studio, or a network executive, can they do it?

Is there a point when doing commercials might be a detriment to someone's career? When should someone stop doing them?

If you're in television and you want to make a move into the movie industry, it can be a detriment to be too well-known as a television personality. It's the same principle with commercials.

If you're building a career, you want to be seen enough to make people want to see more of you, but avoid being overexposed in one medium. Visibility is very important in the beginning; then you want to stop doing things so that people will want to see more of you.

9.

The Auditioning Process

Getting Auditions

FINDING OUT ABOUT CALLS

In the primary markets (New York, Los Angeles, and Chicago) as well as in the secondary markets (Dallas, Miami/Orlando, and Atlanta), the best way to find out about auditions is through an agent. Agents are aware of most of the calls and will set up an appointment for their clients. Trade magazines such as *Back Stage* (New York) and *Back Stage West* (L.A.) also provide information on auditions, but most of the auditions listed are "open calls" or "cattle calls." This means the auditions are open to the public. You will probably have to wait in long lines for what are usually non-paying jobs. Even so, consider these casting opportunities. Many independent films listed cast through these resources. The end result could be that you get some great film on yourself and some valuable on-the-set experience. It can also be a wonderful way to start relationships with up-and-coming filmmakers.

No matter what market you are in, you should be promoting yourself by sending your head shots and résumés to agents and casting directors. In smaller, regional markets, consider sending your promotional materials to local production companies. However, if there are agents in your area, agency representation should be your ultimate goal.

INTERNET SUBMISSIONS

Be cautious when dealing with companies that claim to be Internet casting services. You could get caught up in a new version of the old scam where you are asked to pay money to have your photo(s) appear in a magazine that casting directors supposedly cast from. Every city with agents (who represent talent) and casting directors (who do the initial selection of talent) have an organized means of communication. Casting directors do not scan random websites to select talent.

In Los Angeles, there are (at the time of this publication) two organized online means of casting. One is via Casting Networks Los Angeles (www.lacasting.com), the other is through Breakdown Services (www.breakdownservices.com). These websites offer a minute-to-minute means of photo submissions by agents to casting directors over the Internet. There is a section on each website that is set up to accept open submissions by actors with no agency representation for projects posted by casting directors. These projects are usually for nonunion projects or for talent searches for very specific special skills.

If there is a means in smaller, regional areas to submit talent online, it will be done in a similarly organized way (a communication system between agents and casting directors).

HOW AN ACTOR IS SELECTED TO AUDITION

The typical casting-call scenario begins with a casting director getting a call from a director or producer. The art director, producer, and writer and director present the casting director with a *storyboard*, which is a frame-by-frame pictorial layout of how the commercial is to be shot (fig. 14). The casting director makes a list of people to call in—people she has either worked with before or selected from photographs/résumés that she has on file, or names that she has on a database file. Then the casting director gives the character breakdown to agents.

In Los Angeles, breakdowns go out via an Internet system between agents and casting directors. Internet picture/résumé submissions are sent out by the agents to the casting directors through the system. Selections are made online, then sent back to the agents. In New York and the rest of the country, the breakdown goes out via phone calls, faxes, or e-mails to the agents. Hard copies of the photographs and résumés or lists of names are submitted to the casting director via

OPEN ON A COCO'S CHEF AND A COCO'S MANAGER SEATED AT A CUTTING BOARD TABLE. MANAGER HAS AN ADDING MACHINE, CHEF HAS A PILE OF FRESH VEGETABLES.

MANAGER: Mr. generous Coco's Chef here has created something new for dinner.

CHEF NODS SMUGLY.

Calls it his Three Course Dinner.

CUT TO ECU SLOW TRACKING SHOT OF ENTREES

He gives you a choice of six of our most popular entrees, ...

TRACK TO FULL SCREEN ECU OF TERIYAKI CHICKEN.

like Teriyaki Chicken

SETTLE ON FRESH RED SNAPPER.

or fresh Red Snapper...

Evans Hardy+ Young INC.

FIG. 14: Sample storyboard.

FOLLOWED BY SOUPS AND SALAD,

plus hot soup or salad, ...

THEN A COUPLE OF APPETIZERS

and your choice of four delicious appetizers ...

AND A FEW DESSERTS.

or six tempting desserts.

*CUT BACK TO MEN. AS MANAGER TALKS,
CHEF PUSHES ONE TOMATO FORWARD.*

Then he says to sell it all for just $7.99,
to which I say...

*HE THEN CHOPS IT IN TWO, FORCEFULLY,
WITH A LARGE CLEAVER AND LOOKS
MEANINGFULLY AT MANAGER.*

SFX: Chunck!!!

Good idea. Very good idea.

CUT TO FULL PRODUCT SET-UP.

SUPER: $7.99. COCO'S.

AVO: Coco's Three Course Dinners,: Just $7.99

MANAGER: (VO) Very, very good idea.

messenger, fax, or e-mail. Each agent submits her ideas (people she feels fit the part) to the casting director. The casting director goes through the lists and decides whom to bring in for the audition.

After the selections are given to the agents, whether it be through an Internet service or a phone call, if an agent feels strongly about an actor who was not chosen to audition, the agent may go to bat for the actor (pitch the actor) and try to convince the casting director to call that person in. While you might have all the right elements defined in the character breakdown, it's possible that you won't be selected because the casting director already has enough people for the role.

Having your picture and résumé in front of the casting director helps considerably. Casting people also refer to two union-produced directories to find actors: *The Player's Guide* (New York) and *The Academy Directory* (Los Angeles). These directories are also available online. In markets outside of New York and Los Angeles, make sure that the directory listing you see is a legitimate one.[1]

WHAT TO DO WHEN YOU GET THE CALL

Once the casting director has decided whom to call in for the audition, she notifies the agents. The agents then call the talent to let them know they got the audition and to give them important information about it.

Always have a pen or pencil and paper ready by the phone. It is important to be prepared to take notes the second you receive the call. This is a very fast-paced business. It is a mark against you if you are not prepared to move smoothly and quickly as agents run off the important facts about the audition. Nothing annoys people in this business more than having to repeat themselves (or wait) because you weren't prepared to take their call. And if an agent forgets to tell you something, be sure to ask.

You should be given the following information about the audition:

- The date of the audition.
- The time of the audition.
- The date of the shoot. Never audition if you are not going to be available for the shoot. It is a horrendous waste of everyone's time.

---

[1] Beware of other "directories" produced by people who take your money, claiming casting directors cast from these publications or websites when, in fact, the directory is only produced as a money-making venture and is not a legitimate source for casting directors seeking talent.

- The product the commercial is advertising.

- Any conflicts. In a union commercial, you cannot be under contract for two competing products (such as Tide and Wisk detergents). An advertiser would never want the same person on the air selling a competing product. Never assume what the conflicts are. When you accept the job you will actually be entering in to an agreement where the conflicts are unwritten, yet you are legally responsible to be free of them. Have your agent tell you specifically in what categories of products the ad agency is asking you to be free of conflicts. There can be surprises—for instance, you might not realize that a detergent has a whitener in it, creating a conflict not only with other detergents but with other products containing whiteners.

- If there is any food involved. If so, ask if you will be required to eat the food. Never attend a food-related audition (when eating is involved) if you cannot eat the food. If, for instance, you are a vegetarian and the commercial involves eating a pepperoni pizza at the shoot, you will not be able to pick the pepperoni off.

- How the commercial is going to run. Terms like *network, regional, spot, test, dealer, seasonal, cable,* and *Internet* give you some indication of how much you could make (see Chapter 13: How Much Can I Make?).

- What to wear. If an agent doesn't know, consider the product being advertised and who you are in the spot, then dress for that part.

The Day of the Audition

WHAT TO WEAR

Dressing for the part improves your chances of getting the job. If you're supposed to be at a party, dress up a bit. If you're supposed to be cleaning a bathroom, dress more casually. In general, if your agent doesn't give you detailed instructions, wear casual, clean, and comfortable clothes. Jeans are okay, but stay away from all-white clothing. White causes the camera lens to close down (it perceives white as light, which confuses the metering system), making you look dark and hard to see.

Don't wear all black either. Black is a serious, dramatic color, contrasting with the happy, playful energy of commercials. If, however, black is called for by the character (such as a poet at a reading, or a guest at a cocktail party), *do* wear black. Otherwise, wear colors that enhance your skin tones, making you look fresh and healthy.

Men should stay away from neck chains. Gold necklaces can be interpreted as slick. This would be inconsistent with a character such as a warm dad, guy-next-door, or anyone portraying vulnerability. If you wear an earring, wear one only if you feel the character you are auditioning for would actually wear one—for example, if the character is a musician, slacker, or someone with a "street" attitude.

WHAT TO EXPECT WHEN YOU GET THERE

Be on time, or even better, be ten to fifteen minute early. This will give you time to find which studio your audition is in, relax, warm up your voice, and look over your script (if applicable). Come in with a positive attitude, knowing good commercial technique. Have your head shot/résumé with you. The casting director will not always collect it, but always have it with you. Please note: Do not submit a photograph without a résumé properly attached to it (stapled or glued in all four corners and cut to fit your eight-by-ten picture).

Résumés are important for several reasons. Something on your résumé might catch the casting director's eye and possibly result in a conversation being generated between them and you. Or, there might be a special skill on your résumé that will interest the casting director for another project they are working on.

Many commercial directors also direct film and television. They could look at your résumé and feel you are also right for something else they are working on. To submit a photo without a résumé shows no respect for yourself as an actor and no respect for the casting director as someone interested in talent.

In the reception area, there will be a size card or sheet that you are required to fill out. (See fig. 15 for a sample of a size card and fig. 16 of the SAG/AFTRA Commercial Audition Report for a sample sign-in sheet.) The size cards are referred to during the commercial casting process. Your Polaroid or thermal print[2] and head shot are usually attached to this card. If there is a place to enter your Social Security number or home address, leave it blank. It is not necessary to give out your Social Security number at an audition. The only time you need to give your Social Security number or home address is after you have actually booked the job.

---

[2] A thermal print is a black-and-white still photograph taken directly from an image coming from a video camera printed directly on thermal paper using heat instead of chemicals, as in a Polaroid.

Always keep your safety in mind. Just because you are asked for information doesn't mean you have to give it. You do not want to risk identity theft or other related issues as a result of giving out your Social Security number unnecessarily. Your Social Security number is private, *not* public information. NOTE: After the job is cast, the size cards are thrown into a garbage pail. It has been reported to SAG that garbage disposals have been picked through and the size cards taken by unsavory characters, who then become a nuisance (to say the least) to the actors listed on the cards.

When you get to the reception room, do not sign in right away (fig. 18). Wait until you have had a chance to freshen up a bit, relax, and look over the script.

Expect the waiting room to be full of people who are your type (fig. 19). Expect to see a script and/or a storyboard. Dialogue often will appear on the right, and any direction, on the left. Sit down and wait to be called in. Use this time to go over the script and perhaps get familiar with the other actors. You'll tend to see the same people at many auditions, so becoming friendly may be useful.

TERRY BERLAND CASTING (310) 571-4141

Job _____

Date _____

Name _____

Phone # ( ) _____

Cell # ( ) _____

SAG Membership # _____

SAG _____ AFTRA _____ Other _____

Agent _____ Agent # ( ) _____

Extra Work Yes ____ No ____ Height _____

(Under 18) D.O.B. _____ Weight _____

NOTES:

PHOTO

SIZES: Suit _____ Inseam _____ Waist _____

Shirt _____ Dress _____ Blouse _____

Slack _____ Shoe _____ Hat _____

FIG. 15: Sample size card.

COMMERCIAL AUDITION REPORT

PAGE _____ OF _____

TO BE COMPLETED BY CASTING DIRECTOR

		AUDITION DATE
(X) WHERE APPLICABLE	PRINCIPAL PERFORMER ☐	EXTRA PERFORMER ☐	
ON CAMERA ☐ OFF CAMERA ☐	TELEVISION ☐ RADIO ☐	

INTENDED USE

UNION: SAG ☐ AFTRA ☐

Person to whom correspondence concerning this form shall be sent:
(Name & Phone Number)

CASTING REPRESENTATIVE NAME — COMMERCIAL TITLE - NAME & NUMBER — ADVERTISER NAME

PRODUCT — JOB NUMBER — ADVERTISING AGENCY AND CITY — PRODUCTION COMPANY

INSTRUCTIONS: Circle the name of principal performer if known.

* SPANISH LANGUAGE TRANSLATION SERVICES

TO BE COMPLETED BY PERFORMERS

NAME (PRINT)	SOCIAL SECURITY OR MEMBERSHIP NUMBER	AGENT (PRINT)	ACTUAL CALL	TIME IN	TIME OUT	INITIAL	CIRCLE INTERVIEW NUMBER	SEX (X) M F	AGE (X) +40 -40	ETHNICITY (X) AP B C L HNA	PWD (X)
							1st 2nd 3rd 4th				
							1st 2nd 3rd 4th				
							1st 2nd 3rd 4th				
							1st 2nd 3rd 4th				
							1st 2nd 3rd 4th				
							1st 2nd 3rd 4th				
							1st 2nd 3rd 4th				
							1st 2nd 3rd 4th				
							1st 2nd 3rd 4th				
							1st 2nd 3rd 4th				
							1st 2nd 3rd 4th				
							1st 2nd 3rd 4th				
							1st 2nd 3rd 4th				

Asian/Pacific — AP — Latino/Hispanic — L
Black — B — Native American — NA
Caucasian — C — Performer with Disability — PWD

Mail top copy to SAG OR AFTRA on the 1st and 15th of each month.
WHITE-UNION

The recorded audition material will not be used as a client demo, an audience reaction commercial, for copy testing or as a scratch track without payment of the minimum compensation provided for in the Commercials Contract and shall be used solely to determine the suitability of the performer for a specific commercial.

The only reason for requesting information on ethnicity, sex, age, and disability is for the talent unions to monitor applicant flow. The furnishing of such information is on a VOLUNTARY basis. The Authorized Representative's signature on this form shall not constitute a verification of the information supplied by performers.

AUTHORIZED REPRESENTATIVE SIGNATURE _____

FIG. 16: Sample sign-in sheet.

WHAT TO DO AFTER YOU ARE CALLED INTO THE AUDITION ROOM

In a typical audition room setup (fig. 21), expect to see a camera, a television monitor (which is positioned so the screen is not visible to you), lights, and a *cue card*.[3] Generally at the first call (audition), the casting director or session director would be the only person(s) in the room with you. Many times you may not even meet the casting director. It is the casting director's job to know the talent, and if they are not in the room with you, often they watch the audition at night or after the auditions are over.

Read over the cue card first. Get used to the handwriting and the sentence structure, which may be different from your typewritten script. Keep track of any words that have been changed or added.

THE ACTUAL AUDITION

When you enter the audition room, the person running the session (a casting director or a session director) should give you basic or specific direction regarding the attitude and read expected for the particular situation. He may ask you to rehearse once. This way, the session director can give you any adjustments, notes, or "tweaks" he feels are necessary. Then your audition will be recorded. You may hear the following words and phrases during the process:

- *Take your mark.* There is a mark on the floor; standing on the mark will place you in the proper light and at the correct distance from the camera.
- *Roll camera.* This means the camera is on and recording your audition.
- *Slate your name.* Say your name—with personality.
- *Profiles, please.* Turn slowly, showing one profile of your face and then turn your body and face to show the other profile. Remain smiling, showing personality. Don't go into a serious mug shot.
- *Action.* This means it's time to say your lines.
- *Cut.* The camera is no longer recording.

You may be recorded once or twice. Do not try to determine whether or not the director liked you based on the number of recordings. The creative team has predetermined how many takes are necessary. The next time you'll hear about the job is when (or if) you get a *callback*. Getting

---

[3] A cue card is the script written in large letters and placed near the camera lens. This eliminates the need for actors to memorize copy.

FIG. 17: At a casting facility that has many audition rooms, find your studio listed according to product and casting director.

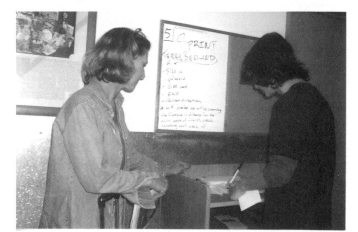

FIG. 18: Sign-in area. Find instructions, storyboard, script, sign-in sheet, size card.

FIG. 19: Waiting room.

FIG. 20: Inside studio. On your mark.

FIG. 21: Inside studio. Session director, casting director, cue card.

FIG. 22: Callbacks with clients.

a callback means that you are asked back to read again for (usually) the director and producer from the production company, as well as for the producer, art director, and writer representing the ad agency (fig. 22).

WHEN YOU CAN EXPECT TO BE INFORMED IF YOU GOT THE JOB

Usually, you will know within a week or two after the first casting session if you got a callback. Generally, the auditions are completed within four to five days, with callbacks taking place the following week, but this varies considerably. There are times when callbacks are within one or two days later.

Two to three days after the callbacks, there is a preproduction meeting at which the choice of talent is shown to the client for approval. The shoot is generally scheduled approximately three days to a week later. But nothing in this business is carved in stone—you could conceivably get a call to shoot the next day.

Seven Elements That Give You the Competitive Edge

Now that you know how the auditioning process works, consider these seven ways to make sure you come out on top:

- KNOW COMMERCIAL TECHNIQUE. Know how to analyze the script quickly and make you and the situation you create in the audition seem one hundred percent real and honest. (Chapter 10 sets out specific techniques for auditioning.)

- MAINTAIN A POSITIVE ATTITUDE. It's not always easy to keep a positive attitude when you walk into a waiting room full of people who look a lot like you and may have more experience. Keep in mind that the casting director needs you—you make her look good. She is expecting you to do a good job because she has either seen you in a show or was impressed by your picture and résumé, or your agent has convinced her that you would do a good job.

Your agent needs you too. He only makes money when and if you book the job. The creative team wants you to do a good job because they want a wide selection of strong talent to choose from. It's like a puzzle, and you are the missing part that brings it all together.

Just by getting the audition, you've already passed a screening process. You've been given this time slot over many, many other people.

So stay positive throughout the audition, even when the unexpected happens.

- **ALWAYS EXPECT THE UNEXPECTED.** Things do not always go as planned in this business. Being able to go with the flow is a crucial trait successful actors cultivate. For instance, you may worry when you see the crowded reception area. Chances are the casting director has set up the audition to run smoothly (not to be overcrowded), but some unplanned event has caused a backup. For example, the casting director may have been asked to bring people in four at a time, then on the day of the audition, the creative team decide to see people two at a time. This will cause a backup. Or, the first group of actors to be auditioned is late, causing a backup.

  Sometimes a backup is unavoidable. The casting director may get a call from the ad agency or production company informing them that the script has changed, or there may be technical difficulties. It is important not to let such happenings affect your attitude. At any audition, you should always seem pleased to be there, from the moment you walk into the room until after you have left the site.

  Also, if you sense any negative vibrations in the audition room, focus on the fact that you are not the cause. It could be that the art director and the producer are disagreeing about something creative, or they just got word from their location scout that they lost their favorite location for the shoot, or any number of concerns. Don't assume that it has anything to do with you.

  You may find it difficult to keep a positive attitude when you find out how quickly the auditioning process goes. You wish you had more time. Realize that what is asked of you in the auditioning room is all that is needed of you. Don't make yourself crazy trying to analyze your performance after you leave the audition. Just give it your best, then go on to the next thing.

- **ALWAYS EXPECT TO BE PUT AT A DISADVANTAGE.** Be prepared for such things as the session being canceled. Maybe the character you came in for has been changed. The cue card may be difficult to read. Props that could make it easier for you to audition may not be supplied to you. Do your best to take each situation as it comes without getting visibly discouraged or frustrated. It's all part of being professional in this industry.

■ **Be flexible.** Be open to change and direction. For example, you've figured out how you're going to do your copy. You get into the room and the casting director gives you an entirely different set of directions. You must be flexible and say, "Okay."

If you aren't flexible, when things change, you'll become frustrated and will not be able to give a good audition. Avoid showing frustration and *never* show anger. Do not present yourself in a negative light.

■ **Convey the feeling that you are intelligent.** Being knowledge-able about the business and knowing commercial technique lets the creative team know that you are an intelligent professional and serious about your career.

■ **Give the feeling that you have an unending well of creativity.** Leave the creative team with the impression that you have much more to give, even after the camera has stopped rolling.

10.

The Technique

Getting Started

ENTERING THE AUDITION ROOM

It is important to realize that you are essentially auditioning from the moment you enter the room. Since commercials are basically playful and upbeat, you should walk into the audition room with a positive, happy energy. You must be comfortable enough to smile confidently.

With film or television auditions, you usually get about ten or fifteen minutes for your audition. You come into the audition room, chat with the casting director, then get into the mood and read one to four pages of copy. In commercial auditions, the pace is much faster. Your auditioning time slot is only about five minutes, depending on whether or not there is copy and how much copy is involved. There is no time to waste. Be ready as soon as you enter the doorway. You must be comfortable enough to smile confidently. You say your hellos (no handshakes) and walk to your mark ready and eager to receive your direction.

If you are auditioning with other people, you want to appear comfortable with them right off the bat. Doing so will create a favorable impression with the person directing you, setting the mood for a positive auditioning experience. You also should appear enthusiastic and delighted to be there—and why wouldn't you be? This is the moment you've been waiting for, the chance to audition for a commercial spot!

To win at the commercial game, you have to *be* the character one-hundred percent. You want to feel as though you are experiencing (or re-experiencing) the situation and avoid appearing "removed." You *must* look completely involved and connected to each commercial scenario. In order to achieve this, the first thing you must be familiar with is the space you are given to work with.

COMMERCIAL SPACE

You have a certain amount of space to work with in front of the camera. It is very different from space used in film, theater, sitcoms, and soap operas. Most beginners automatically assume that the physical space they have to work with is fairly small. It *certainly* is smaller than the space available to you in the other media. But there is a way to expand the space and play in it.

The commercial space is like a sandbox. Its parameters seem small, but you can really play in it. You can bring a friend into it. You can make sandcastles and mud pies. You can throw sand out of the sandbox or up into the air. You can run into the corners, dig holes and tunnels, and jump up and down in your sandbox. All of a sudden, what you thought was a relatively small space doesn't seem so small after all. There isn't much room to walk around, but there is plenty of space to play and to release and reveal your personality.

The following exercises will help you see how you can expand the space you are given and give your performance more dimensions. Have a friend or family member tape your practice sessions with a video camera so you can review your performance afterward.

EXERCISE 1

Pretend you are reaching for something on a table. Try doing it two ways: First, stand firmly in place, extend your arm, and pick something up from the table. This shows one dimension.

Now, reach for something on the table by putting one leg in front of the other and tilting forward. This gives the feeling that you have just walked over from somewhere else and have not quite finished getting to where you are going. You are still "in frame" (visible on the monitor) and have given the space more dimension by this forward movement.

While you are giving this small space more dimensions, you are building in time beats for yourself—giving yourself opportunities to express your personality. This is important since what the client is buying is your personality. There's only one way to give yourself time and that is to be familiar with the space. Giving the space different dimensions helps you gain the edge needed to win in commercials.

EXERCISE 2

While on-camera, try looking over to your side. As you'll see when you look at the playback, you have given the viewer the impression that you are looking over at something. You have now expanded the space to another dimension simply by looking slightly off-camera.

Now, record yourself looking off-camera and laughing at what you see. Playback and see how your mind conjures up images of what might be going on. Record yourself looking off to the side and appearing curious about what you see. Play this back and see how the viewer might be affected by your performance.

To effectively expand the space, you must really "see" what you are imagining. To do this, you must go into great detail as you imagine each scenario.

BODY LANGUAGE

Try leaning forward and saying something to the camera. See how leaning in implies closeness, creating a sense of intimacy with the viewer. The slightest body tilt can change a relationship on-camera.

EXERCISE 3

Work with a friend. Stand next to each other with your bodies facing straight forward toward the camera. Look at the camera, then look at each other. Now, look back into the camera. Because your bodies are facing the camera, your primary relationship is with the viewer.

Turn your bodies in slightly toward each other and look at each other. Your primary relationship is now with each other.

Keep your bodies facing slightly towards each other and turn your faces to the camera. Now, the viewer is your secondary relationship.

Turn your bodies straight toward the camera again. Once again, your primary relationship is with the viewer and your secondary relationship is with each other.

It's important to know how your body position can affect your relationship to the camera (the viewer) because you can use it to enhance your performance. You have control. You can make certain choices.

Now, stand together and nudge each other with your elbows. Something else happened to the relationship—a sense of mischief or fun, perhaps. The slightest movement can mean something different. In some ways, commercial space is microscopic and unforgiving. Everything you do in this space is important to the message you are conveying.

In the Audition Room

TAKING YOUR MARK

There will be a mark (usually a piece of tape) on the floor for you to stand on (fig. 20). This is called *taking your mark*. Ultimately, you will learn to take your mark, then immediately create a specific sense of place and dimension to your personality. The previous exercises will enable you to do that. Your mark will place you in the position for the best lighting and camera focus during the audition.

WORKING WITH CUE CARDS

In any unionized state, a *cue card* is required by SAG. A cue card is the script written out on a large sheet of paper in large print (fig. 21). The cue card should be placed so that it is easy to read while looking into the lens of the camera. This makes it easier for your eyes to sweep across the cue card while looking (often) into the camera.

Sometimes a cue card is placed in a position that puts you at a disadvantage during the audition. If, for instance, someone places the cue card underneath the camera lens, you will have to look down at the cue card, then up at the camera, then down again at the card, etc. Reading a card that is placed next to the camera lens is much easier. The slight back-and-forth motion of your eyes as you read the cue card and look back to the eye of the camera is acceptable and expected. Usually care is taken to place the cue card in a position to make it easiest for the actor to see and make eye contact with the camera. If the cue card is placed much too far away from the camera lens and you see it can be easily moved (if it's on an easel, for example), you may ask for it to be moved. Be aware, however, that your request may or may not be received favorably, especially if the casting director is pressed for time.

The cue card stand would really have to be very far away from the camera to ask this. It is not your job to go in and arrange the room to suit your needs. An example of a time you might understandably ask for the cue card to be moved closer is if you wear glasses, but forgot them. We are all human and sometimes forget to bring everything we need with us, but it is best if you try never to forget something as important as your glasses, especially when going to an audition. Think of the cue card as your friend. You can emote expression toward the cue card as opposed to searching in your memory bank and your eyes looking blank.

As soon as you enter the audition room, look over the cue card. Make sure you can read the handwriting. Look for any changes in the script. A word may have been changed. Being comfortable with the cue card will make it easier to move your eyes smoothly from the cue card to the eye of the camera. Try to look at the camera as much as possible.

Here's what you can do to practice:

EXERCISE 4

On a large piece of paper (a 26½-inch x 34-inch artist's pad, for instance), write down copy taken from a magazine ad. On a separate piece of paper, draw a circle approximately the size of a camera lens and place it next to the copy. Position both sheets of paper at eye level on a wall in front of you. This will simulate cue card copy and the lens of the camera. Practice moving your eyes from the copy to the lens (eye of the camera).

MEMORIZING COPY

If you are auditioning in New York, Chicago, or Los Angeles (where cue cards must be provided under SAG rule), it is best not to waste energy trying to memorize your script. If you memorize the script and words are changed on the cue card, it could throw you off.

Another problem can surface if you haven't completely memorized the material and your eyes go blank as you try to remember the words. The cue card is there so you don't have to be concerned with remembering the script. Your energy can best be put to use preparing your character, analyzing the script, and making your performance as real as possible.

RELATING TO THE CAMERA

Think of a laser beam running from your eye to the center of the camera lens, into the back of the television monitor, and out through the monitor to the person viewing the tape.

The way for you to relate to the camera is to look directly into the "eye" or center of the lens. Relate to the camera the way you would to a long-cherished friend. You want to come across as open, friendly, and approachable. It's easier to avoid being intimidated by the camera if you pretend it's someone or something you feel warm, friendly, and familiar with. The camera is no longer a cold, intimidating piece of plastic and metal—it's your very best pal, your favorite aunt, someone you like very much—someone who likes you too. Make the camera someone you can be vulnerable with, someone you can let your personality out to.

Unless otherwise indicated, talk to the camera as if you are talking to one person. Keep in mind that if you have a background in theater and stage, you may (at first) tend to be too "big," projecting your character and lines the way you would on stage when you are performing for a theater full of people.

In commercials, you need to have a one-to-one relationship with the camera, as when you are talking with someone who is right next to you.

HOW YOU ARE "FRAMED" (HOW YOU LOOK IN THE CAMERA)

For auditions, assume that you are framed from the mid-chest up or waist up. Never ask, "How am I framed?" You do not have to be concerned with the technical aspects of the audition. You should be acting from head to toe, no matter how you are framed.

If, for instance, you are supposed to appear tired, not only should your face look fatigued, your body language should say, "I'm pooped" as well. Your responsibility is to act properly within the context of your mark.

Generally, the person directing you will be standing somewhere near the camera. The monitor will be facing him. He can either look and talk directly to you, or he can look at the monitor while talking to you. The director usually looks at the monitor because things look different on the monitor than they do to the naked eye. Viewing the monitor is the same as viewing the playback auditions.

Before the camera starts rolling, if the director is speaking to you and relating to you by looking at the monitor, the way to relate (or look) back at him is to look directly into the eye of the camera. If the director is looking at you while speaking to you, look at him when you speak to him. However, as soon as the camera starts rolling, begin relating to the camera.

When the camera is rolling and someone is interviewing you from off-camera, ask the director if you should respond by looking directly into the camera or off-camera. Usually, the answer will be into the camera. It's okay to ask, just to be sure.

In two-person auditions, the person running the camera wants to frame you so that both faces can be seen clearly with the shoulder and chest areas visible as well. The chest area indicates the energy of the whole body. In commercials, body language is important. The following exercise will help prepare you for two-person auditions.

EXERCISE 5

Stand about four feet from a friend. Notice that on the monitor you appear to be much farther apart. You appear unfriendly.

Now stand close together, facing the camera with your arms slightly brushing. Generally, this position might feel a bit too close for comfort (perhaps even a bit intrusive). On the monitor, however, you look comfortably close and friendly.

REHEARSING AND TAKING DIRECTION

Usually you will get a chance to rehearse before the camera starts rolling. Rehearse out loud the same way you plan to do the commercial for the camera. That way, the person directing you can give you any adjustments or notes (changes in the way the material is to be presented).

As an actor, it is important that you be open and willing to take direction. Do not comment on or critique any direction you may be given. Be accommodating when you are given adjustments, maintaining your positive attitude the entire time you are in the audition room. Being able to take direction is very important. Be careful that your nerves are not interfering with your listening abilities.

You should be like a piece of putty, molding yourself to the director's instructions. After you do what is asked of you, you may suggest doing it again with an idea you have.

In some cases, you might not get a rehearsal because something totally spontaneous is wanted from you. If this happens, just try to relax and give it your best shot.

SLATING YOUR NAME

The first thing you'll be asked to do after the camera begins rolling is to slate your name. This means to say your name (first and last). During the slate, you should be smiling and looking very pleased to be there. Your personality should already be radiating energy, flowing right up through your body and out to the viewer.

When you slate, look right into the eye of the camera and speak clearly with an upbeat, positive attitude. After you say your name, maintain your smiling, happy persona for a solid beat (moment) while continuing eye contact with the lens.

Staying with the camera a beat or so after slating gives you a moment to collect your thoughts before you begin to deliver the script. It also gives the viewer a chance to hear and register your name and face.

Good Slate. A good slate involves keeping solid eye contact with the camera before, during, and after the slate. It means maintaining a consistent, upbeat attitude. Basically, what you're saying as you slate is, "I'm really pleased to be here."

Bad Slate. One way to get a bad slate is to let your eye dart over to the side. This makes you look nervous, not confident. Another way is to allow your eyes to look down toward the floor and back up. This looks as if you are insecure and don't know how to use the camera.

If you are slating with another person, the second person should wait a full beat before saying his or her name. In a two-person shot, sometimes the person directing you might point to you when it's your turn to slate. Sometimes, on a tighter shot, you'll notice that the camera will be on the first person slating, then move over to the second person.

Here's what you can do to improve your slating technique:

EXERCISE 6

Practice slating in front of the camera. While you are saying your name, dart your eyes off to the side (off-camera). As you watch playback, notice how distracting you look when you do this. If you were to say hello to a friend, then dart your eyes away, it would appear to your friend that you were hiding something or that you were distracted. This is exactly what happens if you dart your eyes off to the side while slating.

TRUTH IN THE EYES

The eyes are very important in this medium. They can make you come across as truthful and trustworthy—a must in commercials. To do this, create active, detailed visuals that give the effect that you are actually seeing something.

EXERCISE 7

Practice looking blankly into the camera, then create a visual that represents something delicious to look at. See every detail of the visual you choose. When watching playback, notice the difference in your eyes when you give yourself an effective visual. Truth in the eyes can give you the competitive edge, making the difference between booking and not booking the job.

VISUALIZING AND REACTING

Your reaction allows you to show your specific, individual attitude and personality. You want to create opportunities for yourself to show attitudes. One way is by reacting to something after you look at it.

Remember to *look . . . see . . . react . . .* whenever you are given the opportunity to visualize something. It is not enough just to *look.* Actually *see* what you are looking at. You do this by using the sensory and visual exercises presented in this section. Then it's time to *react.*

EXERCISE 8

Imagine you're looking at a dog licking a baby's face. See the baby in vivid detail. See him laughing. See what he looks like, what he is wearing, etc. See him sitting on the carpet. Notice the color of the carpet. See the puppy in complete detail. Finally, see the puppy licking the baby's face. React. Chances are, after giving yourself visuals like these, you will be smiling and reacting with certain facial expressions. These reactions let special traits—your unique personality—come out.

Don't be afraid to take the time to really *look* at the visuals you've created. Some people don't take enough time to really *indulge* in that beat. You must allow yourself to get into the moment and really experience it. You want to expand the space you are given. Give it dimension and apply your personality.

It is very important to create visuals for yourself. No matter how much direction you receive from the script or the director, you must keep giving more and more information to yourself. *Sensory practice* involves pulling from memory the visuals and feelings you need to project in order to do an effective job with the script.

Sense memory exercises involve recalling sensations of touching, feeling, and smelling that are stored in the memory. When you recall them, you are recreating an exact experience of these sensations, rather than coming from a purely made-up mental image.

EXERCISE 9

Close your eyes. "See" a glass of water on the table. Sit in front of the glass of water. Create a situation in your mind that will make you feel very thirsty. Maybe you've just finished jogging in very hot weather. You can't wait to quench your thirst with a cool, refreshing drink of water. Now, open your eyes and "see" the water. Reach for it, drink it, and allow yourself to indulge in the feeling of satisfaction. Look, see, react.

Develop your ability to use visuals and sensory work to fine-tune your auditioning skills. Strive to get to a point where you feel you're actually there—jogging in the heat, seeing the puppy and the baby—whatever the scenario.

. Everything must seem honest. If you are miming reaching for a glass, your hand should look as if you are picking up the glass. Your arm should show intention (look like you want the water) and move toward the glass like you intend to pick it up. If you are picking up a piece of pizza, your hand should look like you are actually picking up and holding the pizza. You might even use the other hand to hold up the end of the slice to prevent the imaginary cheese from sliding off.

When picking up something small, like a tiny piece of chocolate, your hand and fingers should be positioned as they would be if you were really doing it. Practice on-camera reaching for many different objects, from very small pieces to larger, bulkier things.

EXERCISE 10

- *Think about sucking a lemon. Close your eyes. See the lemon being cut. Bring it to your mouth and suck on it. Feel your mouth start watering and puckering up from the tart sensation of the lemon juice hitting your taste buds.*

- *Open up a can of cat food. Really smell the odor of the cat food.*

- *Reach for a little piece of candy. Watch how your hand holds it. Think about the way the candy will taste when it gets to your mouth. Put the candy into your mouth and savor the rich, delicious flavor.*

- *The winning lottery numbers were just posted. Pick up your lottery ticket. Begin rubbing off the numbers, one by one. Feel the excitement build as you realize that each of your numbers matches one of the winning digits. React to the realization that you have just become a lottery millionaire!*

  Another way to do this exercise is to build up to the moment when there's only one number left (you have all the others). You rub off the last one (the excitement builds), then react to the disappointment of discovering that you did not win after all.

Analyzing the Script

Now that you are familiar with the camera and you have your sense memories warmed up, it's time to learn how to analyze a script (fig. 23). You need to come from someplace and end up someplace, so you are not performing in a void. You need to make particular choices, have particular intentions, and stay with your intentions.

Every script, every improv, every situation in a commercial audition is an opportunity to express your personality. Do not think of yourself as selling anything. The creative team is looking for a personality to help bring their vision to life. Your job is to let out your personality within a small working space and in a very short amount of time (fifteen, thirty, or sixty seconds).

First, you must understand how the agency uses the script to sell a product. The three main ways are through frustration, put-down, and humor. They are using you as a vehicle to help sell their product. You should use the script or improv as a vehicle for you to let out or apply your personality to the situation. Ask yourself, "Where are the opportunities within the script to show the creative team various aspects of my personality?"

Generally, the outline of a commercial's "story" using the frustration and put-down sell goes like this:

- *Some form of frustration and a problem to be solved are introduced.* Since commercials are generally light-hearted, any frustration shown has humor in it.[1] By adding humor to the situation, you become likable and approachable and the viewer will smile at you.

- *You discover a product.* Life becomes grand and your outlook is much brighter.

- *There is a statement about your discovery* and how it has changed your situation.

- *A put-down or jab is made toward the other competitive product.*

- *Your satisfaction with the product is restated.*

- *A final comment (called a button line) ties up the story.* This final statement provides an excellent opportunity for you to release your personality.

Fig. 23 shows an example of a very basic commercial script. Use the following steps to analyze this script.

- *Read the script over* to get familiar with the material.

- *Identify what you are selling.* In this case, the "product" is National Airlines. It is important to know that you are not expected to "sell" the product. The commercial script is designed to do the selling. All you have to do is let out your personality.

---

[1] As the character, you should choose frustration over anger. An angry person is not approachable or amusing. A frustrated person is approachable. We can laugh at and with a frustrated person. Commercials are like sitcoms in this way. People in sitcoms are frustrated, not angry. They are likeable, funny, and approachable, and we would be comfortable having them in our home. They are not a threat.

My vacation had a very dull beginning./Don't get me wrong,/
Florida's wonderful./But I came down on the airline with no
movies./2 ½ hours of looking out the window –/very boring./
I'm going back on National Airlines./The only airline with
movies in every cabin of every wide-bodied plane./Why be
bored on an airline with no movies/when you can say,
"National Airlines, take me. I'm yours!."

FIG. 23: How the script may look.

The *sell line* is the first line that mentions the product name. Underline this sentence—in this case, "I'm going back on National Airlines." This does not mean you are expected to hit it hard or to sell hard. Underlining the sell line just lets you see where the sell comes in.

Notice also the frustration that comes just before the sell. It builds so that when you introduce the discovery of the product, there is a sense of relief from your frustration. This sets up the sell. The delivery of the sell is relatively simple. You simply become delighted and brighter or have a feeling of conviction because you have discovered this wonderful product.

- *Find any specific "sell" information.* Don't fall into the trap. You will notice that there is not a lot of sell information in this script. The applicable line in this case is "The only airline with movies in every section of every wide-body plane." The sell information usually comes right after the introduction of the product. Put a box around this area so you can see it clearly. The trap is to lose your personality and start sounding like a spokesperson. Stay in your personality while saying the lines.

- *Find any put-down lines.* In this script, "Why be bored on an airline with no movies" is a direct put-down to those other inferior airlines. Sarcasm would be a good attitude to apply here.

- *Divide the script into "beats," or moments of emotional or attitude change.* Label each beat or attitude change with a slash mark (/).

You will want to show a lot of emotional changes within the context of the script. Think in terms of creating a woven piece of material. Each change of emotion or attitude represents weaving a different color into the material. In this case, the more colors, the prettier the end result. Although you want to make strong choices, it's more effective to make changes with smooth transitions. The arrows indicate emotional changes. Down arrows indicate frustration. Up arrows indicate feeling bright. Forward arrows are a cue to the actor to speak with more conviction. Double underlined words are to be "punched up" (with more personality). Markings are individual. Develop your own markings so that the script has meaning for you.

- *Divide the script into a beginning, a middle, and an end.* Doing so helps you realize that a basic script is not very long. Take it one step at a time. You'll notice that the beginning has only three lines, the middle has five, and the end only two. Tackle each section in the same way you would undertake skiing down a steep mountain. Instead of looking at the enormity of the task of getting to the bottom, break the mountain up into smaller sections, then proceed down one section at a time. Before long, you find that you have accomplished your goal with relative ease.

  Decide where you are physically. Remember to use active visuals, not passive ones. For example, an active visual would be running on a beach and feeling exhilarated. Just sitting on the beach and feeling nothing is passive. You want your audition to feel real—to be multidimensional. If you don't specifically come from someplace and go someplace, you are in a void.

  In this case you could choose the airline terminal. See what it looks like in great detail and hear the sounds.

- *Define your attitudes,* using very strong visuals. Create a very real situation for yourself. It should appear that you are either experiencing what is happening or that you are re-experiencing the situation.

  Make particular choices. Have specific intentions and stay with your intentions.

- *Establish relationships.* Know who (or what) you have a relationship with in the script. Give them (or it) a detailed history. Remember to stay playful (unless the script clearly calls for something different).

In this script, relationships are with (a) National Airlines, (b) the people you were with when you were in Florida, and (c) the person you are telling your experience to.

It is best to choose one particular person to speak to—someone you are extremely familiar with and with whom you can be loose and playful.

Remember that the creatives are looking for an opinionated person, a definite personality. If an idea comes to you that is not consistent with your personality, don't stop yourself. Use it. Be open to discovering and exposing the many layers of your personality.

The following are examples of active visuals that will help you prepare for attitude changes. The script has been broken down into beats.

My vacation had a very dull beginning/

The first line expresses a sense of frustration. Think about how you will create that sense of frustration within yourself. And even though you are frustrated, you must also give the viewer the sense that you are likeable and playful.

For instance, think about the way you would feel if you planned a vacation in Florida and it didn't go the way you had envisioned. You were going to surf in crystal-blue waters. You could actually *see* yourself riding the crest of the waves with the sun reflecting off your fabulously tanned body. This was your dream vacation and you couldn't wait to go, but when you actually got there, it *rained.* You found yourself in your hotel room with nothing to do. What a bummer.

Visualize the entire scenario. *Be* there. Coming from this visual, you can really say the line with frustration. You can *feel* the frustration.

Don't get me wrong/

Make your attitude a little brighter. You are coming out of frustration, relating directly to the viewer.

Florida's wonderful/

Your attitude is even brighter now. Visualize what you like about Florida—the huge waves and the beautiful, clear water.

But I came down on the airlines with no movies/

You're going back into a sense of frustration. Think of it raining. Sitting in the hotel. You are stuck inside. You have one week of vacation and it's *raining.*

2½ hours of looking out the window/

Now you're going deeper into frustration. Think of yourself sitting in the hotel room. Think of all the things that are going wrong. As you say the line, look three-quarters away from the camera as if you are looking out a window. *Look, see, react.* Then turn back to the camera and react with humorous boredom and frustration:

Very boring/

Your frustration is deepening. Your whole vacation is ruined. It's so bad, it's funny. Now, you're setting up the typical sell—frustration right before the discovery of the product that will make everything right again.

I'm going back on National Airlines/

This is your sell. This is brighter. You have your solution. You've made a discovery. Keep in mind that brighter doesn't mean louder or even "big" and happy. To hit hard on the sell line is old-fashioned. In this case, you can be empathetic, knowing, or enlightened.

To prepare your attitude, you might imagine that you are trying to book a flight to sunny Florida. You call one airline and get a recording— you can't get a human being to come to the phone. You call a different airline and are cut off in the middle of the call. A third attempt to yet another airline finds you put on hold indefinitely. Finally, you call National Airlines and a customer-service representative picks up the phone and helps you right away. Life becomes so much easier.

The only airline with movies on every section of every wide-body plane/

This statement reinforces the prior statement.

Why be bored on an airline with no movies when you can say . . . /

Here is the put-down. You are being condescending to the other airlines.

National Airlines, take me—I'm yours! (end)

This is the button line. You can make it coy, big, embarrassed, shy—whatever you want.

These techniques can be applied to almost any script. In short, when you're working through a script:

■ Find humor.

■ Use active visuals.

- Experience and re-experience the situation.
- Find visual references—*look, see, react.*
- Deliver the script as though you are talking to your best friend.

Don't beat yourself up if you didn't get every word right during the audition. Although you should try to get the words right, that's not what the audition is all about. You can make a mistake and still book the job. It will be obvious to the people selecting you that you are good, but your tongue got tied. You will probably be asked to do it again. Now, if you keep messing up again and again, you probably won't get booked. It would be obvious that you are unable to do what is asked.

Leaving the Audition Room

Be sure to leave the audition room the same way you walked in—looking confident, positive, and happy to have been asked to audition. Thank everyone for bringing you in and don't criticize yourself. You have performed; you let it out, now let it go. You've given a good audition. Now it's time to find out how the selection process works.

11.

The Selection Process

The Creative Team

It's time to meet the creative team and find out what part they play in the selection of talent for commercial work. It takes at least eight people to decide who gets the job. Here's who they are:

The producer is responsible for putting together and keeping together all the elements that make up the production of a commercial. These elements include budgeting, selecting the director, coordinating the decisions of all the people involved, and making sure the production is on schedule, including editing of the final spot.

The producer is one of the people on the team who actually has a say as to who will be booked. If a producer knows your work and requests that the casting director include you in the audition, the casting director will definitely do so. It is a big plus when a producer is familiar with your work.

The art director is the person who visually conceives the spot and makes it come alive through drawings and visuals. In short, he or she is responsible for the way the commercial will look. The art director works very closely with (or is part of the team with) the writer.

The writer puts the message of the commercial into words. The writer and art director have to be in total alignment as to the message they want to get across.

The creative supervisor oversees the activities of the art director, writer, and producer.

The creative director is responsible for the work of all creatives in the advertising agency, and thus sets the tone for the entire agency. (Various agencies are known to be "on the cutting edge," "hip," conservatives, etc.)

The director, of course, directs the spot. The director is hired for his creative input—his ability to enhance the spot. If a director has worked with you before and feels you are right for the project at hand, he will most likely make sure you are called in to audition. This gives you a chance to work with people who were previously unaware of your work. Many times, at the end of the creative selection process the director ultimately decides who will be presented to the client.

The account executives from the advertising agency serve as the liaison between the client and the agency. It is their ongoing responsibility to talk directly to the client. Their agreement that the client will probably "buy" the actor at the preproduction meeting is essential.

The client(s) are the executives who represent the product being advertised, be it Pepsi, Dell Computers, or Discover Card. All selections of talent are presented to them at a preproduction meeting and they have final approval. (The talent and the account executives are sometimes called "the suits.")

How the Talent Are Selected

The creative team collectively decides who would be best for the job, and the client makes the final decision (fig. 22). The casting director has very little to do with the actual selection process after the auditions are completed, although she might be asked to comment on a specific talent's acting ability and performance ability.[1]

Realize that the creative team is trying to be just that—creative, and turn out a nice piece of film. At the same time, they need to sell the product, meet legal specifications, and anticipate the client's tastes—knowing that, ultimately, it's the client they have to please. The client has to approve the final look and production of the spot as well as the actor(s).

---

[1] In film, television, and theater, the casting director is more actively involved in the selection process.

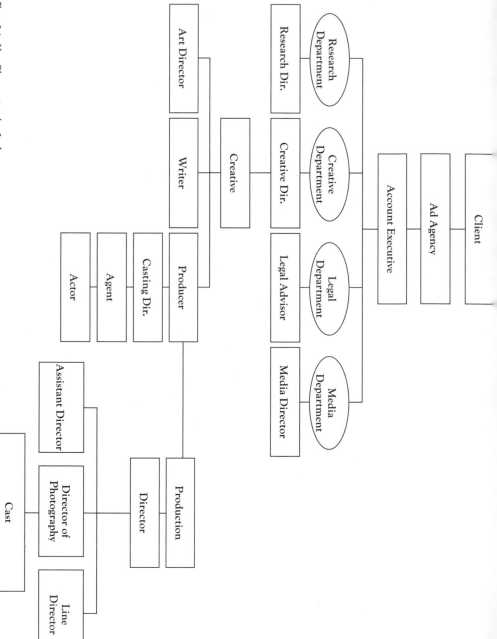

Fig. 24: Key Players in the Industry.

Always keep in mind that the decision-making process is very subjective. The writer, for instance, might think that your type of face is not the type that would be cleaning floors in the kitchen—that you would more likely be dressed up at a cocktail party. In his opinion, you look too upscale to be used in a commercial cleaning floors. The producer, however, might feel that your face *doesn't* look upscale. Or perhaps the producer may not want you simply because you look like his ex-wife. It happens.

All you can do as an actor is give a good audition. Once you've done that, it comes down to a "look" and people's subjective opinions. The final choice could come down to a "look" or it could come down to acting ability. But one thing you have control over is your ability to audition well, and this is the factor that will give you the competitive edge in the long run.

Many times, the way you are asked to audition has very little to do with how the final spot is done. You may be asked to do a broader range of emotions at the audition than when the spot is actually shot. The team needs to know that you are capable of handling whatever they throw at you. The day of the shoot is very demanding, so the creative team shies away from booking actors who are fairly one-dimensional. Thus it pays to expand your technique to show many dimensions.

Who Sees the Auditions During the Selection Process

After the audition, one copy of the audition is viewed by the creative team. A copy is also made or *dubbed*, and sent to the director to view. The selection process occurs and the actors are then called back.

The selection lists of the agency and director are generally compatible. It is possible, however, that if you weren't on the agency list but you *were* on the director's list, you will be called back. If the two lists are significantly different, the agency will realize that the director is envisioning the commercial in a way that is not consistent with theirs and will call the director to discuss his choices. The director will explain why he picked the actor. Generally, the agency will go with the director's choices, agreeing that the person should be called back.

Here's a scenario of how you might be eliminated from a callback list for reasons that have nothing to do with your performance: The agency and the director are going through their lists of actors selected for callbacks. The director is interested in seven people whom the agency has shown no interest in. Both sides discuss six people, and then the agency gives in to the director on each person and agrees that each will get a shot at callbacks.

Now they discuss the seventh person on the list (which just happens to be *you*) and the agency is beginning to feel that they are losing a bit of control. At this point, the agency argues against the seventh person (you), saying that they don't think you are right for the job.

Maybe the agency feels you're too quirky (different) for the spot. The director argues that the quirk is actually good for this particular job. The agency says they already have two actors for the spot who are quirky and would prefer that more of the people called back be more conservative. The agency argues strongly, expressing an interest in gaining more control. Ultimately, the director "gives you up" because he already got most of the people he wanted for the callback.

The Callbacks

All callback choices are auditioned again. The director is there to direct the actors. The writer, art director, and producer are also there to experience the actors' performances. They want to see how well each actor takes direction, to envision how the actor fits into the original concept, and to see what the actor brings to the concept. Final choices are made. Following is an example:

The commercial involves a family consisting of a mom, a dad, and two teenaged daughters. Polaroids of each actor are laid out on a table as a quick visual reference. The two daughters tentatively chosen are blond cheerleader types. Next to those two choices are two alternate teenaged daughters. One is blond, the other is brunette and "edgier" than the blondes. The art director says, "Look what happens if we replace one blond teenager with the brunette." Because of the differences created by the alternate daughter, the family dynamics have changed. The team decides this combination of teenaged daughters is more interesting, so the brunette gets booked instead of the second blond.

The decision was not based on the actress's performance. All performances were good. The final selection came down to a viewpoint concerning the feeling the creative team wanted to project with the look of the family.

Selected callbacks are sent back to the ad agency for approval before presenting to the client. At the end of the callback, the number one choices for each character are edited on a DVD or streaming video and sent back to the ad agency for final approval by the creative supervisor, creative director, and the account executive.

Presenting the Callbacks to the Client

Finally, the preproduction meeting takes place, with as many as twenty-two people present. Every aspect of the production day is discussed, including the final selections of talent for the commercial. The creative team presents their first choice of actors to the client, showing the callback on a monitor. With luck, the client nods and the producer calls the casting director, giving the okay to book the talent. All personalities involved in the selection process are satisfied. Whew! What a feat.

Time Between the Final Selection of Talent and the Shoot

Casting is the last element to fill before the shoot. Usually, casting begins the week before the actual shoot date. Callbacks could be two days after the first call and the shoot three days after the callbacks. However, there are no rules. Many times the shoot will be the day after the callback. If there are multiple spots with many characters to cast, the time between your first call and the callback could be a week or two.

Understanding the History of a Commercial

As an actor, you must realize that each commercial has a "history" that the creatives help to develop. The history might consist of where the family in the commercial comes from, as well as their interests, relationships, and economic state. The type of furniture the family would own (including the type of fabric) is indicated, along with the type of clothing each family member would wear, and how they relate to one another.

It is amazing how effective commercials can be, especially since they are only fifteen seconds to one minute long. In that short span of time, a commercial can create a myriad of emotions—sadness, envy, joy, humor, and curiosity.

In many ways, the commercial is the ultimate form of storytelling. In extremely short form, we meet characters, identify with their struggle, then watch them change and grow in a narrative complete with introduction, climax, and resolution—all in thirty seconds. Moreover, the advertiser accomplishes the task of showing us that, like the characters in the story, we too can solve our dilemmas by purchasing the product.

Now that you are familiar with the people who create, direct, and produce commercials and have an understanding of how talent is selected, it's time to give you a more extensive look at what to expect concerning callbacks, bookings, and commercial shoots.

12.

The Callback, the Booking, the Shoot

The Callback

Congratulations! You have given an impressive audition and the creative team has called you back to have another look.

Callbacks may consist of as many as ten to twenty people per character. The good news is there are more opportunities to get called back. The bad news is there is more competition.

Keep a positive attitude. Keep feeling special. You *did* get called back. Now the selection process begins again, and the same subjectiveness applies as in the auditions.

INFORMATION YOU SHOULD BE GIVEN WHEN YOU GET THE CALLBACK

When you get the phone call to notify you of a callback, you should receive the following information. If you don't, *ask*.

WHEN AND WHERE THE AUDITION IS BEING HELD: If you do not know how to get there, ask for directions or get the zip code, go to your computer, and log on to the Map Quest website (www.mapquest.com). You don't want to be late. It's a good idea to get the phone number of the place you're going to so if you *do* get lost, you can call to get instructions.

THE SHOOT DATES: You might be put on *avail* (availability) or *first refusal* for the shoot dates, travel days, and weather days.[1] An avail or first refusal is a handshake agreement between an actor, agent, and casting director by which the actor guarantees that the client will have first option on his time on the specific dates set aside for the commercial shoot.[2] This way, when the creative team sells the actor to the client at the preproduction meeting, and the client says yes, the casting director can book the actor with every confidence that the actor will be available and will accept the booking.

If another client wants to book the actor for the time of the avail or first refusal, the agent has to go to the casting director who has the actor on avail or first refusal. The casting director then goes to the client, giving him first choice of either booking the actor or releasing him. If the client releases the actor, the actor is then free to accept the other booking.

WHAT TO WEAR TO THE CALLBACKS: You do not have to wear the same clothes as when you first auditioned, even if the wardrobe description is the same as for the first call. If, for instance, the first call was casual and so is the second, you would still wear casual clothes, but you could wear a different outfit. Of course, if you are asked to wear the same thing you wore for the first audition, do so.

Sometimes, however, the situation changes. For example, the creatives might have chosen you for a different character from the one you first auditioned for. You could be asked to dress differently.

HOW THE SPOT RUNS (IS AIRED):[3] You should have been told at the original audition how the spot was running. At this point, the information should be reiterated. You might hear terms such as *national, network, spot, dealer, cable, seasonal, regional,* and *Internet* (see Chapter 13).

TYPE OF CONTRACT: You might also hear that a *standard contract* is desired by the client. This means the contract remains as written with nothing crossed off the back. On the back of your contract (in small print), there is a section that gives the client the right of use for theatrical (movie theaters), foreign, and cable usage as scale payment. This is a very acceptable practice and should not create a problem for the actor.

---

[1] If it is an outdoor shoot, you can expect to be put on avail for a "weather day." This means if the shoot is rained out (or if any kind of bad weather occurs to delay the shoot), you have reserved the day specified to reschedule the shoot. There are also rules pertaining to payment for such a day depending on how many hours in advance the shoot is canceled due to weather. These rules can be found in a SAG guidebook or by calling your local union office and/or your agent.

[2] In New York, the procedure is referred to as first refusal; in Los Angeles, avail.

[3] The places it runs are also referred to as markets, the places the spots will be shown on the air.

MONEYS AND PAYMENTS INVOLVED: If there are moneys involved other than scale (basic union fees), this is a good time to confirm the amount to avoid possible misunderstandings at the time of booking or at the shoot, when you are signing your contract.

There are, for example, situations in which monies are guaranteed per *cycle* for the actor. A cycle is thirteen weeks. This means that the actor would receive an agree-upon amount of money (guaranteed) every thirteen weeks. For more on talent payment, see Chapter 13.

CONFLICTS: The actor cannot be under contract for a conflicting product.

WHO WILL BE AT THE CALLBACK

Part or all of the creative team will be at the callback to direct and observe the actor. Among the people who might be present are the *producer* from the ad agency, the *writer*, the *art director*, the *director from the production company*, and the *production company producer*.

It is common to have at least five people watching you audition at the callback. The person who will actually be directing the shoot will most likely direct during the callback. This gives the director the opportunity to see how flexible you are and to see if you and he can get along well. It also gives the director a chance to see how his concept of the direction is actually going. It's unlikely that he'll go heavily into this at the callback, but he will get a sense of what is (or is not) working.

Many times, the director will pick something unique to your personality from your performance and build on that with you. Something special in your audition that sparks interest from the director could be the deciding factor in whether or not you get booked.

HOW YOU SHOULD CONDUCT YOURSELF AT THE CALLBACK

As always, it is important to be on time for the callback. Your appointment was scheduled specifically for the director to have a certain amount of time to work with you (and another person if you are paired up with someone for the audition).

You will be escorted into the room by the casting director or the session runner and be shown where to stand to take your mark. Do not approach the creatives in the room and shake each person's hand and introduce yourself. Go to your mark, say hello if the creatives are paying attention to you, smile, be open, and wait for your direction. Many times the creative team pays no attention to you until they are ready to watch your audition. Many times, the director will have the casting director direct you and, after your first performance, will then get involved in communicating with you. It is important to take direction, be flexible, and amiable. Give a good audition, say your goodbyes (don't go up to anyone and shake their hands), then leave the room with a positive attitude.

WHAT THE CREATIVES ARE LOOKING FOR

What is the purpose of a callback? It's another chance to see how actors perform. Naturally, something in your performance may be slightly different from the first time. Callbacks give the creative team time to work with actors to see how flexible they are and how broad a range they have. If there are two or more actors in the commercial, the creatives can observe the chemistry (or lack thereof) between them. They can see if there is something special and very personal the actor brings to the performance, and they can watch the actor apply new ideas that the team may have come up with since the first call.

The team gets to determine how much they like the actor personally. Would *they* feel comfortable working with the actor all day? Is the actor cooperative? Do the actor's eyes have life and sparkle? Does the actor seem intelligent? Does he seem to understand the script? Does she appear natural and genuine?

Don't put pressure on yourself to do anything particularly different. Remember, if you understand the script and the circumstances of the spot you're appearing in, and know your technique, your focus will be on being the character in the scene. As with real life, something a little different might happen—perhaps a slightly different inflection in the voice, a slightly different attitude, or a slightly different movement. You are not expected to be exactly the same as the first audition. So just be yourself and *do* be spontaneous at the callback.

If the situation calls for two or more people to work together, you might be mixed and matched. You may be called into the audition room with one person, then asked to wait and come back in the room with another person. Take notice of how your energies and chemistry change with different people.

Sometimes what you are doing will work better with one person than the other. This is normal and expected. If you are called in with someone you do not work well with, it doesn't create the best possible experience. But is also does not mean you won't get booked. If you are doing well and the other person is not good for the spot, the creatives can see it.

Many times, one person is booked and the other is not. No matter what occurs, keep doing your best at the audition. Don't play into the negative energies (or the bad choices) of the other person. Work with the person as much as possible without bringing yourself down. In fact, within the scenario, try to bring the other person's performance up to par.

The Booking

HOW MUCH TIME ELAPSES BETWEEN
THE CALLBACK AND THE SHOOT

It can take anywhere from one day to two weeks from the callback to the booking, but there are unending variables. In a standard situation, the creative team at the callback will make their selections, then present you at a preproduction meeting approximately three days later. Final approval is left to the client (the executives who represent the product). The ad-agency producer quickly calls the casting director after the meeting and informs her of who should be booked. The casting director quickly calls the agent and books the talent. No time is wasted; the sooner the casting director gets the actor off of avail or first refusal and booked, there is less chance of losing the actor to another booking.

INFORMATION YOU SHOULD BE GIVEN WHEN YOU ARE BOOKED

The actual booking call consists of the time, date, wardrobe fitting (if applicable), and the location you should report to. An actor is not allowed to be called by wardrobe until he is booked. The terms of agreement and conflicts (if there are any) should be gone over too.

WARDROBE

After the official booking call, the wardrobe person (or stylist) will contact the actor and set up an appointment for the actor to be wardrobed. The stylist already has the actor's sizes from the size card filled out at the audition. Several different outfits will be tried on the actor at the fitting. Usually the fitting takes an hour. According to the SAG contract, the actor is paid for a wardrobe fitting. If you are asked to bring and wear your own clothing to a shoot, you are compensated for doing so. If you are booked for a nonunion commercial, you could very well not be paid for a wardrobe fitting, or you could likely be asked to bring your own clothing to the shoot. Remember, your rights to payment for services are protected more under the SAG or AFTRA contract.

The Shoot

WHAT IS EXPECTED FROM ACTORS ON THE SET

An actor must have an understanding of the script. He must appear genuine and natural. Sometimes an actor is chosen because she interpreted the script better than anyone else.

When you arrive on the set, you might find you have been made the core of the scene and the cast will have been built around you. The creative team will have the actors spend a lot of time together on the day of the shoot before they actually start rolling the camera to see what might happen between them. They might then use this relationship for the commercial.

Actors must be cooperative, prepared to listen, and take direction well. You should come to the shoot with a sense of involvement and energy.

An actor should be aware of the totality of the spot, not just what their little piece involves. You need to know what you are trying to convey and whom the client is selling to. Actors should have their lines memorized beforehand. It's up to the agency producer to get the material to the actor ahead of time so they can memorize it. The script might be given to you at the wardrobe call.

Flexibility is important. Actors must be prepared to make adjustments in their interpretation of the script. In situations where the actor was hired because of his creativity, there will be times your unique spin on the situation will be welcomed.

There are two main ingredients in a successful spot—the finest director and the best talent you can get. The spot is nothing if you have a great director and poor talent (or vice versa).

WHAT GOES INTO THE PREPARATION FOR A COMMERCIAL SHOOT

The creative team does a lot of preparation before the shoot. The ad agency draws up a storyboard, then gives it to the director for his interpretation. Next, a shooting board is drawn up, which is a tightly scripted, tightly drawn board laying out all the shots for the commercial. This is done after considering the input of the clients, the agencies, the account executives, and the director.

The creative team, with the director, blocks out the shots with a more precise interpretation. There are hours and hours of meetings regarding locations, props, and how to shoot the commercial while capturing a theme. Nothing is left to chance. The team also discusses the types of plates, food, clothing, and other props they are going to use. The director will make up the shooting board based on all these elements.

WHAT IS THE USUAL LOCATION OF THE SHOOT

Actors can be called *anywhere* to shoot. Travel arrangements will be made with their agents. Be on time. If, for instance, you will be traveling by van with the production company and the departing time is 7:30, don't get there at 7:35. Time is crucial on a commercial shoot.

There are times you will have to travel to a shoot out of town. Travel arrangements to fly to a location are made between you and the producer. Under the SAG and AFTRA union contract, you will be compensated for airfare and travel to and from the airport by the production company.

WHAT HAPPENS THE DAY OF THE SHOOT

On the day of the shoot, dozens of people are present: the director, producer, copywriter, art director, film/shooting crew, makeup person, stylist, script supervisor (who is responsible for accuracy in keeping with the scripted words), and the clients. Expect to see up to six of the client's people on the site, including marketing managers or product managers.

Remember, the client is an ally; all of his needs should be met. Monitors are set up off to the side so that everyone can watch the monitor instead of standing around and watching the actor. This helps sharpen the team's eye for what is seen on the TV screen.

WHAT HAPPENS WHEN THE ACTORS FIRST GET ON THE SET

The producer usually introduces himself to the actors first. The agency producer or the second AD (assistant director) will give the SAG contract to the talent at the beginning of the day. This will confirm the start of a particular job. Then, a photo is taken of the actors in their wardrobes so the team can refer to it later on.

WHAT IS EXPECTED OF ACTORS IN TERMS OF THE CONTRACT

The contract is given to the actors to be signed. They should be aware of the provisions beforehand, including how the commercial is supposed to run. All this information has been given to their agent.

Occasionally, the contract could look different from what the casting director discussed with the agent. In this case, the first thing an actor should remember is to maintain a professional demeanor, to call the agent, and to explain the situation. The differences are then worked out by the agent and the producer.

AT WHAT POINT THE PRODUCT IS INTRODUCED TO THE ACTORS

The actors should be familiar with the product being used so that when it is put into their hands, it is not foreign to them. They should be asked at wardrobe whether they have worked with the product—for example, a particular type of razor. If not, they are given the product to become familiar with before the day of the shoot.

A technical advisor will be on the set. If the product is gum, the actor will learn how to load[4] and chew gum; if it's a soft-drink spot, she'll learn how to swallow and use the product in the correct way.

THINGS ACTORS SHOULD AVOID WHILE ON THE SET

First of all, when there is down time, the actors should observe what is going on, staying within the confines of the set and developing some camaraderie. The worst thing that can happen is for an actor not to be accessible because he is on the phone or out eating somewhere. Actors should let the assistant director and the agency producer know where they are at all times. If a shot comes up and an actor is not around, it creates a problem. Also, no family members, pals, or kids should visit the set. In short, the actor should always be there and committed.

---

[4] A technical way to put gum into the mouth for a commercial.

Actors should be polite and courteous, relaxed and comfortable with everyone on the set. After all, they are the ones who are presenting the product. All the focus is on them.

Finally, actors should not ask for things on the set. Do not ask, for instance, if you can have the clothing you wore on the shoot. If someone offers to give something to you, that is different.

HOW LONG A COMMERCIAL TAKES TO SHOOT

There is no standard time; a shoot can run eight to sixteen hours a day. How the commercial is being shot is a primary consideration. Factors such as location shooting and special needs (like a sunrise or sunset) all affect shoot time. Consideration must also be taken for children (see Chapter 17: Kids in the Business).

There is also a union rule requiring a twelve-hour turnaround for the crew. This means that twelve hours must elapse from the time you wrap (end) until you can start again. This may result in a later call for the next day's shoot.

Usually, on a stage, you might have a crew call at 6:30 A.M. with the actors arriving at 7:30 to be put into wardrobe. The shoot might start at 8:30 or 9:00, once lighting is set. A shoot is over when it's over.

If the shoot goes beyond twelve hours, people begin to get tired and wear down. Sometimes, the shoot is scheduled to go into an additional day, but that is not always possible. The agency producer has the responsibility of keeping things going.

There is always a lot of waiting around on the sets. Different camera setups and shots are required, which result in a lot of down time for actors.

IS THE COMMERCIAL SHOT IN SEGMENTS?

An actor may shoot the spot from beginning to end in its entirety, or the commercial may be shot in segments. For example, the *master shots* (wide shots that show the entire scene) may require the same kind of lighting, in which case, the actor would be involved. Then the director might jump to a shot that would appear third or fourth in the commercial. All the close-up shots might be done at the same time because afterwards all lighting and lenses must be changed. It's pretty rare for a commercial to be shot from the beginning straight through to the end.

HOW MANY TAKES CAN AN ACTOR EXPECT?

Ad-agency creatives want several different interpretations of the commercial script because they have a lot of people to satisfy. A shoot may involve anywhere from a couple of takes to twenty or thirty. A good actor can endure many takes of specific direction. At some point, though, he hits his performance peak, then it goes in a different direction.

WHO DIRECTS THE ACTORS? DO THE ACTORS HAVE ANY INPUT?

The director has primary contact with the actors on the set. The director is the sole focal point—the sole voice that actors should be hearing. If someone on the set wants to request something from an actor, the request should go to the director.

Whether or not actors can give suggestions to the director during the shoot involves a lot of tact. There is no protocol on the set. Actors should let the director direct, *then* they may be allowed to offer other interpretations.

Actors should *not* tell the director that they don't like something or don't want to do it. An actor could possibly say, "How about this?" or "Can I try something?" Remember, the actor is hired for his uniqueness. Therefore, his interpretation might very well be welcome, especially in comedy.

13.

How Much Can I Make?

The commercial industry is one of the most lucrative in the business. Performers from all over the country have financed college educations, upgraded lifestyles, and catapulted themselves into other areas of the business as a result of working in commercials.

A long-running national commercial can net over $200,000. Even a small regional spot pays hundreds of dollars for single day's work. An actor was in a network commercial for Wrigley's that ran for three years, and he made $90,000. That's for a single day's work. This sort of thing happens a lot. More often than not, each commercial spot will make considerably less. Your commercial may not even run at all. The commercial could be shot, you get your shoot-day payment, and the commercial may not run at all.

Payment for commercial work is determined by factors such as:

- How often the commercial runs.
- Whether it runs locally, regionally, or nationally.
- Whether it is a union or nonunion commercial.

The nonunion agreements can buy you out in perpetuity or for a specified limited amount of time. When you sign an agreement for a nonunion commercial, you should be informed as to the time you are agreeing to allow your image to appear in the commercial being used.

If you are doing nonunion work in a smaller region, you get "bought out," which means you get paid a certain amount of money, and the client owns the spot and can play it as much as he wants. You don't get residuals (payments made to the talent every time the spot runs). Obviously, the potential earnings from this kind of commercial are limited.

With union commercials, however, there are payment rules and regulations that protect the talent. Professional "talent payment" people, whose job is to handle payments to actors, follow an elaborate system and are checked by tracking methods that make sure everything is handled correctly. The following is an extensive look at how performers are paid for work on television and radio commercials.[1]

Television

SESSION

When a commercial is filmed or taped, the performers are paid a session fee as compensation for an eight-hour day of work. The session fee also provides the advertiser with the right to use that commercial for thirteen weeks and prevents the actor from doing spots for competitive products for the same length of time. To maintain the rights to use the commercial and to "hold" the actor, the actor is paid an additional holding fee every thirteen weeks (see Holding Fees/Exclusivity below).

A session fee for an on-camera performer is $535.00 for an eight-hour day.

A session fee for a TV off-camera performer is $402.25.

Performers receive a session fee for each commercial produced or each day of work, whichever is greater. For example, if five commercials are recorded in a two-hour session, five session fees must be paid. Session fees are usually fully creditable against reuse fees.[2] "Special provisions" cover any agreed upon details that do not appear in the standard contract. These include money above scale and special travel arrangements.

EXTRAS: Extras are paid a single fee, or *buyout*, entitling the advertiser to the use of that extra in the commercial for its broadcast life. In other words, extras do not receive residuals.

---

[1] Payments cited here are based on statistics available at the time of publication.

[2] Reuse fees are paid every time the commercial runs (airs) or is used again after the initial run (airing).

A session fee for an extra performer is $291.80 for an eight-hour day. The current hand model[3] buyout fee is $445.30 for eight hours.

OVERTIME

SCALE SESSION FEES (regular union session fees) cover one eight-hour day. If the performer is required to work for longer than eight hours, overtime is paid as follows:

- The ninth and tenth hours are paid at 150 percent of the scale session fee for one hour (the hourly rate is equal to one-eighth of the eight-hour-day session fee). The current rate for the ninth and tenth hours is $100.32. This is called "time and a half."

    For example, one hour of overtime for an on-camera performer is:
    Hours 9 and 10: $100.32 per hour.
    Hour 11: $133.76.
    1/8 of the 8-hour session fee ($535.00) divided by 8): $66.88
    Plus an additional 50 percent of the hourly amount: $33.44
    Total amount: $100.32

- The eleventh hour and beyond are paid at 200 percent of the scale session fee for one hour. The current rate is $133.76. This is called "double-time."

- An additional 10 percent must be added to the above hourly rates for performance between 8:00 P.M. and 6:00 A.M. This fee is called a "night premium." The hours subject to the night premium for extras are slightly different.

- Performers are paid 200 percent of scale for weekend and holiday work. Recognized holidays include New Year's Day, Martin Luther King Jr.'s Birthday, President's Day, Memorial Day, Independence Day, Labor Day, Thanksgiving, and Christmas Day.

TRAVEL TIME

When performers spend time traveling to or from a location, they are compensated for the time at the same rates by which they are paid for session time. Hourly or half-day rates may apply depending on the time of travel. On a travel day when no services are rendered, the talent is due a minimum of $535.00. When services are rendered on a travel day, they are paid for each quarter hour ($16.71) if such work time exceeds the eight-hour work day.

---

[3] A hand model is a person whose hands (only) are in the shot—for example, in a close-up of a hand opening a jar.

CONSECUTIVE EMPLOYMENT

Performers who have traveled to shoot at a location for any one commercial and cannot return home for the evening are paid for intervening time when they are not used. For example, if performers work on Monday and Wednesday but not Tuesday, they are paid a scale session fee for Tuesday in order to hold them for performance on Wednesday.

FITTINGS/WARDROBE

Time spent by a performer in fittings is considered to be session time and is paid as such. For example: If a *principal* (primary) performer spends one hour in a fitting, the payment due would be one-eighth of the scale session fee for an eight-hour day ($66.88).

Performers are compensated for use of their own wardrobe at the following rates:

1. $28.20 for evening wear.
2. $16.90 for non-evening wear.

HOLDING FEES/EXCLUSIVITY

Advertisers must pay principal performers a holding fee every thirteen weeks in order to retain the right to broadcast the commercial during that thirteen-week cycle. The holding-fee amount is equivalent to a session fee. The *holding-fee cycle* begins with the earliest date that an on-or-off-camera principal works and lasts for thirteen weeks. At the end of that time the next holding fee is due and a new thirteen-week cycle begins.

Holding fees also provide the advertiser with *exclusivity*, meaning that as long as an actor is being *held* to a certain product or service, she may not accept work in any competitive television advertising.

When a commercial is no longer held, the advertiser loses the right to broadcast the commercial and the performer is released from her employment contract and is free to accept competitive work.

Holding fees do not compensate the talent for any use of the commercial. However, holding fees are fully creditable against the use fees of a commercial.[4] For example:

Network use fees due:	$1,436.50 (10 uses)
Less holding fees:	$ 535.00
Total amount due:	$ 901.50

---

[4] Holding fees may not be credited to cable cycle.

MAXIMUM PERIOD OF USE

The life of a commercial contract is twenty-one months with additional use periods obtained through *contract renegotiation*. During the twenty-one-month period, the rights to continued usage are obtained through the payment of holding fees every thirteen weeks (as described above).

REINSTATEMENT AND RENEGOTIATION

At the end of the twenty-one-month maximum use period, the performer has the right to request a new rate. This process is called *renegotiation*.

In the event an advertiser wishes to use a commercial after the employment contract(s) runs out, the talent agreements must be reinstated. This process includes reinstating the conflict and negotiating a new payment agreement.

RESIDUALS FOR TV COMMERCIALS

In addition to session fees, principal performers are compensated in *residual payments* for the use of commercials in which they appear. There are as many use types as there are ways to broadcast a commercial. Different and complex rate structures determine talent payments for each type, including network use, syndication use, wild spot use, cable use, foreign use, dealer use, theatrical/industrial use, and Internet use.

NETWORK USE. Residual payments for network use are based on the frequency of use. Performers are paid for each telecast during a thirteen-week cycle. The first network use date commences the thirteen-week network cycle. Rates are structured on a decremental scale, with the first use being the most expensive and use rates beyond the first decreasing in price per use.

WILD SPOT. Residual payments for wild spot use are based on market weightings attributed to the cities in which the commercial is being broadcast. The unit weightings are based on population. New York, Chicago, and Los Angeles are referred to as *majors*, and because of their populations, they are more heavily weighted. The presence of majors, if any, plus the unit weightings of any additional cities, determines the dollar amount due to the performer. This payment covers unlimited use of the commercial in those markets for thirteen weeks. If additional markets are added mid-cycle, the payment must be upgraded to cover additional units.

CABLE. For commercials used on cable networks, each principal performer is paid for thirteen weeks of unlimited use based on the total number of television households/subscribers receiving the cable broadcast. The rates for an on-camera performer range from $535.00 to $2,581.00 for each cycle of use. There are lower rates established for use on local cable systems with one million or fewer subscribers.

DEMOS/NON-AIR COMMERCIALS. There is no exclusivity required of performers in demo commercials. The rates are $401.25 for an on-camera performer and $201.15 for an off-camera performer. Because there is no exclusivity, no holding fees are paid. In the event a demo spot is upgraded to a broadcast commercial, the talent must be re-contracted under the appropriate scale.

INTERNET USAGE is $353.00 x 3.

Radio Commercials

SESSION. The session fee to voice a radio spot is $235.40 + 10%. Session fees are fully creditable to use fees. NOTE: AFTRA does not allow agents of performers to deduct their fees from scale earnings. As a result, most radio announcers are paid at scale plus 10 percent for session fees and residuals.

EXCLUSIVITY/MAXIMUM PERIOD OF USE

There is no exclusivity for radio performers. Radio performers do not receive holding fees and are free to accept work in competitive advertising during the course of their contract. The maximum period of use or *life* of a radio commercial is twenty-one months from the session date. Additional use periods are obtained through contract renegotiation.

RESIDUALS

Payments to radio performers are made when the commercial airs. As with television, there are several different use types and each type has its own rate structure. Some of the different use types are *network, wild spot,* and *dealer use.*

NETWORK. Residual payments for network radio are based on the length of the cycle. Network radio cycles can be one, four, eight, or thirteen weeks in length. During the cycle unlimited use is allowed on any network programs on any and all radio networks for a single advertiser. There is also a limited use for thirteen weeks for either twenty-six or thirty-nine uses during the cycle.

WILD SPOT. Residual payments for wild spot use are based on market weightings attributed to the cities in which the commercial is being broadcast. The unit weightings are based on population. The presence of majors (New York, Chicago, and Los Angeles), plus the unit weights of any additional cities, determines the dollar amount due the performer. The payment can be made for either an eight-week or a thirteen-week cycle. The rates for a thirteen-week cycle are slightly higher than those for eight-week cycles. The eight-week cycle is designed to give advertisers a price break for those commercials intended for a shorter term of use.

DEALER USE. This is a flat rate for twenty-six weeks (six months of use) for broadcast time contracted and paid for by the dealer or distributor of a product (versus media buys made by the manufacturer).

The next chapter discusses the pros and cons of working in regional markets and commuting for work, and how to tell when it's time to move on to a larger (or different) market.

14.

Working in Regional Areas

Advantages and Disadvantages of Working in Regional Areas

Small, regional markets are important places to develop and nurture a fledgling talent career. Opportunities to appear in local commercials exist in all regional markets with a varying degree of work in national commercials, radio, industrial/corporate videos, voice-overs, commercial print, films, and television (including national searches for lead characters)—see fig. 25.

One reason a national commercial will be shot in a smaller region is for its location. These commercials are usually cast locally, with simultaneous casting in the larger markets such as New York, Chicago, and Los Angeles. Actors beware: You are up against some stiff competition. Producers don't mind flying someone in from a larger market to do the job. The best man will win.

In every state of the country, you can now find a high degree of professionalism that has evolved from sophisticated communications systems and mobility. In addition, many directors, producers, and ad agencies have relocated from larger markets to smaller ones because the latter suit their lifestyles better. Actors often make the same move, bringing with them new ideas, new photos, and a greater competitive edge. Agents and casting directors in all markets are communicating to a greater degree, and anyone who is interested can become more savvy to the workings of the industry, thus becoming more competitive commercially. Agents can quickly e-mail photos when they are needed to casting directors around the world.

One of the benefits of working in smaller markets is less competition, which makes it easier to get an agent, book a job, build your résumé, and get your SAG card. In many regions, you can keep busy providing you are willing to audition in all areas of the business. One day, for instance, you might be working in a film, and the next day on a print job.

Gregory Bouldin, a talent agent at the Gregory Agency in Wichita, Kansas, says: "There is so much more competition in a larger market. By starting out in a smaller market, talent people have a greater chance of being a big fish in a small pond and have more opportunities to build that résumé. Because the talent pool is so much smaller than in a larger area, local agencies and production companies will depend on and trust a good local talent agency. Instead of auditioning against a hundred other people in a larger market, there are times an actor can be booked directly without an audition.

"The Internet has been a valuable tool for our agency as it has cut down a lot on the steps we typically went through before. Some of our clients (production companies and ad agencies) go directly to our website and pick the people they want from there. They can trust the images are current and that the talent they see are reliable."

Heather Laird, a casting director at Wright/Laird Casting in Kansas City, Missouri, adds, "You can gain a certain level of confidence working in a regional market that I think is *really* valuable. So many people end up in the L.A. market with very little experience, hoping to get 'discovered.' If people have an opportunity to work in a regional market, they are going to be a step ahead of ninety-nine hundred other people who just decided they want to be famous and walked out the door and went to L.A."

There can be some disadvantages to working in smaller markets as well. There is less work than in New York and Los Angeles, it's harder to find good coaches and classes, and you may have to invest a great deal of time scouting for opportunities to network and to find auditions. Savvy talent people make the most of their regional market by creating their own opportunities to build their résumé and get experience and exposure. Kay Tanner, an agent at Genesis Talent in Atlanta, suggests that actors in smaller regions form their own theater groups. "There's puppet theater and other forms of theater that people can do to make a living. It's not a great living, but it can be done. It's a way for actors to express themselves creatively too."

The reality is that there may not be much happening in your area. If you love where you live and don't want to leave, you will have to find another means of financial support. Commercials and other industry work can simply become an enjoyable part-time outlet for your talents and creativity. Be sure to set yourself up with a job that is flexible and allows you time to go to auditions and do commercials.

Commuting

Another option is for actors to commute from smaller markets to larger ones. There are a lot of people commuting from places like Milwaukee, Indianapolis, and even Detroit to Chicago for work, for instance. Some actors travel to and from Washington, D.C., Philadelphia, and Pittsburg, or between Atlanta and Wilmington, North Carolina, for film opportunities. Actors in Florida travel as much as four hours for an audition. Actors from New York will go to Los Angeles for pilot season[1] or episodic season.[2]

Others actually relocate temporarily in another market—for instance, actors from New York will go to Los Angeles for pilot season. Of course, while they are there, they also audition for commercials. These actors are known as *bicoastal*.

By networking with other actors, you can find markets that would be viable for you. You would then want to find an agent in the other markets. It is accepted practice to have a different agent in each market. If the market you are commuting to is very close to your home region, check with your agent to make sure your agreement with him does not cover the other market you are interested in. Doing so will avoid unnecessary and potentially messy contractual issues with the agent you sign with in the new area.

---

[1] A pilot is the first episode of a potential TV series. If accepted, the show is given a time slot and the production company produces more of the series. Generally, pilots are cast January through mid-March. They are finished and delivered by the end of April to be considered to be picked up, with final decisions made between May and June.

[2] Episodic season is when the television series are up and running. Casting is being conducted on a weekly basis to fulfill all the supporting acting roles. Episodic season runs from late July to the end of March. There is a period of time that the shows are on "hiatus." This is the time frame that no casting or production is being done. If you are an actor focusing on a television career, this would be a good time to go home to visit or take a vacation.

Commuting can be expensive, so some talent managers suggest setting money aside for the year to cover the cost.

Moving to a Larger Market

If you have reached a point where you feel you've done all you can within your base area and want to do more—and if you're willing to relocate—it's time to consider moving to an area where you can get more work. The market you pursue depends on where your aspirations within the industry lie.

If your primary focus is on film and television, you will want to consider moving to Los Angeles, since that is where most of those projects are done and there are many more opportunities to audition on a daily basis. There are auditions in New York, Chicago, and other places in the country for a national search, but if you *know* you want to make your living in film/TV, you should be based in L.A.

If your passion is theater, your base should be New York. There is also a good deal of work in soap operas and commercials in New York. Chicago is a regional market that is known for good theater as well as film and TV opportunities and many searches are conducted in that area. There is clearly no one "right" place to be. Go where you feel most comfortable and content. It is important to balance your aspirations for your career with the rest of your life.

Before making the move to a larger market, make sure you have gotten as much experience as possible in your local area. A good time to move to a larger market could be when you have exhausted all of your options—when you were going hot and heavy and interest in you has cooled off because you've become overexposed. The creatives who are making the selection decisions are looking for the "new" idea, the "new" person.

Actors tend to move on to a larger market when they become bored with what is available to them in their home market, or they outgrow the kinds of parts they are getting and move to an area where more opportunities are available to them. They also leave for markets with more choices of training. Actors may feel instinctively when it is the right time to leave.

Heather Laird, Missouri casting director, adds, "People who want to be actors get involved in their regional market and they do well so they don't stay. However, there are an awful lot of people who go to L.A., get some time in, and come back to their original market. It is definitely a plus to have joined SAG (or become SAG eligible) before leaving for a larger market. Expect competition to be much stiffer. In New York and Los Angeles, it is not unusual to be competing against 125 other people for the same role, in comparison to 15-25 in a smaller, regional market. Also be prepared for more competition for agency representation. An agent in a larger market may not want to represent you because doing so would create competition within her own agency. They don't want too many people who, in their opinion, are too similar."

Lori Wyman, a Florida casting director, points out some of the hard realities of moving to a larger market: "Actors are enticed by the fact that they will have more of a chance to audition for a lead in L.A. or New York than in Florida. But if you can't get an agent and don't get auditions, what chance do you have? Everybody comes from somewhere. Your regional market can be a great place to get your feet wet, learn the business, learn the rules.

"I have heard it said that in Florida, we are the barracudas and in L.A., they are the great white sharks. Smaller markets are not as aggressive or as brutal. Actors get a little taste of it out here, but out there it is thrown at them. Here, a strong talent might go out on every single casting that they would be right for. In L.A., that won't happen all the time. Actors come back frustrated."

In smaller, regional areas, local TV stations, ad agencies, and film production companies do their own casting. You can look up who they are over the Internet or the Yellow Pages and get your photo and résumé over to them. Call and speak to an assistant or receptionist and ask whom to address your information to. Write a note attached to your info telling the person what you are interested in doing. (See Chapter 2, Résumés and Cover Letters, for tips on sending out your promotional materials.)

Despite the challenges relocating to a larger market presents, if you are acting and hoping to etch out a full-blown career, eventually you might make the move. In the meanwhile, making the most of your regional market is a valuable part of the process.

Interview With Tom Jourden

Tom Jourden started out working with a business degree in Sales Management in Atlanta, Georgia, for a Fortune 500 company. He wanted to make the transition into acting and started studying it in Atlanta. He moved to Los Angeles in 1999 to expand his studies and opportunities in acting. He is now one of those rare actors who has a career acting in television, film, commercials, voice-overs, and hosting

(Tom is well-recognized as the host for *Amazing Vacation Homes*). He not only made a move successfully, but also transitioned successfully into a new career. He offers some valuable insights into the issues facing performers who are considering the move to a larger market.

Secondary markets are great for learning about acting, studying, and getting some work. Atlanta is a perfect example. It's not as competitive in the area of industrials and commercials.

If you work in a secondary market first, you're going to understand what agencies do, what casting directors do. You're going to learn a little bit about taking head shots, hitting a mark, and how lighting works, and hopefully you'll get your union card and book some jobs. Even though it's not like the big markets, the experiences you have in a secondary market serve as training wheels. They give you a start.

In a secondary market, it's much easier to book work at different levels—nice little parts in films, parts in industrials, and commercials. You might be competing against eight or ten decent people in a smaller market, whereas in a larger market, you're competing against thousands and thousands who all look like you and might be better than you, especially if you're coming out to Los Angeles without training and experience.

After doing a certain number of industrial films and local commercials, you may feel like there isn't a whole lot more you can do without simply repeating yourself. At that point it may be time to move on, take the bigger risk and challenge—to learn and grow as an actor.

The worst thing that can happen in the big market is not having enough money. You end up getting to a place with great opportunities for commercial work and training, but you can't take advantage of them because you're working as a waiter somewhere forty hours a week and you don't have the time or the money to pursue leads.

I read a lot about acting in the area before making the move, and I talked to people who either were living in L.A. or had been there. I've learned that it's important not to put a time frame on your success. If you say, "If I don't make it in two years . . .," you're not really committed to staying with it for the long term, and that kind of commitment is absolutely necessary in this business.

When I first moved to Los Angeles, whenever I would go home or talk to friends, they always want to know either when I'm going to do something they can see or, even if I've just done something, when I'm going to be in something else. People not in the business have absolutely no idea how incredibly difficult it is just to get an audition, let alone a booking. When leaving a secondary market, you've got to expect those questions and be prepared to say, "I just met an agent . . .and that is a big deal." Make your victories a little different than they used to be.

One of the most surprising discoveries I found when I moved to L.A. was that there are a lot of *bad* actors in the big market. Yet for all the bad actors, there is an enormous amount of good actors. In some cases, I observed actors pick up three pages from an Oscar-nominated scene or an Emmy-winning scene and after twenty minutes give a polished performance. It's hard to find the same level of competence in the smaller markets. But no one expects you to be that good, that quick, in smaller markets.

OPPORTUNITIES AVAILABLE

STATE	NEAREST MARKET	ON-CAMERA	VOICE-OVER	RADIO	CORPORATE VIDEOS INDUSTRIALS	COMM. PRINT	THEATRE	FILM	TV*
ama		x	x	x	x	x	x	x	x
ka		x	x	x		x	x	x	x
ona		x	x	x	x	x	x	x	x
nsas	GA, LA, OK					x	x	x	x
fornia		x	x	x	x	x	x	x	x
rado		x	x	x	x	x	x	x	x
necticut	MA, NY				x	x	x		
ware		x	x	x	x		x	x	x
ida		x	x	x	x	x	x	x	x
rgia		x	x	x	x	x	x	x	x
aii		x	x	x	x	x	x	x	x
o		x	x	x	x	x	x	x	x
ois		x	x	x	x	x	x	x	x
ana	IL, OH, KY	x	x	x	x	x	x	x	x
a		x	x	x	x	x	x	x	x
sas		x	x	x	x	x	x	x	x
tucky		x	x	x	x	x	x	x	x
isiana	TX	x	x	x	x	x	x	x	x
ne	MA				x	x	x	x	
yland	NY, Wash DC	x	x	x	x	x	x	x	x
sachusetts		x	x	x	x	x	x	x	x
higan		x	x	x	x	x	x	x	x
nesota		x	x	x	x	x	x	x	x
sissippi	LA, TX	x				x	x	x	x
souri		x	x	x	x	x	x	x	x
ntana	ID, UT, WA	x	x	x	x	x	x	x	x
raska		x	x	x	x	x	x	x	x
ada		x	x	x	x	x	x	x	x
w Hampshire	MA				x	x	x		
w Jersey	NY, PA				x	x	x		
w Mexico		x	x	x	x	x	x	x	x
w York		x	x	x	x	x	x	x	x
th Carolina		x	x	x	x	x	x	x	x
th Dakota		x	x	x	x	x	x	x	x
o		x	x	x	x	x	x	x	x
ahoma		x	x	x	x	x	x	x	x
gon		x	x	x	x	x	x	x	x
nsylvania		x	x	x	x	x	x	x	x
de Island	MA, NY				x	x	x		
th Carolina		x	x	x	x	x	x	x	x
th Dakota		x	x	x	x	x	x	x	x
nessee		x	x	x	x	x	x	x	x
as		x	x	x	x	x	x	x	x
h		x	x	x	x	x	x	x	x
mont	MA, NY	x			x	x	x		x
ginia	MD, Wash DC	x	x	x	x	x	x	x	x
shington		x	x	x	x	x	x	x	x
st Virginia	NC, PA	x	x	x	x	x	x	x	x
consin		x	x	x	x	x	x	x	x
oming		x	x	x	x	x	x	x	x

evision includes sitcoms, Movies-of-the-Week, and/or national searches for TV series.

. 25: Percentage of opportunities vary with size of the market.

15.

Voice-Overs

Voice-over is another area in which you can find many opportunities to develop your talent, make money, exercise your acting ability, express yourself, and have a lot of fun.

What Are Voice-Overs and Who Does Them?

A voice-over is the audio portion of a commercial (or other filmed or taped material)—the voice you hear. Talent fall in love with this medium because it doesn't matter what they look like, and there are significantly fewer restrictions in it than in other areas of the business. Women can go to auditions without makeup, it doesn't matter what kind of clothes you wear, and age is not a deterrent—you can be fifty and sound thirty. There are no ethnic restrictions. If your voice sounds nonregional, you are eligible for any and all nonregional-sounding parts.

Another plus is that when you record a spot, it usually doesn't take all day. In theory, you can record a commercial (which usually takes two hours) and have the rest of the day to go on other auditions or do whatever else you want.

Voice-over talent for television commercials receive residuals for the run of the spot. They tend to have less of a chance of becoming overexposed. Because on-camera actors are visibly recognizable, clients may feel

reluctant to use the same people too much and choose new ⌐
for their commercials. This is not a problem for voice-over t

It can be a plus for certain types of talent to be able ⌐
or cartoon voices. A grown man can do the voice of a magic rug or a
wild animal—even a spoon, a shark, or a clock. An adult woman can
even do the voice of a little boy. The voice of Bart Simpson is done by
an adult woman.

Many newcomers to the field have the misconception that having "a
nice voice" is enough. This is not true. A voice is your instrument, but a
professional voice-over is a combination of several elements—of how well
you play the instrument as well as its tone and quality, your interpretive
skills, personal point of view, and your performance.

Voice-Over Markets

The three major markets for voice-over are New York, Los Angeles, and
Chicago. Secondary markets are Dallas, Florida, and Atlanta, with limited work in other states.

Types of Opportunities in Voice-Over

Television, radio, film, industrial and corporate films, video games,
voices in toys, and the Internet all offer many opportunities for voice-
over work.

TELEVISION
Television offers opportunities for network announcers, promos (promoting a show), animated cartoons, sitcoms, and action voices (any
voices not appearing on-camera: for example, a talking parrot or voices
coming out of a TV set).

In television, the picture is completed and edited first, then the creative team goes into the studio with the voice-over actor and lays down
the track (records the voice-over) to the picture. At this point the voice
must fit the time and mood of the finished (visual) commercial.

RADIO

Radio and television are very different media. Voices for television have the support of the visuals, whereas in radio, the voice is the only thing that conveys the message; it must create the mood and produce a reaction, whether it be humor, frustration, intimacy, or curiosity.

Radio has no visual restrictions. This allows the creative team to be more flexible in the studio. They can change ideas as they go along. Because of this, flexibility and a wider range of performance on the part of the talent are demanded more frequently for radio auditions than for TV auditions. Radio spots allow more opportunities to react and relate with other characters. Technical ability, knowing how to take direction, and having a good sense of timing are essential in both media.

FILM

In film, there are opportunities in *dubbing*–replacing the original voice of the actor with another person's voice. Foreign films, for instance, are often dubbed over with American voices. That way, subtitles are not necessary when the film is viewed in English-speaking countries. A film also may be dubbed if the dialogue needs to be changed. If the original actor is not available, a person who sounds like him or her does the dubbing. The actual technique involves watching the picture and recording the words or sentences in sync with the dialogue being replaced.

Other opportunities exist in *ADR* (additional dialogue replacement), or *looping*. A loop group is where the actors "slug in" background sounds. For instance, in a huge office or crowd scene, the background noises may have to be "sweetened," or enriched with sound effects or music. The actors watch the action and supply additional voices as orchestrated by a director. They have to be very clear as to what the scene is all about and technically correct. For example, if the scene involves a hospital, the actors may have to know some hospital jargon. They have to know regionalisms. If the film takes place in the South, they have to speak with a Southern accent. Actors who do ADR have to be very versatile and have great improvisational skills. They must be able to think and change quickly to coordinate with the visuals.

MISCELLANEOUS USES

Miscellaneous opportunities include voice-over for interactive games, videocassettes, voices in toys and dolls, Internet projects, and books-on-CD. Voices for business applications such as automated recordings on answering devices (like those on automated answering and/or billing services for department stores and utility companies), promos for TV shows, network announcements, and trailers[1] for films offer other outlets for voice-over talent.

What It Takes To Succeed

In every market, there are a handful of performers with the tools to compete nationally. The right tools are training, a professional-quality voice-over demo CD, and the marketing savvy to position yourself properly on the national scene.

The quality of delivery must be solid, sure-footed, and should be defined by the actor's personality. The successful voice-over performer is original and freed-up creatively. Examples of personality-driven celebrity prototypes referred to in casting breakdowns are Robin Williams, Ellen DeGeneres, Janeane Garofalo, Eddie Murphy, and David Hyde Pierce. They have a way of looking at the world that comes through loud and clear, and there's no mistaking their personality—other people will try to be imitators, but it's never quite the same.

A voice-over talent has to know how to interpret copy and then execute it with the right sense of timing and rhythm. A good voice-over talent can take a piece of mediocre copy and make it come alive.

How To Get Started Doing Voice-Overs

The three major markets in the industry are New York, Los Angeles, and Chicago. The process of developing your talent and getting into voice-overs is similar in each market. You need to learn to give a good audition and to perform well under pressure. You also need a good demo CD to use as your calling card.

If you are already doing on-camera work, you'll have an edge. You may already have an agent who knows your work and will submit you for voice-over breakdowns, or a casting person might know you from

---

[1] A trailer is an advertisement for film highlighting selected scenes.

your on-camera work and will call you in to audition for voice-over. Quite frequently comedic actors can make the transition more easily into humorous radio spots.

Training

If you are not a performer, you should take some sort of acting class so that you understand how to play and develop a character. In addition, take a good class in voice-over technique so you know what to do when you get on a microphone. It is important to find your own "voiceprint" (voice personality). From there you want to be able to execute copy with variations on the theme. After several workshops, you should know the difference between TV and radio reads.

Know that one three-hour workshop is not going to make a career. It's going to take a lot of practice time outside of class. You want to get to a point where you can compete with people who do this for a living every day. In order to be successful doing voice-overs, it has to be a passion for you. It can't be just a passing fancy. You have to have the kind of enthusiasm that will give you the energy to see it through the times when it is really tough. Developing a career in voice-over takes time.

Demo CDs

A demo CD is the voice-over performer's calling card. Like the on-camera actor's head shot, it requires careful preparation.

To get a demo CD that sounds professional, you cannot have a friend put it together. Find a professional by getting references from friends who have good demo CDs, or call local talent agents who represent voice talent. The producer of your demo CD will help you choose scripts that are best suited for you and will direct you while recording the demo. They will then edit any glitches out of your demo and finish it off with the proper music.

Always ask about studio costs. You will be charged for the time it takes to record and edit your demo. Your producer will also dub copies that you want to distribute as marketing tools. Meet the producer before agreeing to hire him. It is important that you feel comfortable with this person. Visit the studio. Shop around before choosing a producer. Be sure you choose a studio because it will give you a professional product, not simply because it's the least expensive. Studio time can vary from $25 to $150 per hour. Usually you can get a package deal for the entire recording of your demo CD.

A good demo CD will demonstrate what you do best. If you have only four good pieces and the CD is under a minute long, that is fine. The level of quality has to show that you can compete against people in the market who are working every day. The spots should be produced with music and sound effects. The spots must sound finished and ready to be put on the air.

Each commercial should not be put on the demo in its entirety. Instead, compile short clips of the spot cut off in an appropriate place, so that your demo moves quickly from one spot to the next. Blunt cuts with quick changes into the next piece force listeners to pay attention. Slow fades lull listeners. Your demo CD must start strong, stay strong, and finish strong. Don't try to bury a weak piece in the middle. The creatives want someone who can nail the job and give 100 percent every time. For your first CD, four or five strong pieces are fine. You can build from there as your career escalates.

A demo CD is not only for the performer just entering the field; even the most seasoned voice actors have demo CDs. It is important to keep your demo current by upgrading it annually.

DEMO CDS FOR ADVANCED VOICE-OVER TALENT
A ten-to-fifteen-second clip of a spot is plenty to get across a style. The finished CD should time out to approximately a minute to a minute-and-a-half. The CD should show a range of what you can do. You want to show variety and range. Some examples of range are *real-person conversational, spokesperson, cosmetic, personality-driven, bright, warm,* and *edgy.* Some people have an identifiable style. They do this very well and are booked for it. Examples of such a style is flat rasp, sarcastic, or comedically edgy. Celebrity prototypes are Janeane Garofalo, Eugene Levy, Dennis Miller, Ray Romano, and Bill Maher.

There are different types of voice-overs. There is *commercial, promo, animation,* and *narration.* If you are proficient in more than one, your CD should have a separate track for each type.

HOW TO PACKAGE YOUR CD

Your demo CD should be packaged to create an image of who you are as a voice. The CD case should contain a jacket cover designed for this image. Your name and a contact number should appear on the front. If you have an agent, your agent's name would appear with his or her phone number. You would not put your personal phone number on the package. A photo of yourself is not recommended. It limits people's views of the possibilities of your voice. The CD itself should have a design printed on it that is carried over from the jacket cover. This keeps your package consistent and professional-looking.

It is important that the image created by the CD cover's design reflects your voice style. If your design is bold and strong with lightening bolts as part of the imagery (fig. 26), and your voice is mid-range and whimsical, you have misrepresented yourself. Even if your CD is good, the listener will be disappointed and confused by your marketing. (See figs. 26 & 27 for two samples of CD covers.)

GETTING SOMEONE TO LISTEN TO YOUR CD

This is a business and you are your own salesperson. You have to know exactly what your strengths are and make people aware of them. The more people know about you and what you can do, the better your chances of getting an audition and/or booking. Once you are trained well enough to give a professional-level performance and have put together a well-packaged demo CD, the next step traditionally is to find an agent. There are, however, alternative ways to market yourself.

WHOM TO SEND YOUR DEMO CD TO

If you are in a market with voice-over agents, try to get an agent to listen to your demo CD. You want agency representation. The most effective way to get an agent to listen is to have another one of that agency's clients recommend you to them. If you know a casting director, producer, or anyone else an agent does business with, ask them to refer you. Remember: When someone recommends you, it is a reflection on themselves. Generally, people in the business will only recommend you if they feel that you are competitive and will be able to book work.

Another, more independent, way to market yourself is to find out which trade publications are available in your area and look up local production companies who produce industrial films, animation, local

FIG. 26: Brett Ericson. Packaging portrays strong, intensive, driven, electrifying voice personality (voiceprint).

FIG. 27: Vanessa Marshall. Design of package demonstrates fun, hip, contemporary, energetic, and sexy (voiceprint) type of voice.

commercials, video games, and anything else where they would be in need of a voice. You can go to a bookstore that has a Drama section, call your local union office, or network with other actors. In small, regional areas you can try the Yellow Pages. Another good source in smaller, regional areas is to call local TV and radio stations to find out how they get their talent for local commercials (see appendix for suggested reading).

Marketing and Packaging Yourself as a Talent

In any profession, marketing is everything. From your résumé to the work you do on a daily basis, it's all about marketing. It feels too commercial to a creative person, but the fact of the matter is that you are all in business for yourselves. You are all entrepreneurs. In this particular case, the voice is the product you are offering. The product has to have a unique stand, a unique identity that's presented in your demo.

If you are a beginner, the main thing to do is listen to what's being done to get some idea of general style, then work to develop your own spin on current styles, your own voiceprint. You can hear a demo of all voice actors signed with agents in Los Angeles, New York, and Chicago by going to www.voicebank.net; however, you don't want to design yourself to sound exactly like the voice you think you most admire.

It is actually impossible to learn voice-over technique on your own. Seek the help of a professional who is knowledgeable about the industry to coach you. The better you present what you most individually have to offer, the more rapidly you will move up in the business.

How Long It Will Take to Book Your First Job

It's hard to say. Some people hit it immediately. They take a workshop and within six months they are out there and have three or four national TV or radio spots. Most of the time it takes years to do it. Many times, people don't make it because they don't have the desire to get out there and stay at it. They send out demos, then don't follow up with calls and networking to keep a marketing momentum going. They just sit and hope someone will call. You have to really make it happen. The more you work at it, the quicker you may succeed. It's a numbers game. You have to practice. You have to get the auditions. You have to be good. Sometimes it's just being in the right place at the right time.

Tapping the Regional Markets

In addition to major markets, there are voice-over opportunities nation-wide, even in the smallest markets. Wherever there is advertising of any kind, there is voice-over. The biggest resource in smaller markets is a radio station, where you can work either in the office, DJ (disc jockey), work as part of the production team, or in the department of creative services, which writes and develops ads for the station's advertisers. You can then end up doing the voices for the commercials at the station—a classic example of being in the right place at the right time. As a result of hearing you, agents and companies who want to advertise may call the station or may contact you directly, and use you on a freelance basis to voice their project.

The second route is through small, local theaters. The person looking to hire a voice often contacts theaters because actors have well-developed voices. Acting classes and acting schools are another resource for producers looking for talent. A lot depends on how sophisticated a market is. Another place to get a start is through professional workshops established by voice-over professionals. You can learn the skills, after which you can put together a demo CD and start sending it out to agencies and communications departments involved in advertising and/or narration.

What an Actor Can Expect at the Actual Booking

The producer is one of the principal players who decides who will get booked for a job.

Barbara Goldman, radio and television voice-over producer in New York City, takes us into the recording studio for a look at what happens during a typical voice-over session.

What can an actor expect when he first arrives at a session?
Generally you are given the script a few minutes ahead of time to look over before you enter the booth (the actual soundproof space the talent

stands in to record). Depending on the climate of the session, you will either be sent right into the booth or you will come in and meet the client and everyone else in the room.

At a radio session, where there may be many characters in one spot, the actors may be called in at the same time to record the spot together because an overall timing is needed for the spot. You may then be asked to step aside so the creative team can concentrate on different performances in different segments of the spot. Many times, you'll have to wait around while the team perfects all the technical aspects of the spot—it's not a reflection on how well you're doing. After the spot is timed out, the announcer might be recorded and allowed to leave; then work begins with the other actors.

Who is in the studio for a radio voice-over announcer session?

A radio recording session will run most efficiently if one person talks to the talent. This person is usually the producer, or it might be the writer. The art director, clients, assistant writer, writer, account executive, engineer, and the producer could all be at the session.

Many times radio work is done at the last minute, so all parties involved are needed there to move the process along. Something magical can happen in the recording session, something unexpected, so it's a good idea for the client to be there. Many changes, including ones involving legal issues, can occur, and actors usually have to record over and over again to cover all bases.

The actor can expect anywhere from three to forty takes. All takes are listened to. The first take might be the one actually liked best. It would then be played back for the talent, and the actor might be asked to do it again. You are expected to understand what you did in a particular take so you could recreate a very subtle nuance of it, if necessary.

Who is in the studio for a television voice-over announcer session?

Generally, the producer, writer, art director, engineer, and, in many cases, the editor are present. Ideally, the voice is the last element that is put on the spot. After the spot is shot and edited, the music is edited, and all the pieces put together, the announcer will be called in. Ideally, one person who can convey the message clearly directs the talent.

If the director is not getting the feeling he or she wants from the actor's read, perhaps the actor will have to chime in and help figure out what is wrong. An experienced actor may suggest a solution as simple as projecting a smile into her voice. Interpretation can make or break a reading.

What is expected of the actor in the studio?

If an actor gives one or two takes and that's all he can or will give, then it is not worth having him there. It may be the greatest performance of his lifetime, but if it's not what the client wants, it's not right.

The attitude and personality of everyone involved are very important. The actor should accommodate—not get in the way. An actor may feel he can read the line ten different ways and give them all to the creatives before being asked. That would be totally distracting. On the other hand, if an actor feels a line should be read differently than directed, he can find ways to approach that without resisting or offering too much.

The actor should not feel that he has to be the center of attention. He has to sense the climate in the control room, determine whether it is playful or serious, and whether or not there is room for some levity. Sometimes it's better simply to get the job done and get out of there.

The more people in the control room, the more likely it is to be a tense situation, simply because there are more people who have to be pleased. If it is a tense control room, the actor has to go along, do what's asked of him, and finesse a way to ask, "What if I try it *this* way?"

Actors have to realize that the people in the studio are under a lot of pressure to get the right outcome. It is the producer's job to accommodate the writer and the client. After the creative team finds what they want, actors are welcome to their way of doing it. But they should bear in mind that the creative team in the control room is not thinking just about the voice. They are thinking about all the elements of the production.

What do actors tend to struggle with on their first booking?

They have the ability, otherwise they wouldn't be there, but they seem to feel insecure about the procedure and, possibly, when to talk. It is not expected for a talent to be a time clock, bringing something in exactly on time. With the new technology, performance can be sped up or slowed down to meet time constraints without any change of voice pitch. If the talent and attitude are there, the creatives will have the patience. However, accomplished voice talent have developed internal clocks and can shave or add a second to their read.

Final Tips on Studio Recording Sessions

Too Many Directors. Sometimes there is just one person in the control room; sometimes there is a bank of people. At some recording sessions, they all have input; at others, they just sit there. The most trying time is when five or six people on the creative team show up and each one has a different opinion of how the recording should go. This has to be conveyed to you and you have to satisfy all of them. These people are all part of the deal. Don't try to split the difference and make everybody happy. Communicate with the people who are directing you. Explain to them that you are hearing two different pieces of direction and you are not sure what they want. Suggest doing it one way and then the other way. This business is all about communication.

Too Many Takes. Nick Omana, a voice-over talent, shares his experience of an extended taping session: "There was a time when I had sixty-seven takes. I went out to get a glass of water during a break and the engineer said to me, 'You're doing a great job. These guys do a hundred or more takes.' Producers want to make sure they have every base covered, so they are going to work you every way to Sunday to make sure they have what they want. As talent, we are always seeking approval after two takes. That doesn't happen very often."

To do well in voice-over work, you need a lot of versatility and diversification. Once you are booked and in the booth recording, you want to get the job done right. You should learn to take direction. Listen to the creative team. They are the ones with the idea—right or wrong. Usually a smart director or writer will say, "Is there any other way you hear or feel this?" Then you can put it down the way you feel it should go.

Animation

There is tremendous growth in cartoons, creating expanded opportunities for voice talent. The bulk of animation is done in Los Angeles, the "Mecca of toons."

Charlie Adler is a voice-over cartoon artist who is the voice of Mr. Whiskers in the animated TV series *Brandy and Mr. Whiskers*, three characters in *Pet Aliens*, and voices *Jakers! The Adventure of Piggley Winks* in addition to directing the *Wild Thornberry* series, *Rocket Power*, and winning an Emmy for directing *Rugrats*.

Charlie suggests that animation involves a much more definitive, broader use of acting abilities than acting on camera. With on-camera acting, the actor is seen. The viewer knows if the character is tall, skinny, fat, sloppy-looking, handsome, or sophisticated. In animation, the actor has to paint the picture with his voice—to entirely create the look of the character with it.

"I have done a series called *Swat Cats*: Brock Peters was one of the villains and Roddy McDowall, Tim Curry, Sally Struthers, Brenda Vaccaro, Nancy Travis, and Jim Belushi played various characters. It was a wonderful place for people to come and do real, good work. The only difference between this and other acting media is that you are invisible, so nobody's watching you.

"This is an acting job. It is offensive when people out in the real world say, 'Oh, *I* can do a funny voice. *I* can do cartoons.' It's not about funny voices. You need to have a great ability to act and create characters. You need an incredible imagination and the ability to be very, very free. You must be very flexible, able to switch gears in a matter of seconds. Technically, you have to be very adept at many things.

"Yes, voice is important. Yes, having dialects is very important. The energy level is hyperspace in animation. It's like running a marathon every time you do a show. The ability to commit to a character and to be consistent requires some serious acting skills. Animation's not a medium for people who can't act."

HOW TO GET STARTED IN ANIMATION

There are an infinite number of ways to get into animation. For example, Charlie Adler has always considered himself goofy. He was the brat at school. He was the kid who never shut up, who made fun of everybody and lived in the principal's office.

Luckily for him, he had a talent that could be translated into acting. He went into theater and broke into commercials very early (at the age of eighteen). He learned how to work in front of a camera, which helped prepare him for voice-over and radio.

Adler's agent got him into an audition for an animated special that came to New York. She knew he was goofy, knew he had done a lot of improv and that he was good at satire. He went in, landed the spot, then recorded it in New York. After going on tour in a Broadway show, Adler moved to Los Angeles—the hotbed of animation.

"I told the agent I got in L.A. that I wanted to do cartoons. I had to go in and demonstrate to her that I knew what I was doing. I wrote forty characters, three lines per character, and insisted that I audition for them. They listened to what I had to do. A week later, they got me a general audition for Hanna-Barbera using my material, my characters. I was given five minutes. I ended up doing twelve. Nobody stopped me and a week later, I had *Smurfs*. Two weeks after that, I had another series and three weeks later, another.

"There's a sense that in the voice-over world, as in many other businesses, there is a clique with the same old people getting all the work. This is not true of animation. A casting director in animation cannot hire the same people, so there is room for newcomers in the voice-over field. Creative teams are always looking for new voices. The trick is to be able to execute the technique as well as or better than established veterans."

HOW TO MAKE A CHARACTER COME ALIVE WITH A VOICE
Adler goes on,

> Before the voice-over is done, the talent should be able to see a picture of the character. If a sketch is not available, a monologue in which several actions are taking place is necessary. One should not always expect these to be cohesive.
>
> You have to have a keen sense of the visual—of what is going on. A director or writer tells you what the action is, and you put all that information together—what you believe from the monologue and the piece, the physical characteristics you get from the picture, and what the director and the other people in the control room

tell you they want in the way of sensibility and feeling.

Do they want a mischievous person? A young person? An older person? Full-bodied? Angry? Edgy? A character type? Someone who is aggressive? Shy? Neurotic? These descriptions translate into an energy and sensibility. A good way of hooking into a character might be to imagine you are doing children's theater, musical theater, vaudeville, or characters typical of those in *The Wizard of Oz*. In fact, one could say that those characters were living cartoons.

You have to be very imaginative and very, very free. Paint your character with broad brush strokes. Take all these things into consideration, commit to a choice, and *go*. It's very improvisational and you really, really must fly.

Let's say you finish the monologue and the director says, "Okay, that was interesting but this character has to be a little crankier and he needs to have a little more weight. Look at the picture—he is a little heavier. And look at the upper lip—it's very, very thick and he has buck teeth. We want to get a sloppier sound and a more aggressive character. He is a little angrier."

Then all of a sudden the writer says, "You know what? I think it would be very interesting if we went a whole different way with this guy. Let's try this: Instead of making him fat and aggressive, let's make him very thin sounding and neurotic."

Those are two huge adjustments to make. Now you have to take that monologue and adapt it to a different personality. You have to completely switch gears, and you might have fifteen seconds to make this adjustment. You have to commit to the character and go with it. That's why I say it's very improvisational. That's how you get the job.

Usually, you show up at work for a table reading, which is a rehearsal sitting. Sometimes you rehearse at a microphone. Every studio has a different setup for rehearsal. They have the full script with pictures of the characters. You have a read-through with the director, and he tells you every beat action[2] of the scenes. For instance, you know if there is a physical action. Does the character trip and fall here? Is the character getting up and reaching? Is he screaming here? Whatever.

You do a read-through. You mark your script. This takes about an hour and a half, then you go to tape. It goes like a radio play and it moves like the wind.

---

[2] A beat action is a moment when an actor changes attitude, emotion, or physical movement.

By the way, SAG allows the people booking you to require you to play three characters and get one payment with a ten percent bump up for the third character. That tells you right there that it is cost-efficient for a producer to hire somebody versatile.

Let's say you are playing one character and you have two more that you are required to do. Of those two, you could have rehearsed a sixty-five-year-old Irish elf, which they have decided on ahead of time. Then, in between the rehearsal and the taping they could say, "We never had the drawing, but play him as a fourteen-year-old East Indian boy. Go." There it is. That's how it works.

Bob Bergen, the voice of Porky Pig, is another inspirational source of information for those who want to enter the world of animation.

Since 1990, Bob is one of a handful of actors who voices the Looney Toons characters for Warner Bros. The main character voices you hear him bring to life are those of Porky Pig, Tweety, Sylvester, Jr., Henry Hawk, Speedy Gonzales, and Marvin the Martian. You have also heard his voice in *Fraggle Rock*, *Spider-Man*, *Dennis the Menace*, *Toy Story 2*, *A Bug's Life*, *Finding Nemo*, and *Shrek 2*.

How did you break into Animation?

I wanted to be Porky Pig since I was five years old. My family moved to Los Angeles when I was fourteen and I began taking voice-over workshops. At the age of eighteen, I was introduced to a voice-over agent by another voice talent. Within a week I booked my first cartoon—*Spider-Man and His Amazing Friends*. For the next five years I paid the bills primarily working as a tour-guide at Universal Studios, while slowly adding to my voice-over résumé. In 1990 I auditioned for and booked *Tiny Tunes*, my first gig for Warner Brothers, in which I played Porky and Tweety.

How do you suggest other people get into voice-over? What tools do they need?

Well, the first thing is that you can't get into voice-over by just doing cartoons. You have to do commercial voice-over as well. Commercials are the day-to-day work in voice-over with cartoons being the icing on the cake. Before ever taking a voice-over workshop, I recommend studying acting. Voice-over *is* acting. I'm also a *huge* advocate of improvisation. Improv trains you to get out of your head and make solid choices. Once you've studied commercial and animation voice-over, it's time for a demo. Make sure you have your demo produced by someone who produces demos for today's voice-over talent.

What makes for a good animation demo?

Your animation demo should sound like a montage of real animation clips cut together into a minute-and-a-half demo. Stay away from telling a story. Also, never repeat a voice twice. Once you've established a character, move on to the next. Try to have each character *doing* something, not just *saying* something, in each bite. Give them some kind of action to be doing. This will show off not just your vocal range, but also your acting range. In cartoons they are looking for actors first and funny voice people second, which means that if you are a great actor who can only do a few voices, you have a better chance of booking a job over someone who does dozens of voices, but can't act.

Your animation demo should consist of characters with distinct personalities. Everyone can do a witch. What makes your witch different? How are your kid voices different from the *Rugrats'*? Nancy Cartwright, who does Bart Simpson, had been doing kid voices for years before booking *The Simpsons*. What makes her Bart stand out is her acting. Her personality is as memorable as his voice. Think of a script as a skeleton and you—the actor—have to give it a body.

How do you make a character come alive?

My number one rule in creating a character is if you physically play a character, the voice will follow. What that means is you can't stand at the mic with your hands at your sides just reading the script and expect to give your best performance. From head-to-toe you need to physically play each character, as you would if you were on stage. The only catch is you need to stay on mic! If you are playing more than one character (and my record for one episode is seven), then each character will have not only a different voice, but different facial expressions, different body language, different gestures, etc. By physically changing along with the voice from character to character, you prevent blending voices.

A one-half hour cartoon takes about four hours to record. The direction is fast. A voice-over performance, whether animation or commercial, is basically a cold-read. You won't get much time with the copy, so you are expected to be brilliant without much preparation. In cartoons you'll get direction like, "Let me hear you run, take a leap off a cliff, and slowly get up kind of dazed and out of breath—then say our scripted line." You have to be able to remember all of that while staying on mic and in character. Plus you might be having a two-way conversation with yourself since you are hired for scale to play at least two voices in episodic cartoons. If all of this sounds easy, then you are ready to pursue it. If not, keep studying! Voice-over, especially animation, is very competitive. Each listener gives you one shot, so make sure you are ready when opportunity knocks.

16.

Models Crossing over into Commercials

Why More and More Models Are Getting into Commercials

Models have broken old stereotypes and have become extremely savvy. "All looks—no brains" could hardly describe the streetwise entrepreneurs who work today's runways and appear in editorials and advertisements in major markets around the globe. And as America's baby-boomers reach maturity and approach seniority, the industry has begun to tune into their needs. Whereas models used to have a career lifespan of little more than ten or so years, now a good model can work well into her forties and beyond—a direct reflection of changing demographics relating to the "aging of America."

Well before a model's career begins to wind down, she starts to invest her earnings or develop businesses of her own. Models are opening restaurants, designing clothing lines, endorsing products, and branching out into other areas of the industry. More and more models are exploring film, theater, and television, and one of the primary ways for models to get their foot in the talent end of the industry is through commercials.

Models who expand into television commercial work position themselves firmly inside the industry. An increasing number of models are taking acting classes to increase their chances of getting commercial work. As models become better prepared and well-trained in commercial auditioning technique, they broaden their career and fatten their bankbooks. The residual income from commercial work can come in years after the actual work was done, carrying the model through slow times and/or adding a lucrative financial base from which she can expand in both careers.

Most commercial agencies have separate departments or are affiliated with modeling agencies exclusively to represent and send out models for commercials. Many of these departments have expanded even further into representing their talent for theatrical (film and television) deals. Modeling agencies recognize the fact that models cross over into other areas of the industry and are quick to give attention to this lucrative segment of their businesses.

How Commercial Experience Can Be a Stepping-Stone to Television and Film

Many times a beautiful person is needed in a film. The casting director or the film's director will see a model acting in a commercial and will trace him or her down to audition for the film.

Commercials can be a model's first opportunity for exposure outside the world of print advertising. As the first experience of acting on-camera, commercial work can help models learn to take direction, deliver copy on time, follow blocking instructions, and exercise expressions and emotions on film.

After acquiring some commercial experience, a model often discovers that she likes acting and pursues it more seriously by taking dramatic acting classes. The commercial experience gives her the insight and confidence to expand her career.

How Modeling and Talent Conventions Offer Opportunities to Expand into Other Areas

From Toledo, Ohio, to Hollywood, California, aspiring models and actors vie for the opportunity to break into the business by attending one of the numerous modeling and talent conventions held annually in the United States. These events, running over the course of a few days to one week, draw casting directors, agents, and managers from major markets across the globe, each scouting new faces to appear in print, commercials, television, film, musical theater, and recording contracts.

Talent cannot individually attend one of these events; they have to come with a modeling or talent school or agency. There can be as many as 2,000 contestants and 350 VIP model and talent agents, managers, and casting people scouting for talent, judging, and giving seminars about the business. It would be impossible to meet that many agents in five years' time with no résumé or track record, trying to break into the industry.

A good convention will separate the model and talent competition events. A talent can attend events and competitions in both areas. If you are thinking of attending one of these events, check out the ratio of the number of VIP judges to contestants as well as who the VIP judges attending will be (and have been in the past). Be sure to check out their credentials. It is very easy to do this over the Internet, or by directly calling the person's office.

Go to the convention, not only to be discovered but to learn from the seminars offered and see what it feels like to have a competitive experience. The most important and positive feedback one can hear from attendees of one of these conventions is that it was a self-esteem booster and a great learning experience. Life as an actor and model is competitive. Your experience at the convention will tell you if you can take the heat.

Many minds and career paths are turned around from model to talent as a result of attending these conventions. Wannabe models have also discovered a wider range of opportunities open to them through the talent exposure at these conventions. Participants of modeling and talent conventions have signed contracts with major agents and managers in both Hollywood and New York and have appeared in national commercials as a result of attending, including Halle Berry, who is featured in our next interview.

One well-known and highly regarded convention is the Millie Lewis Actors, Models, and Talent Competition (AMTC), where the average is a 1:12 ratio of VIPs to contestants. The following is a short (but by no means complete) list of talent who became household names after being discovered at AMTC: Mena Suvari (*American Beauty*), Mitch Holleman (*Reba*), Ashley Scott (*AI*, *Walking Tall*, and co-starring as Joey's girlfriend on *Friends* spin-off *Joey*), rapper Infinity (MCA Records).

Models, as a result of attending AMTC, have been featured in major magazines such as *Vogue*, *Elle*, and *Rolling Stone*.

Another well-known, and sizably larger, convention is the IMTA. Ashton Kutcher, Katie Holmes, Elijah Wood, Jessica Biel, Joel West (contracted for Calvin Klein's *Eternity* commercials with Christy Turlington), and many, many more found success at this convention.

It is up to you as to which size convention suits your personality and needs.

HOW DO YOU KNOW A CONVENTION IS REPUTABLE?

Carey Lewis Arban, owner of the Millie Lewis events, suggests that, since the modeling industry is largely unregulated, you should look at four factors:

- **HISTORY:** How long has the convention been in business?
- **REPUTATION:** What do others in the field say about them? What is their BBB record? Are they licensed? Do they have testimonials from their customers?
- **SUCCESS STORIES:** Who has found success as a result of attending their events?
- **GUT FEELING:** How do you feel about what you have heard? Do you feel "pushed" or "promised" anything? Never ignore your basic good sense.

The Role of a Good Manager in Making the Transition

Talent manager Vincent Cirrincione discovered and developed Halle Berry. Halle started out as a pageant contestant while she was still in her teens. She became Miss Teen All-America and was runner-up to Miss USA. A native of Cleveland, Ohio, Halle—who is only five feet seven— moved to Chicago, where she primarily did catalog modeling for various department stores. She had intended to study acting extensively, but when she met Vincent and came to New York, he moved her acting career along so quickly that she wound up getting on-the-job training instead.

"You can't expect to live in a small town and fly to a big city and have people take you seriously, until you're a big star," says Vincent. "I never heard Halle say, 'I can't do this or that.' She just did what she had to do. There was a time after her first movie when she lived on a couch in my office to save money on rent to invest in herself. She took the money and hired a publicist. When I gave her advice, she understood and acted accordingly. Halle went out there to follow her dreams. She didn't just wait for it to come to her. There was a certain amount of strategy and serendipity."

Vincent's strategy included positioning Halle's career contrary to Hollywood's assumption that you can't act if you're a model. Up to this point, Halle had done a stereotypical part in a short-lived TV series about models called *Living Dolls* and guest-starred on weekly sitcoms such as *A Different World*. The new strategy led to her role in Spike Lee's *Jungle Fever* with Wesley Snipes, where she played an unattractive crack addict. This gave Halle a chance to show that she had more to offer than just a pretty face. One thing led to another and she got an Eddie Murphy movie and a TV series called *Queen*. The *Flintstones* followed.

Halle's crossover from modeling into film was made very quickly, and she was able to bypass a television commercial career. But after becoming a Revlon girl, her career had come full circle. She got the Revlon campaign because she was successful in film and television, and she feels her background in pageants gave her the ability to talk to people and express herself well. She has since proven herself to be a truly versatile talent—able to easily transition from her cosmetics contracts to her role as a "Bond girl" in *Die Another Day* (co-starring with Pierce Brosnan), and with an Oscar for Best Actress for her role in *Monster's Ball* (co-starring Billy Bob Thornton). With that Oscar win, Halle positioned herself firmly as one of the industry's most respected actors.

How Fashion Print Work Differs from Making Television Commercials

In some ways, modeling for print is very similar to working on-camera in a commercial spot. You have to be comfortable being in front of the camera, you have to relate to the camera as you would a dear friend, and you have to be able to take direction from the person behind the camera. You have to love the camera, and the camera has to love you.

In other ways, commercials present new challenges for a model. In print work, the photographer is trying to capture a moment. Clients wade through resulting proofsheets looking for a single shot or a strong series of images that will best represent the client and what they're looking for. Movements for print work are exaggerated, free-flowing and stylized, often mannequin-like. A commercial is an active medium from start to finish. For an on-camera commercial, movements and expressions are more natural, usually with more warmth and approachability in the actor's demeanor.

Another consideration is space. Whereas on the runway or for print, a model has ample space to move and express herself, in some commercial work she will have to adjust to the limited space of the television screen. Movements for commercials in this case will be slight, yet expressive.

In print advertising, your primary promotional tool is the portfolio, consisting of a range of photographs containing your strongest images as well as tear sheets[1] from previous work. In the United States, commercially, your primary marketing tools are your commercial head shot, résumé, and—ultimately—a demo showing samples of your work in commercials.[2] In foreign markets, where the trend is to use pretty faces for commercial work, a model may get by without standard talent marketing tools.

---

[1] Tear sheets are samples of a model's published work (print ads, fashion spreads, etc.) torn from the publications to put into a portfolio.

[2] Most of the time, a demo is not requested for commercial work. However, it is always best to request and collect a copy of every commercial you do at the time of the shoot or soon after the shoot. You will then have the material on hand if you wish to put together a demo. This will give you the competitive edge on the rare occasion when a demo is requested.

WHAT IT TAKES TO CROSS OVER

The transition from model to on-camera actor takes more than just a great face. When the model speaks, being physically attractive isn't enough. That's when knowing how to analyze a script and to audition can expand her career.

When you see those good-looking people running down the beach in a commercial, the talent must know how to make choices and handle themselves properly. Whether they are just walking down the street and laughing with a friend or playing with a young child, a definite choice has to be made with the same ease and comfort in front of a camera that is required in print work.

Anything a model has already experienced through print work can be applied to on-camera work for commercials. There are those diamonds in the rough who have an amazing personality that comes across well on-camera. The model who is savvy enough to take some classes will excel.

TRAINING

Although your modeling experience may give you a slight edge, the transition to commercials will be much easier if you invest in a good commercial auditioning workshop. There is a specific technique applied in commercial auditioning. Proper training will help you get comfortable with the procedure and give a good audition. Having commercial training with a good coach listed on your résumé also shows you are serious about learning and applying the craft.

Opportunities in Foreign Markets

There are many opportunities for models, not only in the United States but in foreign markets as well. Clients from all over the world often want someone beautiful to represent their products, and not just cosmetics. European markets can become a virtual gold mine of opportunities for models with acting experience. The trend is to use models instead of actors whenever possible. In Europe, models cost less than professional actors, which saves clients as much as fifty percent in salaries.

The trend toward using primarily models in commercials is evident in many countries. For instance, models from Scandinavia, America, the U.S., Canada, and England go to Barcelona, Spain, to make money in commercials—then go to Madrid to do editorials—using money made in TV commercials to finance other career aspirations.

In Milan, models can enjoy a full range of work, from high-fashion editorial print (as opposed to catalogues) to television commercials. Greece does a fair amount of commercial work, as does Australia and South Africa. England has a strong commercial market. With agents sending photos and portfolios over the Internet, models' photos can be viewed very quickly and inexpensively and decisions can be made very quickly. Worldwide searches can be done quickly over the Internet between casting directors, photographers, and agents. Be aware of Internet scams. There are, for instance, web-based companies that charge money to post your photo(s) on their site, claiming that casting people frequent and cast from these sites. Know that casting directors mainly cast through agents to control the degree of professionalism that is needed by the model.

HOW A TYPICAL AUDITION IN EUROPE DIFFERS FROM ONE IN THE UNITED STATES

In Europe, all commercials are dubbed over, so it doesn't matter if you can't speak the language. If there is a script, you are given a copy anywhere from the night before to an hour before, and someone will help you translate it into English and direct your facial expressions. You are just expected to mouth the words, so that when the voices are dubbed in, the audio and visual parts go together well.

Compensation

WHAT A MODEL CAN MAKE IN PRINT AND COMMERCIALS IN THE UNITED STATES

In the United States, a day rate for catalog print modeling can range from $1,500 to $10,000. As the popularity of the model increases, so does her day rate. Top celebrity models can make up to $20,000 a day.

HOW MODELS ARE PAID FOR COMMERCIAL WORK

In each country, compensation is different. In Milan, for instance, the agent negotiates a set price for the talent, then discusses royalties. If the spot runs for many years, the agent negotiates for more and more money each year. Generally, the model is paid for the day, plus the royalty for the first year. Future royalties are paid to the model by most agencies, even if they are no longer in the country.

Most foreign markets don't have unions, at least not like SAG and AFTRA in the U.S. The exception would be Canada, which has a strong union, ACTRA; England, which has British Equity; and Spain, which has Edicion Premios Union de Actores. Day rates in most foreign markets depend on the model's name and experience—and whether or not it is for a private channel, a local channel, or a national channel. In Italy, for example, day rates range from several hundred dollars for a small spot to two thousand dollars and up (base) plus royalties for a national commercial.

Interviews with Elle Macpherson, Carmen, Tim Saunders, and Patrick Johnson

Following are some inspirational insights and advice from professional models who have made the transition into commercials.

ELLE MACPHERSON

Elle Macpherson is an international supermodel who has done commercials for McDonald's, Biotherm (in Europe), and MCI, and has successfully transitioned into film. In addition to other companies, she has a lingerie company in Australia, where she produces her own commercials. Here's what Macpherson recalls about her start in modeling:

> In Australia I was awarded an opportunity to attend law school. But after graduating from high school, I decided to take a year off before going to college. I held a variety of jobs, including waitressing in a theater restaurant and working in a pharmacy. A friend of mine, who was a model, suggested that I try it and possibly make a lot of money. "No way," I said. "No way ever. I could never do that." My friend then bet me twenty dollars that if I went to the agency with her, they would take me on. I thought, okay, that's twenty bucks, the equivalent of three or four hours' work. So I went.

When you are sixteen, you have weird perceptions of beauty. You haven't grown into yourself. I was a long drink of water, very tall. I didn't look like what I thought models looked like.

I gave the agent a snapshot taken by a friend. The agency sent me to have more photographs, and the next thing I knew I was being booked for jobs. I worked for a year and a half in Australia. While on a skiing trip in America, I called an agent from Click in New York who had been pursuing me, started working for them, and never left the States.

I always had more of a commercial look than a high-fashion look. I really didn't do a lot of fashion. I didn't work a lot for the magazines, except *Sports Illustrated*. I did a lot of advertising campaigns and TV commercials. I guess I work well on-camera. I feel like I need to move and I'm freer when I'm moving, so I'm better on-camera than when I'm in stills.

I never wanted to act. It was just one of those weird things. A script for *Sirens* came to my manager's attention, and he suggested that I read it. I didn't want to read it because I didn't want to do film. I couldn't see the point. He suggested I read it anyway. The director was in town and wanted to meet with me. He said, "I think *you* should be the one to tell the director you are too lazy to read the script. That you don't care about doing a movie in Australia about a famous Australian artist and spending two months in the mountains with Hugh Grant. You should be the one to tell him that you won't even consider it."

So I read the script and changed my mind. I thought it would be really good for me to spend a few months in Australia and do something different. Working very hard in modeling made me feel burnt out. I did the film. It led to others, and my film career seemed to propel itself. Now I love making films, and that's all I want to do.

CARMEN

Carmen is known for her longevity in the modeling world. She has been with Ford Models since they opened their doors approximately fifty years ago. Carmen has appeared in every magazine from *The New Yorker* to *Vogue* and is known for her work with Revlon and for the classic *Vanity Fair* lingerie advertisements as "the girl with no face." She is trying to help people redefine themselves at every age from fifty to seventy and beyond. Her longevity in the industry lends itself to some interesting insights. Here's what she has to say about it:

I take good care of myself. Life's a challenge as a human being, not just for models. It's a long trip. One has to have an overview of the whole trip. I eat when I'm hungry. I try to keep some balance in my life. I drink a lot of water. I am always mentally prepared. I make sure I get good nutrition and maintain a high energy level. If you stay up all night at nightclubs, it's going to come out of your hide in the long run. And smoking is the worst thing you can do for your skin. Forget smoking. You have to opt for healthy choices.

Doing commercials takes natural ability, being able to apply one's inner life and imagination to the craft of acting. So I didn't find it difficult to move from print work to commercials. I found it challenging. The timing and what I am asked to do on the set is different. Television commercial work is not as intimate as photography in a studio because there are so many people around. It is a different process. The hours are different. When you are used to one and you like the area you are moving into, you just pay attention and learn the trade.

Make sure that you keep on educating yourself because the work does not come to you. You have to keep developing your lust for life in general so that you have some inner life to bring to a job. What makes the difference between someone who gets work and someone who doesn't is the amount of passion you bring to your craft.

I would advise young people to stay in school. School really teaches discipline. It's very hard to pick up self-discipline on one's own. Reading is the single most important thing for youngsters to get into. Once you can read, you can learn by yourself.

It's very tricky for young people starting out to understand the personality of some of the people they come in contact with. For instance, if you are hired for a job and you know you are going to make some money, and the photographer is on drugs and offers or insists you take the drugs to "make you more expressive," it's important for you to remember to do the right thing. It takes a lot of guts to gracefully get out of the way of something that is self-destructive, but it must be done.

TIM SAUNDERS

Tim has been modeling with Ford Models since 1966. He got his start in London a year before signing with Ford. Tim is represented by several commercial agents in New York and has done more than 200 TV commercials, including ones for Sominex, Promise margarine, United Airlines, Cadillac, Bahamas Tourism, and Prell shampoo. He describes the differences in shooting print and television commercials:

> They are very different jobs. In commercials you must be able to walk, talk, and chew gum at the same time. With print, you don't. Each print job and commercial is different depending on what you are trying to sell. With fashion modeling, you are usually selling a garment and you are trying to make the clothes look good while giving them an attitude. In modeling you either look right for the job or you don't. You don't have to go deep down to any acting abilities to come up with a special look. You were chosen for the job because you look the way you do and the client wants you to be yourself.
>
> In television commercials, you are acting more. You are relating to either the camera or to another person you are working with. In both, you have to have a presence. When you are booked for a print job, you are booked for a certain specified number of hours or days. With a commercial shoot, the hours never end. If you are booked nine-to-five, you might work nine-to-midnight, and you are obliged to stay until the job is done. Print is not done this way. You are very often booked for one job from two-to-three and another job for the afternoon from three-thirty-to-four. You can say your time is up and go on to the next job. Commercials very often have more down time while sets are being lighted or camera angles are being changed. You very often are shot and do your scene at the end of the day."

PATRICK JOHNSON

Patrick has done more than fifty commercials, including ones for Lever 2000, Gillette, Centrum vitamins, Head & Shoulders, Schweppes, Close-Up toothpaste, and Sears. He is also an acting coach and motivational speaker. Here he shares some of his insights into what it takes to do well in the industry:

> Growing up, I never had any real interest in modeling or acting, unlike many young people today, until a good friend encouraged me to enroll in a modeling/talent school while I was a sophomore attending Arizona State University. A few months later, the school asked me to meet with Eileen Ford, who was in town on a scouting

trip. (At the time I had absolutely no idea that Eileen Ford was the owner of the most prestigious model agency in the world!) She encouraged me to find a way to get to New York to try modeling. So, in the summer of 1980, I attended a modeling convention in New York City, was awarded its Model of the Year award, and signed with none other than Ford Models. I must say that if it hadn't been for the convention, I *never* would have ventured to New York to pursue a career in modeling. The thought of going to such a big city on my own was terrifying, and the convention provided me a convenient opportunity to meet with many New York agents in just a few days.

Even though I was lucky enough to sign with Ford Models and quickly get a few breaks in the modeling world, it wasn't until I discovered commercials that a passion was born. Modeling came pretty naturally. On the other hand, trying to read and perform commercial scripts was like learning a foreign language. I had no idea how to move, speak, or even look relaxed in an audition. Thank goodness I discovered on-camera commercial classes! I learned how to give commercial directors what they wanted, learned about the commercial industry itself, and learned a great deal about me as well.

With time, I began to enjoy and relish the working environment of a commercial set. I found it more challenging and stimulating than the average modeling shoot, and commercials helped me escape the dreaded "Golden Handcuffs" of the modeling industry. Don't get me wrong: averaging two-to-three-thousand dollars a day, while taking a trip half way around the world to some exotic location, is not a bad way to spend your life. However, when you are constantly at the mercy of the modeling industry's "Golden Handcuffs," it leaves you with no time to explore other venues of the industry.

Commercial success was a springboard into other areas of the industry for me. My experience motivated me in co-founding a theater company, performing in late-night, prime-time, and day-time shows, and working in feature films as both actor and/or producer.

Modeling got my foot in the door and, although I am not "famous," the commercial industry has kept me busy and happy for over twenty-four years. Find your source of discipline, get ready for some hard work, be prepared for any challenge, and dive in to classes and workshops. If you've got the desire, you can make things happen."

17.

Kids in the Business

In commercials, kids are big business. Appearing in commercials can create scores of extraordinary opportunities for children, including:

■ Significant income potential.

■ Business opportunities that can be carried into later life.

■ Personal development in communication, presentations, and teamwork.

■ Visibility, which can help the child move into other areas of the business.

What Types of Kids Do Well in Commercials?

New York children's agent Karen Apicella describes children who are suited to the business:

> Kids who do well in this business are naturally outgoing. They don't have to be "rehearsed" or "energized" [by parents] before they go in to meet an agent or casting director. They're just fun-loving young people who are not afraid of strangers and can talk without being coaxed or coerced.
>
> Children can't be afraid to leave Mommy. I look for children who will talk, who can keep their attention focused, who can answer questions. Someone who is very spontaneous, very

uninhibited, and not at all shy. All this is as important as looks.

We get a lot of moms who say, "Look, I have this beautiful child," but Susie is very shy. She gives one-word answers. She is always looking at the ground. She fidgets and is clearly uncomfortable. Seven-year-old Susie is not going to work because there are other children who are sparkling, outgoing, and lots of fun. They enjoy themselves. They look like they're having a good time. They respond to you. They're funny.

It's important that you not only have a cute child (*everybody* has a cute child) but that you have a precocious child. That's what the agents look for, the one who stands out and is remembered.

Los Angeles children's talent agent Judy Savage discusses specific requirements:

> The first thing I look for in a child is the passion. A child who wants to do this comes in for the interview and he's just so excited and "alive"—he *loves* the idea of being in the business.
>
> I look for size. In L.A., we look for forty-two-inch six-year-olds to play four-year-olds and fifty-four-inch ten-year-olds to play ages eight, nine, and ten. We also look for twelve-year-olds who are not over five feet tall, thirteen to fourteen-year-olds who are five-one to five-two. If they're thirteen and five-seven or five-eight, they have to play fifteen to sixteen-year-olds because they're taller than everybody. It's almost always preferable to have older children who look younger.

Children who do well in the business read well. The earlier they learn to read, the better they'll do. Child actors who are very successful are always smart. Usually, the smarter they are, the more they'll work. They also have to have charisma. Kids who are suited for the business light up the room when they come in. Even with a three-year-old, the conversation during the interview should be so interesting that you'd rather be with the child than anyone else.

NOTE: Never beg, bribe, or bully a child to get him to perform. Having to resort to such tactics indicates that the child is not interested in doing this. Children will always be better at something they enjoy doing.

Getting Pictures

To get a child under 5 or 6 started, all you need is a couple of snapshots to send out to agents to peak their interest. It is highly impractical to spend $300 on professional headshots to search for an agent. The child's looks will change before you find that agent. In addition, an agent usually likes to have final say as to which picture or pictures they would like to have to represent you.

In a snapshot, agents look for the same things as in a professional head shot. You want a picture that looks like your child. No hats, makeup, big bows in the hair, Halloween masks, or food on the face— just a nice, clean picture of your child looking like a child. Make sure the face is smiling or looking like she's having a good time. Don't send in "crying baby" shots.

Once you find an agent to represent you, it is time for that professional head shot. A good commercial head shot is your child's most important marketing tool. The agent submits the head shots to casting directors in order to secure auditions for the child. As with adults, your child's head shot is his calling card.

In Chapter 1: Getting Head Shots, you learned how to go through the process of finding a good photographer, selecting the right shot, and getting mass reproductions. That process is almost identical when preparing children for the business. However, you have one additional question to ask every photographer before you go to see their work: Do you specialize in photographing children for the industry? There is a big difference between commercial head shots for the industry and pageant pictures (figs. 28 & 29). Whereas photographs intended for commercial are done with simple lighting, simple clothing, no noticeable makeup on pre-teens and younger kids (and very light, clean makeup if any on teens), in pageant competition photographs, it is perfectly acceptable, depending on the pageant system, to use glamorized photos using makeup at almost any age, fancy dresses, and hats and accessories; gimmicky photos (using special effects, diffusion or soft focus, and "theme pictures") are also appropriate. Some pageants are judged by modeling and talent agents, so it is best to ask for guidelines before submitting entries. Agents and managers frown on traditional pageant pictures. Agents and managers have stereotyped views of pageant kids, seeing them as little automatons, too

Morgan Thrush

FIGS. 28 AND 29: There is a big difference between a commercial head shot (fig. 28) and a pageant photo (fig. 29). PHOTO CREDITS: FIG. 28: Rich Hogan. FIG. 29: Old School Photography.

poised or rehearsed (lacking normal childlike spontaneity). Pageant moms have also gotten a bad rap in parts of the industry ("stage moms").

Know that each style of photograph has a specific purpose. You would not wear a ballerina's tutu to a rodeo audition; neither would you use a typical pageant photograph for a commercial audition. To look professional, become clear as to the uses of each type of photograph and use the right picture for each circumstance. It's important to find someone who knows what agents and casting people want in a child's head shot.

Not all photographers relate well to children. Try to find someone who photographs lots of kids and *loves* doing it. When you go to the interview, watch the interaction between the photographer and your child. If they don't seem to be hitting it off, it might be better to look for someone else. You're paying for these pictures and a successful outcome boosts the child's chances of getting work in the business. A great head shot is a collaboration between artist and subject; the result of the shoot depends on the existence of a very positive chemistry between your child and the photographer.

Tips For a Successful Shoot

- *Kids look best in simple, kid-type clothes.* Denim shirts or jackets, overalls, and textured sweaters look great on kids, and they love wearing them. Stay away from busy patterns, frilly things, hats, bows, and large accessories that get in the way. Avoid distracting jewelry or props. Avoid glamorous hair styles and don't have your child wear makeup (other than corrective). Teens should look clean (not made-up). Trust the photographer and the stylist to suggest what's best when it comes to preparing for the shoot.

- *Make sure the child comes to the shoot well-rested.* No sleepovers or late parties the night before a photo session. Do not let little ones fall asleep in the car on the way to the studio, or they will look sleepy or puffy during the shoot. (They may also get crabby if they weren't ready to wake up.) If you have a long ride, plan ahead for activities that will help the child stay alert and excited about the shoot.

- *Bring some quiet project to keep the child occupied in the waiting room.* Avoid letting her run all over the studio, and never leave a small child unattended.

- *If the child is not well or having an off day, call and try to reschedule the shoot.* Your child will not photograph well if he's not into it. Give as much advance notice as possible as a courtesy to the photographer. Not showing up without calling to cancel is a definite no-no.

- *Don't bring any negative energy to the shoot.* Leave problems at home. Children absorb emotional energy, positive and negative. If you have been lecturing the child or engaging in nonproductive conversation on the ride over, or especially in the waiting room, it may affect the child's session. Commercials are happy and energetic. It is important that your child feels that way when performing in front of the camera.

After the shoot, thank the photographer and assistants. When your proofs come in, the photographer will usually help you select the best ones to enlarge. Reread Chapter 1 for help in selecting your pictures, retouching, and getting mass reproductions of your prints for distribution.

Résumés for Kids

Résumés for kids (fig. 30) are set up pretty much the same way as adult résumés (see Chapter 2)—a single eight-by-ten page (which you will attach to the back of the head shots) that summarizes your child's statistics and experience in the business.

Unlike an adult résumé, children's résumés include their date of birth (never age; it dates the résumé) and eye and hair coloring. An early résumé also includes school productions (these show the child's interest in performing), achievements that imply drive and ambition, and any special skills the child may have (for a three-year-old, special skills might include reading and having a long attention span; for older kids, skateboarding, roller-blading, and scuba diving may be listed as special skills). With a little imagination, even a rank beginner can put together an attractive, interesting résumé.

Never lie on a résumé, especially about a special skill. Says Karen Apicella, "Anything you list on the special skills portion of the résumé, you'd better be able to do and do *well*. If you get called into an audition and you're asked to do something you listed as a special skill, then you can't do it, that leaves a terrible impression. Make sure your résumé is honest.

"Also, I don't like to see modeling or pageant experience on talent résumés. Many casting directors feel that pageant kids are over-rehearsed automatons, and they feel so strongly about this that if they see it on a résumé, they will tend *not* to pick the child. I think pageants and modeling are wonderful accomplishments, but being in a pageant really does not connote being a well-rounded actor. On the other hand, acting experience of any kind is good.

"Mom may say, 'Well, Susie has only played a tree in the school play.' I want to see that. It shows she wants to perform, and performing

Talent Agency

YOUNG TALENT DIVISION

www.cedtalent.com

10635 SANTA MONICA BLVD. / SUITE 140 / LOS ANGELES, CA 90025 / (310) 475-3336 / FAX (310) 475-6127

CODY ARENS
SAG/AFTRA
D.O.B. 11-8-93

Hair: Brown   Eyes: Blue

FILM

Shadow Man	Kevin	Creation Pictures/David Benullo
Riding in Cars with Boys	Jason	Columbia Pictures/Penny Marshall
Meet the Parents	Little Boy	Universal/Jay Roach
Anger Management	Cody	Columbia Pictures/Peter Segal

TELEVISION

Punk'd	Boy	MTV
Detective	Jason	Hallmark
Plainsong	Bobby-Lead	CBS-MOW
The Division	Casey (at 7)	Lifetime
Sunset (Pilot)	Mike Stackhouse(Recurring)	NBC
Malcolm In the Middle	Young Malcolm	FOX
The Shield	Mike Jr.	FX
Grand Pa's Place	Jason	Pilot
Passions	Christmas Carole Boy	NBC
Lucky	Adam	FX
Family Affair	Dunkin	WB
Cedrick The Entertainer	Police boy	FOX
Becker	Boy in Park	CBS
Sex and the City	Martin	HBO
Third Watch	Richardson's son	NBC
Spin City	Featured	ABC
Now & Again	Little Boy	CBS Pilot
Law & Order	Jackie Bender	NBC
Guiding Light	Jason/Recurring	CBS
One Life to Live	Ben	ABC
Late Night with David Letterman	Kid Telling Jokes	CBS

COMMERCIALS/VOICEOVERS

Current list of conflicts available upon request

SKILLS/INTERESTS

Follows directions, Reads above grade level, Friendly, Excellent memory, Gymnastics, Singing
Chess, Baseball

FIG. 30: Sample of a children's résumé.

is what it's all about. A child's ability to get out and act, whether in front of a camera or on stage, is precisely what I'm looking for. Include any experience of singing, dancing, or acting classes in the training part of your résumé."

Once you put together your (typed) résumé, print it on good quality paper. Attach one to each of your head shots. If necessary, trim the résumé to the exact size of the head shots. (Use a paper cutter, not scissors, for a cleaner look.)

Finding an Agent

Now you're ready to start mailing out head shots to children's agents. Refer to industry books for legitimate talent agencies. First, send your child's snapshots or professional head shots to agencies that indicate they have a children's division. If you want to send to more agents, and a children's division is not indicated in your industry reference book, call the agent and ask if they have a children's division. If you have a friend who already has an agent, ask if they would speak to their agent about your child. Referrals are always the best means of introduction.

Stay away from the Yellow Pages as much as possible. If you do choose an agent from the Yellow Pages, or an Internet listing, check them out with the Better Business Bureau before you approach them. In smaller, regional markets, call community theaters and the nearest SAG office to find talent agents in or near your area. Be sure to enclose a cover letter (see Chapter 2) with each submission, requesting an interview. Generally, agents only respond when they'd like you to come in for an interview. If you don't get a response within two weeks, call each agency to make sure they received your mailing.

Once you've secured an appointment, the following tips may help you and your child get through the interview/audition process:

- Review Chapter 8: What You Need to Know About Agents, Managers, and Unions.
- Make sure the child is well-rested and fed before going in.
- Do not coach the child about what to do or how to behave at the interview. Let the child answer questions addressed to her and do not answer for her.

- Dress the child casually, preferably in clothes she likes. The same choices and advice given for photo shoots apply to interviews and auditions for kids.

- Resist the temptation to critique or analyze the child's performance during or after the interview. After the interview, the agent will either offer to represent your child or tell you why he isn't interested at this time. He may suggest waiting until the child is older or suggest that the child take a class or workshop that will make her more marketable.

Typical Scams

You do not want to get involved with an unsavory agent. The most popular industry scam involves a so-called agent who will only offer to sign you if you pay to take a class or use his photographer. You should be able to choose any training you want and use any photographer you want. It is common for an agent to have a list of several good photographers and classes.

If you are from a smaller, regional area with limited options for access to good industry training and photographers, do as much research as possible before deciding who to work with. (See Chapter 1 and Chapter 4 for more information on finding a good photographer and/or talent coach.) Be aware of packages and contracts that run thousands of dollars. Check out your options. Do everything possible to avoid being taken advantage of (see Chapter 5 for more information on scams). An agent should only be making a percentage of the money you make on the jobs booked through their agency.

Another scam you want to avoid is where a so-called "agent" sends you out on auditions, collects payments from your bookings, then does not pay you for your services. Unscrupulous agents may dangle you on with excuses such as "they have not yet been paid for the job" for extended periods of time. Reporting such treatment to the Better Business Bureau would be your recourse. An agent must pay a performer who has worked on a job under SAG or AFTRA union contract within fourteen days from the day of the shoot. If they do not, the actor can report the situation to the union, and fines and penalties are involved in accordance with the situation.

Managers

Whether or not to hire a manager is a personal decision. For a child, having a manager can be an asset. Good managers tend to nurture and develop a child's career. For children four and over, it is the job of the manager to introduce the child and get them signed to an agent for TV, film and commercials. However, agents do not generally sign children three and under. It is the job of the manager to have good relationships with several agents who will call the manager for audition times.

While agents work hard to find jobs for your child (and many others), they are generally too busy to educate parents and kids about the business, to monitor the child's progress, or to teach the family how to deal with frustration, rejection, or success. Many people, especially beginners, find that having someone mentor parents and child as they learn and develop is well worth paying the extra fifteen percent.

Parents might consider hiring a manager at the point where the child has done many commercials and the family decides it is time to expand into film and television. The manager will guide the growth and movement of the child's career just as he would for an adult.

There are many managers who represent only children. Some handle both children and adults. Others represent infants. Many agents will not sign infants as clients because they change too quickly in looks and behavior. Another problem with representing infants is that parents often change their minds about the business when they discover the cost and time involved in launching and maintaining a child's career. An agent is reluctant to invest time and energy in a client who is not in it for the long haul. Dealing with overzealous or unmotivated parents or trying to educate them about the professional expectations of the industry can be time-consuming. Rather than sign on infants himself, the agent will contact managers who represent them.

The best ways to find a manager for a child is to ask other industry parents or your agent for names of managers in your area. Call the National Conference of Personal Managers in New York City or Los Angeles. It is not a good idea to look for managers in the Yellow Pages.

Training

When children are young (four to seven), they can pretty much get by on their personality and charm. But by the time they're eight or nine, they really have to begin to know what they are doing.

Judy Savage elaborates: "I always say that if you are an incredible six-year-old—you read, you're smart, you're small, you're outgoing, you have the personality—your competition in the whole town is only about ten other kids who are that special [at that age]. By the time you're ten, there are about two hundred competitors, and by the time you turn eighteen, there are about two thousand.

"What happens is that everybody who turns eighteen and has a passion for acting comes to California from all over the world to try to break into the business, and your competition absolutely magnifies. These other kids might have been taking acting, singing, elocution, speech, and every other kind of lesson you can think of since they were six years old. Also, when you turn eighteen, the competition comes from the legal sixteen- and seventeen-year-olds who have graduated from high school as well as from good-looking twenty-five-year-olds, so it's tough."

A class or workshop[1] in on-camera commercial technique will help your child get comfortable in front of the camera while learning how to audition. You want your child to stay natural and spontaneous. Never get to the point where he is slick and polished.

Once the child starts getting calls for auditions, on-the-job training serves as the best teacher. Exposing kids to improvisation classes, acting classes, community theater, and school drama programs can help them round out their talent and develop confidence.

---

[1] A workshop for children should bring out their individual personality and eliminate inhibitions. It should not try to mold or change a child or, worst of all, take away from the child's natural spontaneity.

Tips on Auditions

DO'S AND DON'TS

Do:

■ Respect your audition appointment time. Casting directors have a schedule to keep. Coming late causes confusion and creates a backup.

■ Sign in upon entering the reception area. Casting directors use this sheet to call performers into the studio. Forgetting to sign in could put you at risk of losing the opportunity to audition.

■ Take your child aside and begin going over the script after signing in. Resist the temptation to socialize with other parents and children in the reception area. You are better off attending to the business at hand. Concentrate on preparing your child to give a good audition.

■ Have your head shot and résumé ready to hand to the casting director.

Don't:

■ Over-rehearse the script. It is important to become familiar with the material while maintaining spontaneity.

■ Wait until your child is called into the audition room to begin grooming him. When the casting director calls "Next!" the child should be fully prepared to go in and give a good audition.

■ Bring extra family members, friends, boyfriends, or performers to the audition.

■ Put makeup on your child. *Please!*

OTHER CONSIDERATIONS

■ Food auditions: Many auditions for children are for food, especially snacks, fast foods, and cereals. You will be told at the time of the audition call what the food is. If your child cannot eat the food because she doesn't like it or is allergic to it, please make sure to ask if the actor will actually have to eat the food. If the answer is yes, don't waste everyone's time by going to the call. Your child will be given the food at the audition to make sure she actually likes it. She *will* be expected to eat the product enthusiastically, take after take, and will have to eat more than the usual intake. If your child cannot eat the product, it's to everyone's advantage for you to say so *when you are called for the audition.* You may have to bow out of the audition.

- Parents are not asked to come into the audition room. Part of the casting process is to see how a child behaves without a parent in the room. If a child is shy or insecure, or cries when his parent is not with him, he is not good commercial material. Always be nearby, however, either just outside the door or in a reception room.

Sometimes parents are allowed to "assist" when the audition calls for babies and toddlers. You should be aware that for very young children (age four and under), backup kids are always booked for shoots, just in case one or more children get tired, cranky, or otherwise unable to cooperate. Twins or triplets have good booking rates because they provide instant backup that is identical or similar in looks.

Common-Sense Safeguards for Showbiz Kids

In a world where parents must take every precaution to assure their child's safety and well-being, it defies logic to watch how quickly well-meaning moms and dads throw caution to the wind when it comes to working in show business. The industry requires children to talk to people they don't always know well and to do so without their parents in immediate sight, so it's very important for families to keep their feet on the ground (and the stars out of their eyes) when making decisions that affect their child's immediate and long-term future.

Common sense is essential to guard against unscrupulous vultures who prey on showbiz kids and their families. For instance:

- Know that a minor (fifteen years or younger) *must* have a guardian at a shoot. If there is travel involved, the production company must also arrange (and pay) for the guardian to accompany the child.

- Be alert if you are called to hotels, unsafe neighborhoods, out-of-the-way buildings, or any location late at night. It's not that auditions are not held under these circumstances. Just use common sense when dealing with these conditions.

- If you are going to an unknown casting office, be alert to the surroundings. Are there a lot of other guardians and kids there? Are other kids coming out of the room happy? Are the people who bring the children into the room friendly to them and their guardians?

- Teenagers going to auditions alone must be alert. Females are not asked to wear less than a two-piece bathing suit at a legitimate commercial audition. No one should be asked to change into a bathing suit in the audition room. If an actor needs to change clothes, some kind of changing room should be provided. There have been instances in which Peeping Toms hid behind a two-way mirror and taped clothing changes.

- Males *and* females should be aware of advances or threats by people who audition or hire them (people who seem to be in a powerful position). *No* job is worth compromising yourself, and no legitimate job would ever involve unsavory behavior. You would *never* have to go to a producer's house or go out on a date with him.

- *Trust your instincts.* If something doesn't feel right, *leave.*

When to Consider Commuting or Relocating to a Larger Market

Most agents and managers agree that children should get as much experience in their own market (however small) before deciding on going to a larger market. Karen Apicella advises to audition as much as possible at home so a child can acclimate as quickly and as easily as possible in a larger market. "Also, the child should perform and learn the many disciplines involved before going to a larger market."

The child must listen to his parents. He must be able to move swiftly and in an organized manner, getting to appointments on time. He must tolerate the tedium of traveling from one audition to the next, waiting in the reception room until it's his turn to audition. At the callback, he may be asked by the director to do something over and over again. He may walk into a callback audition and have to perform in front of six clients. The child must be willing to come in early for a booking if need be, and he must be able to handle the pressure during tense moments on the set.

The demands on children in the industry can be considerable. They range from travel demands to disappointments when they don't get the job. It is certainly not for everyone. Yet some kids love the challenge, the demands, and the rewards that come with them. Inevitably, parents of serious child actors will decide whether or not to take the child to a larger market. They need to decide which market to come to and what time of year is best. A typical time to try a new market is summer, when your child is on school vacation.

Deciding between the two larger markets (New York and Los Angeles) is a matter of personal choice. If the focus is entirely on commercials (which is a good way to get your feet wet and to get comfortable with the industry), there are as many opportunities in Los Angeles as there are in New York. Look at both lifestyles and decide which you prefer. New York is a big, congested city where you would use public transportation. Los Angeles has a more outdoorsy atmosphere, and you spend a lot of time in your car driving from place to place. Look into the costs of living in both locations. Is climate a consideration for you? One place won't have the magic answer—so do your research on both markets, then go where you feel most comfortable.

When regional kids come to New York or Los Angeles for the summer, they find themselves competing against hundreds of other kids from all over the country, some of whom have several summers under their belts. Then there are kids who live in the area you will be moving to who were practically raised in the business. If your child is booking most of the jobs she auditions for (or is consistently called back) in her own market, she may be ready for a summer in a larger market. But competition will be stiff. The better prepared children are, the more experience they have, the better their chances of booking in places like New York and Los Angeles.

You will also hear, "Come to Los Angeles for pilot season." Generally, pilots are cast from January through mid-March. They are finished and delivered by the end of April to be considered to be picked up, with final decisions made between May and June. Episodic season is when the television series are up and running. Casting is conducted on a weekly basis to fulfill all the supporting acting roles, "under fives," the co-stars, and guest stars. Episodic season runs from late July to the end of March. May and June, television series are on "hiatus," which means that no production is being done. If you are focusing on television, this is a good time not to come to Los Angeles.

All experiences in your local market will prepare you for the larger markets. In the larger markets every aspect of the business is in larger proportions. There are many more agents, actors, opportunities, and disappointments.

Sue Schacter, a New York-based manager, advises that:

Summer is the best time to come to a larger market so as not to upset the family structure or the child's life. A summer in Los Angeles or New York should be like a vacation.

They shouldn't come with the intention of working. The attitude should be, "Let's go to New York for the summer and have a great time and perhaps while we're there, we'll get some work," because the ones who come with the intention and the compulsion to work never have a good time and never get enough work. It is generally an eight-week commitment. Parents will have to find housing. I try to encourage parents to bring the other children to keep the family together. All too often, because of the money involved and whatever visibility is involved, the mother becomes focused on the one child and forgets the husband and their other children.

My first questions for the mother are, "Do you have family you can stay with in that market?" "Does your husband have the ability to come and visit at least once or twice during the stay?" Often the answer is that he cannot because the family is financially stressed, so it becomes difficult because the mother, of course, gets lonely. The children get lonely too, so we try to create more of a vacation atmosphere for them. But whenever possible, I always encourage them to bring the siblings.

What Parents Can Expect

Judy Savage is the owner of one of the leading children's agencies in Los Angeles—The Savage Agency: "Most people come here not prepared enough, not trained enough, and with high expectations," says Judy. "They think that in three months of a pilot season, they're going to make it. The general rule is that it takes about three years to make it. There may be an exception. They may get a little thing here and there, but to get on a series or to get a movie, the time frame we're looking at it generally wider."

Judy Savage adds, "The parent and the child have to become partners in this. There's never been a successful child actor without one committed parent (or relative; somebody who literally has to give up her own career for ten or twelve years and devote all her time to this child (or children), because they have to be ready to go at any moment.

"So the mother has to be on call. You have to realize that it's going to be really hard on the rest of the family. You can expect not to get much respect on the set. When a child is hired, the mother has to be there, within sight and sound. They would rather have you be a mute and sit in the corner and not know you're there. I did it for fifteen years and I know the feeling. You feel like you don't belong. You feel like a vegetable. You feel like you don't have a purpose. And yet, you know in your heart that this is something your children love and it's an amazing way (for most) to be with your children, and make some money for them. Some kids pay for their braces, cars, college, and houses, and a lot of them don't stay in the business, but they have all that by the time they're eighteen or nineteen. A lot of these parents could never have afforded to give them that kind of lifestyle."

And whatever the time frame involved, the child always needs a parent or parents around. "It's very thankless to be a show biz mom," explains Karen Apicella. "Moms in this business don't get enough credit. You have to be very organized to be a good industry mom. If, for instance, you're with several agents and don't have a manager, you have to keep your facts very, very straight because if you don't, you could wind up in a mess.

"Say, for instance, you go out on an audition in the freelance New York market, and book the job but can't remember which agent the call came from. The client will not know who to send your check to—and if it winds up going to the wrong agent, you will create an uncomfortable situation for all concerned."

"The more you are available, the better your chances of getting started. Most of the time, we get a little bit of notice—a day, or we get the call in the morning, but there are a lot of last-minute calls where they say, 'Be there in an hour.'

Compensation

Because of the many opportunities for children in commercials, a great deal of money can be made, depending on how many commercials the child books and how the commercial runs (see Chapter 13 on talent payments). The amount made can be as little as $535 or in excess of $100,000 a year.

HANDLING THE CHILD'S MONEY

It is very important to know exactly what you are going to do with the money your child earns in the business *and* what the law says you *must* do to protect the child's interests.

In California, for instance, the Coogan Law (named after child star Jackie Coogan, who wound up penniless when he came of age because his parents had spent all his money) was set in place to protect young performers from their parents' or guardians' lack of knowledge, inexperience, or outright greed. The Coogan Law mandates that twenty-five percent of a child's earnings must be placed in trust so that when the child comes of age, he will have something to show for his efforts.

Even if there are no specific laws governing the way a child's earnings are used, know that when children reach the age of maturity (eighteen in most states), they can ask for an accounting of the money they earned while under-age. Parents risk being sued by their children for mismanagement of funds if they cannot adequately account for the money.

In cases in which a child becomes the primary breadwinner for the entire family, courts tend to look with disapproval upon parents who charge the child's estate excessively for such things as chaperoning/chauffer fees, food, rent, and schooling. Such expenses generally fall under a parent's normal responsibilities (most folks don't expect their kids to reimburse them for such things). If a child's money is used to buy property (like a bigger house, for instance), the youngster may even be able to sue her parents for the home, since it was her earnings that paid for it in the first place.

Aside from the obvious legal and financial problems that can arise from failing to launch a sensible financial plan for a child's earnings, the emotional and psychological damage done when children are put in the position of having to sue their parents to get what is rightfully theirs is nothing short of catastrophic. Wise parents will discuss financial planning with their accountant and their agent or manager and put a proper trust/investment package into place.

What It Takes for Kids to Make It in the Business

Judy Savage comments:

> It's going to take absolute passion, total belief in yourself and your child (it works both ways), and the ability to do it for the love of doing it—and not taking the rejection personally, which is such a hard thing. You have to get to the point where you can go into an interview for the pure joy of showing your work to the casting director. You get a high out of that. When you get to that point, you won't take the rejection seriously. And you can never let success go to your head. You have to stay humble and grateful because the minute you start becoming a legend in your own mind, you're almost destined to find yourself moving back the other way.
>
> Most of all, remember to hang in there. Some people struggle for four or five years without something significant happening in their careers. I represented Barry Watson for seven years, traveling back and forth from Dallas to Los Angeles. He started studying regularly and finally in the eighth year, he booked *7th Heaven*. He had to wait until the right part came along at the right time.
>
> There are hard types. The harder you are to fit into something— the more unstereotypical you really are—the more likely you are to become a star one day. Because it's taken them much longer to get started, they've had to spend many more years in theater and in training and in improv groups, so when they do get a role, they are ready to just blow the world away.

WORKING PAPERS

To actually work as a child actor, the child must have good grades. To work in a commercial, a minor is required to have a work permit from the state. The state issues the work permit based on the school approving it. The state will issue the work permit if the child has a "B" average and above. In Los Angeles, the permit is good for up to six months. However, every state has its own rules regarding the length of time the work permit is good for.

How Your Child's Acting Career Coincides With Their Education

ALAN SIMON

Alan Simon is the owner of On Location Education, a company that provides tutors for children in the business while they are on the set. (Alan was previously an actor who supported himself by substitute teaching in the New York City school system.)

The education of children in the entertainment industry is important and definitely not overlooked. On Location Education provides teachers, studio teachers, and educational consultants to work with production companies employing child actors in television, film, theater, national tours, commercials, industrials, and circuses. Children who have alternative lifestyles must work their schooling around their production day. On Location Education helps them form an educational plan of action with their home schools.

Legally, at what age does the actor fall under the "child" category?
In the SAG commercial contract, the definition of a minor is fifteen years and younger, which means anyone older technically is not considered a minor, and provisions that apply to children under the SAG contract cease to apply. Local and state labor laws may have certain provisions pertaining to the needs of sixteen- to eighteen-year-olds, and those can be found through the local departments of labor.

How do parents find out about specific child labor laws?
A complete set of guidelines is available to all members of either union from the local office (ask for the SAG-AFTRA *Young Performers Handbook*, 3rd edition). Parents should check their local labor laws. No producer is going to tell you. You have to read the code or whatever information you can find for your area.

Are there occasions when you are called to give education on the set?
Absolutely. In California, education is required on the set. There must be a welfare worker present at all times. That person, called a studio teacher, functions in the official capacity of a welfare worker empowered by the state of California to speak for the child's health, education, and welfare. Welfare workers serve many roles. They are there to educate the

child and to insure that the physical surroundings are not in any way negative or harmful. They also make sure the wardrobe area is properly situated for boys and girls.

If indeed welfare workers feel that a child is being worked by the production company even five minutes over the proper amount of time, they have the right to virtually stop production and call it a day on the child's behalf. In other states the parents will need to have the forethought to negotiate with the producer and request a teacher in advance.

How is education approached on the set?

There are two ways to answer this question. On Location Education or an individual studio teacher can be responsible for finding out the specifics of the curriculum at a child's home school. We contact parents and make sure the kids bring the material they are supposed to cover, be it the textbook, handouts, or whatever. But when there is no teacher provided, then it is up to the parent to get work from the school and, if necessary, hire a teacher to oversee instruction. The ultimate goal is for the child to return to school on par with his classmates.

If a child is booked with only a day or two's notice, does that give you time to set up the education requirements?

It's the nature of the beast. These things happen very quickly. Kids who work rather frequently know they have to be prepared to bring their materials with them. Parents who do this frequently are ready for it. Parents who are novices are not. Parents need to have a tutoring support network in place. They should know where to find a teacher while maintaining a positive relationship with their home school. If they are working outside of California, they should never assume a tutor will be provided.

A good agent, at the time of the booking, is always going to tell the parent, "There will be a teacher on the set. Please make sure you bring your books." We are also given the child's phone number, are authorized to contact the family, and will do whatever we have to do to ensure that the books and materials are there.

What personality traits do you notice in kids who do commercials?
Kids who are successful, who do this regularly, tend to be bright and have a lot of energy. They tend to know how to budget their time. They know what it's like to sit in that green room[2] and keep themselves occupied.

What is the crucial information parents must have before their children get into the business?
I would say that if you want to make this a career, it would be important to cultivate a good relationship with your home school. Make sure the principal knows that your child is doing this and that there are going to be periods of time when, with very little advance notice, your child is going to be called to the set and will be out. Make sure the school staff know that the child's absences are not a reflection on the teacher or the school, that you really want to work with the school, and that you will hold your child responsible for the workload missed. In fact, you will always see to it that the child is tutored on the set, a teacher will be provided, and the work will get done.

You have to look into the issue of excused absences. If your child is going to be out two days here, three days there, all of a sudden that adds up to ten days' absences; before you know it, you have reached the legal limit of absences you can have before your child is considered truant. You need to deal with these issues up front. It is very, very important.

I think most parents are overwhelmed once they get a job on location. I don't think they realize the implications that an acting career has on their kids, on themselves, and their families. For instance, if they get booked and have to travel to another location, usually a father or another parent is left behind, and maybe other siblings as well. Parents have to create a support system in order for this to work. And I think they need to know who to go to in terms of guardianship if that becomes an issue because they both work or are unable to travel. Who are they going to get to travel with their child? What kind of questions should they ask ahead of time? Who on the set will look out for their child's best interest if they are not working in a place where there is a studio teacher empowered to act as the welfare worker?

I think parents don't realize what working their child regularly means in terms of wear and tear on the family, as well as on themselves and the child.

---

[2] A green room is an offstage theatrical waiting room, traditionally painted green.

Specific Issues and Experiences that Young People and Their Families Go Through While Working in the Industry

Parents and guardians are the ones who have the bulk of the work to do when getting their children involved in the business. The following series of interviews are with parents who know what it takes to do well in the entertainment industry. Through their experiences you will gain knowledge to help you prepare for a successful child talent career.

First, a few introductions:

DEBBIE BOYD is the mother of two children in the business: Jenna Boyd (fig. 31), who has done commercials and stars in the films *The Missing* and *Sisterhood of Traveling Pants*, and a son, Cayden, who stars in *Mystic River*.

JENNIFER ARENS is the mother of Cody Arens (fig. 32), who can be seen in commercials and the films *Shadow Man, Riding in Cars With Boys, Meet The Parents,* and *Anger Management,* as well as in television series (partial list) *Punk'd, Malcolm in the Middle, The Shield, Passions, Becker,* and *Sex in the City.* (See résumé in this chapter.)

KAREN TANK, mother of Hayden Tank (fig. 33), is a mom who has two kids in the business. Hayden Tank has done commercials as well as (partial list) *Freaky Friday, Momentum, The Perfect Storm,* and television series *Gilmore Girls, CSI: Miami, Six Feet Under, Drew Carey,* and *The Young and the Restless.*

KIMBERLEE LUCAS is the mother of Jack "Bean" Lucas (fig. 34). Jack has done commercials and has had two of his own "made for TV" cooking shows called *Bean and Sugar Show* and *What's Jack Cooking.* Mom has four children. Two of the four are active in the business.

DAVID REIVERS is a working actor with four kids in the business. His oldest son, Corbin Bleu (fig. 35), has appeared in numerous commercials with television film credits including (partial list): *Catch That Kid, Gallaxy Quest, Mystery Men,* and has been the guest star in *The Amanda Show, Malcolm and Eddie, ER,* and *Cover Me.* His daughter, Hunter Grey, has booked many commercials as well as co-starring in the television shows *Felicity* and *Love & Money.*

Jenna Boyd

FIG. 31: Jenna Boyd. PHOTO CREDIT: Kelsey Edwards Photography.

Cody Arens

FIG. 32: Cody Arens. PHOTO CREDIT: Studio D Photography.

Hayden Tank

FIG. 33: Hayden Tank. PHOTO CREDIT: Shultz
Bros. Photography.

Jack "Bean" L

FIG. 34: Jack "Bean" Lucas. PHOTO CREDIT
Gary Tice

CORBIN BLEU

FIG. 35: Corbin Bleu. PHOTO CREDIT: Nancy Jo
Gilchrist.

HOW DID YOU GET

YOUR CHILD INVOLVED IN THE ACTING BUSINESS?

JENNA BOYD: We started our "journey" in this business in 1995. I read an ad that was promoting a model search in the Dallas-Ft. Worth area. The ad stated that talent agents would be judging the competition. Being skeptical and fearful that this was simply another pageant, I researched and called the company that was sponsoring the competition. I asked them to specify the names of the agents. I called those particular agencies and got confirmation that they would be participating, seeking out new talent. So, I entered Jenna (age 2) in the model search. That's when and where we got our first local agent. Cayden was an infant, so he became a baby print model with little or no input in the matter. The kids worked in commercials and print in the Texas market.

My husband's work moved us to Georgia, where the kids worked with a very "connected" agent. They worked in more commercials, print, and a couple of independent films. Before long, the Georgia agent advised and arranged for us to meet an agent in Los Angeles. We did so, and as a result of that meeting, we decided to test the waters in L.A. We were under the impression that we were coming for a few weeks—that was almost four years ago! We realized it would have been a waste of time and money to leave after a few weeks. The following year was torture as we went month to month trying to decide if we should stay or go.

My husband would commute and stay for long periods of time. On one of my husband's trips to L.A., I made it a point to take him around, meet agents, and hear feedback. We made a joint decision to relocate to Los Angeles. Families will face the financial pressures of living in two places at one time, and for families to stay together, husbands have to have flexibility to travel and relocate if necessary.

It has been a very slow, transitional, evolving process that has led us to L.A. Each step has better prepared us for the next, and while it may have been small print jobs in the beginning, I never realized it would amount to anything more. The kids have never been taught to weigh one appointment with more intensity or preparedness than another—whether it be print, film, first-call, or screen test. I wanted to do the best with what we had and did not anticipate where we are now. Each step along the way, I was determined to be educated and be creative about how we handled the business. This determination prepared me for the next step (Texas to Georgia) and that step prepared me for the next step (Georgia to L.A.). I was able to learn and make mistakes in the smaller markets that would save me a lot of time and energy in the major market.

JENNIFER ARENS: I got Cody involved in the business through a modeling contest in Connecticut, where one meets managers and agents, and ended up signing with a manager in New York City when Cody was six months old. Mom and Cody have now been in the business for ten years. Cody also has a younger brother and sister also in the business.

There are stages of maturity/knowledge that you go through. I remember going to Cody's first audition not knowing I had to sign in and asking a million questions without trying to seem brand-new.

KAREN TANK: Not knowing anyone else who was doing this, I started off going about it in the wrong way. First, I answered a newspaper ad and paid $900 for nothing. I then did more research, read books, and got a SAG agent list, and then found an agent the correct way.

KIMBERLEE LUCAS: Jack got into the business because of a cooking show we developed and filmed. It was seen by an agent and he was interviewed.

DAVID REIVERS: Corbin and the rest of my children were exposed to the business being that I am an actor.

WHAT IS THE ROLE AS A PARENT AT THE AUDITIONS?

BOYD: I believe the role of a parent/guardian cannot be defined in some "one-line" description. I've always tried to exercise my "stage mommy" muscle at home during the coaching or preparations. Then we usually talk things through on the way, in the car. Once we enter the casting office, I've always attempted to take off my "stage mommy" hat and let our hard work come to life on its own. Obviously, I have to play the role of mom and insist that they (my children) sit down rather than run up and down the hallways. I have to remind them to focus if I believe it's necessary and I have to remind them that we are here for a specific purpose. I keep a low profile and we take care of business and we leave.

ARENS: Sign in, fill out your size card, pull your head shot and résumé, have your child's Polaroid taken, look at the storyboard, have your child learn the copy, hand the paperwork and stapled picture and résumé to the casting assistant, make sure the child's hands and face are clean, and that their clothes are neat—and after all of this, relax. Let your child make new friends and make an effort to meet some of the parents. Although intentions are often questionable, over the years I have learned that these "friendships" are not like typical ones. You learn to balance your trust.

TANK: After my son is signed in, I sit and wait and speak to other mothers. I know there are some parents who make themselves known and try to become friendly with casting directors. The fact is that I have been doing this for over eleven years and there are some casting directors that I could not point out in a crowd.

HOW DO YOU PREPARE FOR AUDITIONS?

BOYD: In regards to film, my kids have spent a lot of time in acting classes in general and have worked with a lot of acting coaches. I believe there are basic skills that have to be learned. I think it is very important that a parent pay close attention to what is happening in group classes. A family can spend a lot of money on classes. Some are far more worthwhile than others. Only recently have I felt comfortable coaching my own kids. I spend time talking them through a scene (sometimes for hours) in order to paint a picture that might help them understand and better connect to the character. Often this requires me to read through a script to get a true feeling for what is happening in the sides and spend a lot of time digging beneath a single scene to try and figure out where the character is coming from.

ARENS: The day begins the night before, writing down all the auditions that your agent has given you. Not only do you need the address and time, but the attire and copy if any (FAX machines by age five or six to receive copy are imperative). Then you need to pull the wardrobe for the next day. Is it P.J.s, baseball, business, geek, etc.? We have nerd glasses and cool glasses, cowboy to casual attire. Bring quiet games to keep kids occupied while waiting to audition. Gameboys, hangman, tic-tac-toe, and drawing are the quiet games of choice.

Before the child is reading independently, you have to sit and help them memorize the script. It could be as little as one line . . . one word even—or several pages. In commercials you get the copy when you arrive at the audition. In film and television, you normally get a day's notice, so it is not much time. You want your child to learn their script while keeping it fun and fresh in the process. You don't want them to stress out because then it's not fun for anyone.

By age seven, you can normally hand off the script to them. I normally will read a couple of times with them after they are off-book just to make sure they understand the dialogue and are portraying the character description appropriately. As with any parent/child dynamic, it is often difficult for a child to hear constructive criticism from their parent. And truthfully, often what the parent thinks the writer/director is looking for is wrong. Having your child coached is expensive, but very helpful in assuring that your child is on track and limits anger/resentment between parent and child. However, it is important that you find a reputable coach that is referred to you by your agent or by several parents in the business. I have found it important to get referrals from several parents as one may steer you to a coach who has not worked well nor gotten positive results.

As far as preparing babies and toddlers for auditions—as with any outing—you want to make sure that you have extra outfits, diapers, clean blankets, snacks, and quiet toys. Don't forget to bring a snapshot. You do not normally need professional pictures until around age four as a child's look changes so rapidly before then. Try to coordinate naps so that they are at their best for the audition. You don't want them auditioning just after they have woken up or are ready for a nap. Also try to acclimate your child to different situations between auditions. They should be comfortable with strangers, abrupt noises, water, and animals, just to name a few. Arrive early so that if your child is fussy when you get to the audition, you can reverse their mood, change diapers, feed them, etc. . . . before being seen.

LUCAS: Preparation for film can take more time than showing up for a commercial audition. For one, film projects often ask for several pages of a script to be memorized. Some roles might deem the need for a coach. Seeing a coach benefits your kid in knowing they understand the character and refined the audition.

My son will spend time memorizing and adapting the role to a given character, then the family has to spend time listening to those lines. I recommend not acting them out with him. It is best to sit on the couch and let the actor stand. It plays more realistic in terms of how the child will experience it in the actual session. If he needs to spend more time, try encouraging him by saying, "Really good! Keep going. Spend fifteen minutes and we'll take a break." It keeps making it more his. It takes more time, but he is still working on his skills.

TANK: Most commercial auditions have no preparation. You can drive an hour to the audition and have your child in the audition room for thirty seconds. A theatrical audition usually has dialogue that your child must learn prior to their audition, so there is more preparation.

NOW YOUR CHILD IS SUCCESSFUL AUDITIONING FOR FILM, TELEVISION, AND COMMERCIALS: HOW DO YOU JUGGLE AND PREPARE FOR IT ALL?

ARENS: For film auditions there are sides (selected pages of script) to learn and coaches to see. You will become more emotionally connected. As with any audition, if you are lucky, you will get twenty-four hours' notice. Twenty-four hours' notice for a commercial is a piece of cake. If you have several auditions miles apart (which can happen often), you have to get them to the auditions and fit in school, homework, rearrange play dates, and find time for whatever lessons they have to learn, rehearsals, and games they had planned. In addition to, and most important of all, is making sure they are well fed, rested, and happy. All this can make the most seasoned auditioning parent feel as though they are teetering between sanity and lunacy. Often there may be several films, or TV shows, with pages of scripts and different character dynamics on top of commercial auditions—or worse yet, callbacks on the same day. Obviously you can't do it all, so you need to prioritize. Although it is a thorn in their side with many parents and managers calling agents with similar issues all day long, you can ask your agent to work on trying to arrange times and sometimes even dates to better accommodate your schedule. Often it is impossible and you will miss out on some auditions. It is hard to swallow, but just know that if you are that busy, your agent and a multitude of casting directors love your child, and it is a good position to be in.

BOYD: Having two kids in the business has made for logistical night-mares on more than one occasion. Fortunately, my husband's job is somewhat flexible and we have minimized this as much as possible. Be good and gracious to your family and friends.

TANK: In order to be able to pursue this as an option, you need to have support at home, especially if you have other children not in the busi-ness. It can feel like a full-time job, and without the support of others, it would be very difficult. There are times you will have to choose which audition you are going to make. Callbacks are first priority and theatri-cals are second priority for our family.

LUCAS: Juggling the auditions is really about what my agency can work out for us. If I am double-booked, I notify the agents. The agent knows the casting houses and should make the arrangements. Always! A parent should not call the casting house to change an appointment. I always have everyone with me, so if I am called on the road with a last minute audition, I will be able to make it. I like to take advantage of car time. We play games, talk about issues, dreams, plans, parties to attend, places and people to go and see. Singing your hearts out and just good old-fash-ioned joke-telling are such memorable times. The times we are juggling auditions can either be miserable or we can make it a good time that we are all together.

Being "on the road" does not help get things done at home. Sometimes we stress about dinner for ourselves and the rest of the family. Stock up and cook ahead of time. Use weekends to plan and prepare a few crock-pot meals for the coming week. I enlist my kids to help around the house when asked. The deal is we have to ask. But our motto is, "You are not passengers on the flight; you are crewmembers and we need you!" A sense of belonging is felt.

REIVERS: Time management does become a very large task when you are trying to coordinate everyone's schedule. You need total cooperation from both adults and kids. When it comes to children in the business, there are many times that they will have to miss out on participating in sports and dance. The desire to be in this business must be met with the flex-ibility to give up other things. There must always be an adult available to run with a child to an audition at any given moment. Since my wife is a stay-at-home mom, we are able to balance this task between the both of us.

When many things start going on at once, we seek outside help. Things can definitely get a little crazy. An example being, my daughter got booked on a job that shoots either the seventeenth or eighteenth of the month, she has elementary graduation on the sixteenth, her senior school party is on the seventeenth, I then booked a job on the eighteenth. Here's where we call upon our resources of baby-sitters, friends, and family.

If I have a booking at a location away from home for an extended period of time, I try to come home during the weekends. If it is one of my children, my wife travels with them and, depending on my schedule at the time, we may hire some help to be at home with the other children.

There is actually a Set Sitting Service that has been developed due to situations of families not having enough help with numerous kids in the business; one parent to take the child and the other parent has an inflexible job. This service provides a responsible adult to accommodate the child on the set.

WHAT IS IT LIKE FOR A PARENT ON A COMMERCIAL SET?

TANK: You must learn how to blend into the background. You never want to interfere and get in the way. Directors do not want you as a distraction in any way. As the parent you must make a point to be there for the protection of your child, to make sure nothing is happening that you feel is inappropriate, but you must be there in an invisible way.

LUCAS: I am there to be supportive and informative. Aside from school time and recreational time, my child should grow in a sense of ownership to the project. I will give you the analogy of a baseball player: If you want to play ball, you watch great ballplayers and you practice and get involved in every aspect of that sport. All this to say, if your child is on the side-lines waiting to be on deck, teach him to be an observer. Spend time getting into the environment provided for his role, which allows your child to be a part of it all. So far, every director has spent time showing Jack equipment and playbacks because of his interest in the filming process. Some actually had Jack shadow them for the time he was on set. A child who is out of control and thoughtless to the surroundings of the set is a nuisance and trouble to the crew and themselves.

Set your rules before you go on set. We have no soda or candy until we leave set—rule. No running on set. Explain why before you are on set, not later. Give them a sense of having a job by teaching them how people handle jobs. Discuss people you know and the businesses they are in. "Can Dad go running around the office screaming and jumping on the furniture?" Do not drag down or embarrass your little actor on the set, but prepare them for the things they can look forward to experiencing when they arrive there.

ARENS: As a parent you automatically feel as though you are in the way no matter how nice everyone is to you. And if you don't, you should. It will keep you out of trouble. Arrive early and you can catch breakfast from craft service. Have all of your child's paperwork with you (I-9, Coogan and work permit paperwork, and your child's schoolwork). Keep quiet and out of the way. However, while your child is shooting, you have the right to view them either via a monitor or off-camera. For toddlers, they let the parent be right near them while shooting, and a treat can be given to them as leverage and reward between takes. Be careful that their hands and face do not get messy. Also make sure that the treat is not too big, or it will stick in their teeth. Be aware of foods that will color their tongue such as an Oreo or a colored lollipop or popsicle.

Sometimes they will be able to run to you; other times you will be able to run to them. This is a question for you to ask your chain of command. For older children, limit their visits to craft services.

School-aged children have schoolwork to do on set. Bring their schoolwork. Younger children should have quiet toys to keep them occupied during down time. Laptops are helpful for educational games. Bring a book for yourself.

When you leave the set at the end of the day, make sure you sign out. Also make sure you ask for a call sheet. This will have the commercial name and ID as well as the client and ad agency information so that you can inquire about a copy of the commercial (which you can receive only after it has aired). It will also have talent names and phone numbers in case you want to keep in touch.

WHAT IS THE CHAIN OF COMMAND YOU SHOULD FOLLOW ON THE SET?

ARENS: The studio teacher is there to teach, but also to ensure the welfare of the child. This is the first chain. The second chain you may talk to is the second AD (Assistant Director). *Never* speak directly to the first AD, director, producers, or ad-agency members. Always go through your chain of command. The only exception is if they speak to you first, or when you are leaving and want to thank them for the opportunity.

WHAT IS THE DIFFERENCE BETWEEN BEING ON A COMMERCIAL SET AND A FILM SET?

BOYD: The time difference (or lack thereof) to make relationships. In the case of a commercial or short-term commitment, everyone understands that "we're working together for a very short time and then we may or may not ever work together again." For that reason, it's very "business." A child doesn't always understand that, and it sometimes comes across as impersonal and indifferent. Children get attached quicker than adults, and my kids have struggled with this on occasion.

We work very hard to be prepared before going on the film set. If there are questions, we try to get them answered at the lowest level possible. There is no point in me asking the director a question that the PA (production assistant) can answer. I go to great lengths to give the directors, producers, etc., their space. I want the relationship to be between my child and them. I do not want to be the buffer between. My ultimate wish is for our hard work to pay off, for my kid to shine, and for the project to be a huge success. In order to increase the likelihood of that, I invite and encourage the decision-makers to feel free to discuss how "this scene or that" might be improved and what my child should or shouldn't be doing to help in that process.

This is not about me, and I usually go to great strides to make sure that set people see that I recognize that. If I notice that a particular adjustment should or could be made to improve the performance, I may or may not say something. There are times I have asked to speak to the director or my child, but those instances are far and few between—and typically not before a basic level of respect has been established. I do not advocate that you sit back and turn your head if rules are being broken and your child is being taken advantage of. Those rules, and how to handle the bending or breaking of rules, should be discussed between parent and the set teacher/welfare worker. I usually have a conversation early on so that the set teacher/welfare worker understand that I am not there as one who will "sacrifice anything and everything" in the name of work. I believe in the team concept, and we are all there to work together for a common goal. However, I will not do so at the expense of jeopardizing my child's protection and the laws that were put in place as a direct result of abuse by the system.

HOW DO YOU DEAL WITH JEALOUSY ISSUES BETWEEN SIBLINGS?

LUCAS: We encourage our children by exposing them to their strengths and let that direct their steps. We cannot measure ourselves against another's success. We are successful in so many ways every day. We are about getting behind each other and helping them to be effective human beings. We have to example that and live it. On the flip side, we need to be gracious when we are given an awesome opportunity. We want to have our brothers and sisters happy for us. We need to tell our working actor how he/she can enlist the help of the other siblings. Even offering to bring back some goodies from the craft service table will help them feel like the brother/sister cares for them. Encouraging an individual's success is a team effort. Parents need to help the other sibling, if there's a problem. They need to be supportive and cheerful for the child.

TANK: You have to point out that even though one may be working a little more now, the other has also had great accomplishments at another time. Other achievements need to be stressed and commended like sports and school achievements.

REIVERS: We as a family are very supportive of each other. The children have been taught from a young age that the success of one is the success of all. When one person's career seems to be moving slow, we always take time to make sure they are involved in something that they love to do and feel is their own. That way no one feels forgotten and we can all be proud of each other's accomplishments as well as our own. We have been blessed as a family to have had success in this business while still being able to keep in perspective what is most important, each other.

WHAT ADVICE WOULD YOU GIVE IN HANDLING "REJECTION"?

BOYD: I believe this is a situation that must be handled delicately. I do not compare my two children in any aspect of their lives. I have taught my children to focus on their own personal best and not the end result. We have emphasized the things we can control, and minimized the things we cannot. We have treated "positive feedback" as a victory in and of itself. I celebrate my children's differences. We also try to celebrate success as a whole family and celebrate each other's victories. We're in this together, we've achieved success together, and we've all had to make sacrifices for such. It's a team effort. I have never fretted over the status of a project—at least not in front of the kids. I focus forward. I do not assume or pretend that either child is "right" for every project. Your handling rejection will have *everything* to do with how your kids handle the rejection that is sure to come.

TANK: I was fortunate as Hayden was never a child to ask about an audition after it was over. He never asked if he got a callback or if he booked the part. When we were fortunate enough to book a job, I would let him know and it became an exciting moment. We always realized that you have to go on many auditions before booking something, so we just waited until it was Hayden's turn.

LUCAS: The disappointment is met with understanding, but also with our faith. Jack knows his job is to give 200 percent to every opportunity. He does. He has no regrets and does not take it personally when he is not chosen. Looking back at some of the things he had set his heart on, he realizes they may not have been for him considering what he was able to go off and do instead. You know the saying, "When God closes a door, He opens a window."

HOW DO YOU FIND TIME FOR YOUR CHILD TO HAVE ACTIVITIES OUTSIDE OF WORKING?

ARENS: The longer you are in the business, the more your children will replace their school friends with friends who are also auditioning. Since it is hard for children and their auditioning parents to make play dates, it is nice to have spontaneous play dates with other auditioning children and parents after an audition. There are opportunities to go to a park and play, a movie, or dinner.

REIVERS: Due to the nature of this business, extended vacations always become difficult to plan. We have learned that spontaneity and short weekend trips work very well. There are many times that we don't have any idea what we are going to do or where we are going to go until that morning. For us, having fun doesn't involve a long thought process.

WHAT ADVICE WOULD YOU GIVE OTHER PARENTS?

BOYD: Get educated as quickly as you can. No one has all (if any) of the answers for success. If any one agent, manager, casting director, acting coach, director, or producer had "the" answers, we would only need one agent, manager, casting director, acting coach, director, or producer in Hollywood. Through time, effort, and education, each of these may bring an educated opinion to the table, but you should regard it as just that. None should be expected to work harder for your kids than you do. None will care about your children like yourself, and none will be willing to make the sacrifices that you may or may not be willing to make. Therefore, your opinion or input should be added to the "pool of opinions" that are sure to flood you. The only way that you will ever feel comfortable and confident about trusting your own judgment and intuition is if you have worked to educate yourself. Read, ask, discuss, experiment, explore, evaluate—do whatever to get educated as quickly as possible.

TANK: Make sure your child truly has an interest. I truly believe that you cannot make a child succeed at this who does not want to be doing it. It is a lot of work if it is not fun. Also, keep trying. We know many people who went years without any success, only to have big success later on.

LUCAS: It takes commitment from the parent. Starting with a support system of family, extended family, or friends will be very helpful. Be prepared to drop what you are doing—with a good attitude—or call part of the support team to get your kid to the audition. It is important to understand that the casting houses are the ones requesting your child to come in. A good agent works hard to facilitate information back and forth to get you on the casting schedule. Do not take these two entities lightly. Casting houses do not appreciate no-shows, and agents can work years to get your child exposed to this industry for next to no pay. Treat them with respect and kindness and do your best never to say, "Sorry, I can't make it." It could take a month or it could take a couple of years to really have your child doing good solid auditions, ownership of role development, and getting jobs. As I see the kids engage in the aspects of auditioning and working, along the way we learn life lessons.

REIVERS: The Screen Actors Guild is a great place for a parent to start for information. Make sure the child understands the entire process and the length of time it could take before actually booking their first jobs. Teach them that they should go over their scripts and always be prepared for every audition. Also, to always focus on getting the next audition and not to worry about the last one. Remember, they are still children, so make it all a fun experience. Otherwise, it's not worth it.

SECTION 3

WRAPPING IT ALL UP

18.

What It Takes
to Make It in
Commercials

Congratulations! You're nearing the end of what we hope has been a wonderful journey through the process of breaking into commercials. To wrap things up, we've summarized tips from agents, managers, coaches, talent consultants, and casting people from all over the country. Their combined wisdom and experience could be instrumental in propelling you toward a successful career in the commercial industry.

We interviewed more than seventy-five industry professionals in every state in the United States in the course of researching this book, asking what they looked for in an actor, what misconceptions newcomers have about the business, what their "pet peeves" about talent are, and what words of advice they could offer. Below are the results of our findings:

What Do Agents and Casting People Look For in an Actor?

- First impressions are important. The personality, the drive, the motivation, the talent, the look—*must* be presented.
- Your personality should be pleasant and outgoing (but not domineering).
- Charisma, determination, energy, and a solid work ethic are requisites for the successful actor.

- Integrity is essential. You *must* present yourself honestly at all times.
- Quality head shots and résumés.
- Good training.
- How you handle yourself at interviews.
- If you are nice and easy to work with.
- If you are easy to direct.
- Availability/flexibility.
- Confidence (but not arrogance).
- Magic in the eyes (expressive, animated, with an obvious love for the industry).
- Eager to work hard.

What Are Common Misconceptions Newcomers Have About the Industry?

- That this is not work. That it can be done as a hobby.
- That you can suddenly be "discovered"—as the tabloids imply.
- That agents will be able to get you every job.
- That being "pretty" is all it really takes.
- That it doesn't take time, persistence, and a lot of hard work.
- That if you work hard, sooner or later you're going to get what you want.
- Newcomers underestimate how much competition there is in larger markets, as well as:
- How impersonal it is outside a smaller, regional market.
- How tough it is to get a decent agent in a larger market.
- That they are eligible for every part that comes up.
- That it's going to happen overnight.

Pet Peeves

WHAT ARE THINGS ABOUT TALENT THAT ARE REALLY IRRITATING?

- Being overly fussy (appearing difficult or uncooperative).
- Not being available (especially after indicating you would be).
- Obvious retouching of photographs.
- Not listening.
- Old photographs that don't look like you anymore.
- You think you know it all.
- You talk incessantly.
- Not being prepared for an interview (not having head shots/résumés and/or demo CD out and ready to give to the agent or casting director).
- Padded résumé that's not realistic or believable.
- Not having your résumé attached to the photo when you hand it in to the agent or casting director.
- A lack of patience.
- Not being realistic about what can be achieved in a given period of time.
- Not following directions.
- Big egos and prima-donna attitudes.
- Wearing perfume or cologne.
- Not showing up on time for an interview, audition, or shoot.
- Not being knowledgeable about the industry and/or not conducting yourself in a professional, businesslike manner.

Words of Advice:

- Have a sense of humor.
- Be prepared.
- Take classes.
- It's a business. Treat it as such.
- You are the product.
- Don't expect your agent to get work for you. They get you auditions; you get the job.
- Get everything you can out of your regional market before moving on to a larger one.

- You can't take no for an answer. Be persistent in your efforts.
- Learn the language of the industry.
- Keep active in workshops and other opportunities to train and network.
- Have your professional tools together.
- Theater is very valuable to your development as an actor.
- Know your strengths and work toward them.
- Be careful of scams.
- Get into productions and showcases.
- Have good head shots—and keep them current.
- Set realistic goals. Be willing to adjust them as necessary.
- Actively market yourself.
- Be as objective about your abilities and limitations as possible.
- Be open to criticism.
- Be persistent, honest, and hardworking.
- Know that it's not a business for everyone.
- Be willing to pay your dues.
- Have some kind of trade you can fall back on.
- Develop a philosophy that will take you through the hard times.
- Be willing to go the extra mile.
- Expect the unexpected.
- If this is something you really, *really* must do, then GO FOR IT!
- Realize that success is built on a concerted effort over an extended period of time.

Whew! That's a lot of wisdom to take in at once. We hope that you've learned about what it takes to make it in the business, and that we have been able to make your transition into it a little bit easier. You know how to prepare a winning promotional package, how to prepare for and give a great audition, and how to follow through after you book the job. By reading this book and acting on the principles herein, you have taken great strides in creating a successful, lucrative career in the exciting world of commercials. Congratulations on completing a journey with us that will enrich your life for years to come.

Here's wishing you a long and prosperous career in the business!

ONLY ONE LIFE
THAT SOON IS PAST
ONLY WHAT'S DONE
WITH LOVE WILL LAST . . .

Glossary

- **Account executives** – Serve as the liaison between the client and the advertising agency.
- **Action** – Director's command to start.
- **Actor's Equity Association (Equity)** – Union governing performers and stage managers in live theater.
- **AD** – Assistant Director. In charge of crew; runs set.
- **Ad lib** – Speech or action that has not been scripted or specifically rehearsed.
- **American Federation of Television and Radio Artists (AFTRA)** – Union with jurisdiction over live and taped television shows and commercials, soap operas, disc jockeys, and other radio performers.
- **Agent** – Functions as a salesperson with *you* as the product. In exchange for finding you work, the agent is paid a commission (usually ten percent of your earnings).
- **Apple box** – Wooden box, the size of an apple box, that is used for various purposes on a set. For example, if the camera is too high, the cameraman will stand on an apple box.
- **Art Director** – The person who visually conceives the spot and makes it come alive through drawings and visuals. The art director is responsible for the entire visual concept of the commercial—the way the commercial will look.

- **Audition** – A tryout or chance to perform for the people who are in a position to give you a job.

- **Avail (or first refusal)** – A handshake agreement between the actor, agent, and casting director in which the actor guarantees that the client will have first option on his time on the specific dates set aside for the commercial shoot.

- **Barn doors** – Metal flaps in front of lighting instruments that control the direction of the light beam.

- **Beat** – A moment when an actor changes attitude, emotion, or physical movement.

- **Blocking the shot** – Carefully working out movement and actions of actors and mobile television equipment; done by the director.

- **Booth** – Enclosed, soundproof area with a microphone where the talent record their words. It is separated from the creatives by a glass window.

- **Cable** – Specifically for cable usage.

- **Callback** – Request for an actor to read again for (usually) the director, producer, art director, and writer.

- **Camera left (or right)** – Directions given from the camera's point of view, facing the audience or the camera.

- **Camera rehearsal** – Full rehearsal with cameras and other pieces of production equipment.

- **Casting director** – Person who selects and auditions the actors they feel properly fit the criteria of a character description. The casting director does not work for the actor and does not receive commissions from actors.

- **Catch lights** – Reflections in the eyes caused by the photographer's lights.

- **Cattle call** – An audition in which hundreds of people may try out for a part on a first-come, first-serve basis.

- **Cheat** – To angle the performer or object toward a particular camera; this is not directly noticeable to the audience.

- **Client** – The executive(s) who represent the product that is being advertised.

- **Close-up (CU)** – A shot of the product, actor's face, hands, etc., taken at close range.

- **Cold reading** – An audition at which the talent is asked to act out a script without having adequate time to rehearse.

- **Conflicts** – Being under contract for two conflicting products (such as Tide and Wisk detergents). This is prohibited for union commercials. An advertiser would never want one person on the air advertising both his product and a competitor's.

- **Coordinator** – Assistant to the line producer.

- **Cover letter** – A letter of introduction.

- **Craft service** – Food set up all day long on the set.

- **Creative director** – Person responsible for the work of all creatives in the advertising agency.

- **Creative supervisor** – Person who oversees the activities of the art director, writer, and producer.

- **Creative team (the creatives)** – The producer, art director, creative supervisor, creative director, director, account executive, and the client(s).

- **Cue** – Signal to start or stop any type of production activity or talent action.

- **Cue card** – Card with the script written on it in large letters. It is placed near the camera lens so actors don't have to memorize copy.

- **Cut** – Director's signal to stop action.

- **Dailies** – The film of each day's shoot; the film is developed and printed at the end of the day and is usually seen the following day. Also referred to as **rushes**.

- **Director** – The person who directs the spot.

- **Dissolve** – Short double-exposure between the two scenes in which the first scene is replaced slowly by the second scene.

- **Dolly** – Tripod on which the camera is mounted and can move about.

- **Dry run** – Rehearsal without camera running during which the basic actions of the talent are worked out. Also called **blocking rehearsal**.

- **Dubbing** – Replacing one voice or dialogue with another.

- **ECU** – Extreme close-up.

- **Fade** – *Fade up* means coming from black and fading up into the scene. *Fade down* means fading out of a scene into black.

- **Fitting** – Trying on of clothes.
- **Flap (mouth flap)** – In animation, movement of the mouth. If the talking stops and the character's mouth keeps moving, an actor will be called in to redo the dialogue to match the mouth flaps with the rhythm of the visual picture.
- **Gaffer** – Chief electrician.
- **Gaffer's tape** – Electrical tape used to hold things together on a set.
- **Generic "look"** – Neutral, classic, all-American look.
- **Gofer** – Person who does odd jobs (goes for), such as getting coffee, running errands.
- **Grain** – In film, exaggeration of the tiny dots that make up the image, which produces an unacceptable print. This is generally caused by overexposure or overdevelopment of the film (high-speed films are naturally grainy). NOTE: The digital equivalent of grain is referred to as "noise."
- **Green room** – Waiting area (historically painted green).
- **Grip** – Crewmember who moves equipment.
- **Head shot** – An 8x10 photograph that serves as your commercial calling card.
- **Hero** – The best-looking product on the shoot.
- **High hat** – The lowest platform on which to place a camera, usually about floor level.
- **Industrials** – Promotional films used either to educate employees or to promote companies. They can be produced strictly for in-house use or to be shown at promotional events such as trade shows.
- **"It's a wrap."** – End of shoot.
- **Line producer** – Director's producer from the production company.
- **Lip-sync** – Synchronization of sound and lip movement.
- **Load** – A technical way to put gum in the mouth for a commercial.
- **Long shot** – A shot seen from far away.
- **Looping (loop group)** – Group of people who work together providing additional dialogue for a scene.
- **Manager** – A talent representative who guides the talent's career.
- **Martini shot** – Last shot of the day.
- **Master shot** – A wide shot that shows the scene in its entirety.

- **Meter reading** – Light reading.
- **Milk-her-down** – Use dulling spray to get rid of unwanted reflections.
- **MOS** – A silent take (from a European director's instructions "mit out sound").
- **Network** – Broadcast all over the country, including the three major markets (New York, Los Angeles, and Chicago).
- **On bells** – When shooting sound, a bell rings to indicate there should be quiet on the set.
- **PA** – Production assistant. Does odd jobs.
- **Pan** – Horizontal turning of the camera.
- **Parent union** – The first union you join.
- **Pilot** – The first episode of a potential TV series.
- **Playback** – To replay (on a monitor) scenes that were shot.
- **Print it** – Scene marked to be printed.
- **Producer** – Person responsible for overseeing all the elements that make up the production of a commercial, including budgeting, selecting the director, coordinating all decisions of the people involved, and making sure the production is on schedule, including final editing.
- **Props** – Short for properties. Furniture and other objects used for set decoration.
- **Read-only CD** – A "read-only" CD allows you to view the contents of a CD, but you cannot make copies of it.
- **Residuals** – Payments made to the talent every time the spot runs.
- **Résumé** – A one-page summary of your vital statistics, experience, training, and special skills. Used to attract the interest of an agent, manager, or casting director.
- **Retouching** – Work by a photo artist (retoucher) on prints to minimize minor flaws in the image by "touching up" temporary blemishes, stray hairs, and scratches or dust spots (white spots caused by dust enlargement on the negative [film] or from shooting with dust on the camera sensor [digital]).
- **Right to work** – In a right-to-work state, companies cannot refuse to hire someone because he does not belong to the union or does not want to join the union.

- **Room tone** – The sound on the shoot in total silence.

- **Rough cut** – The first unfinished edit of the filmed scenes.

- **Run-through** – Rehearsal.

- **Screen Actors Guild (SAG)** – Union governing actors in film. This includes motion pictures (whether shown on television or in movie theaters) and television commercials.

- **Script supervisor** – Crewmember who reads and times the script as it is shot.

- **Seasonal** – Shot specifically for a particular holiday or season that must be identified as such in the commercial. For instance, if it is going to be run during the Christmas holiday, some Christmas decorations or a Christmas tree would be in the scene. There are no conflicts for seasonal commercials.

- **Set** – Arrangement of scenery and properties.

- **Slate** – to identify verbally and visually before each take. A little blackboard (or white board) upon which essential production information is written (such as title, scene date, and take numbers).

- **Slugging** – Inserting.

- **Speed** – Camera is running.

- **Spot** – Placement of a commercial in different spot markets around the country other than the major markets.

- **Standard contract** – Contract used as written with nothing crossed off the back.

- **Stand-in** – Another person or product used for testing the lighting.

- **Statistics (stats)** – On a résumé, your name, union affiliation and agent (if applicable), height, weight, eye and hair color, and a phone number (cell phone, service, machine, or pager) where you can be reached.

- **Sticks** – Tripod on which the camera can be mounted in a stationary position.

- **Stylist** – Designer or purchaser of wardrobe.

- **Sweeten** – To enrich the background, often with music or sound effects.

- **Sync sound** – Synchronizing sound with picture.

- **Taft-Hartley** – A waiver that allows you to work on as many union jobs as you want within a thirty-day period, after which you become a "must join." This means that you must be prepared to join the union for the next job you get after the thirty-day waiver.

- **Take** – Each time you shoot a scene, it's a "take." A take can also be a surprise reaction by an actor.

- **Teamster** – A member of the International Brotherhood of Teamsters labor union. On the set of a union-authorized production, teamsters are hired to drive trucks and load and unload equipment.

- **Tear sheets** – Samples of a model's published work (print ads, fashion spreads, etc.) torn from the publications to put into her portfolio.

- **Teleprompter** – Electrical device that displays the script in large letters that roll by in front of the camera lens at the speed of the actor's delivery.

- **Test** – A commercial that will run for a limited time in a specific market to be tested for product recognition. The time of usage would be agreed upon at the time of booking the talent.

- **Thermal print** – Black-and-white still photograph taken directly from an image coming from a video camera printed directly on thermal paper using heat instead of chemicals, as in a Polaroid.

- **Trailers** – Advertisement of a film previewing selected scenes.

- **Two-shot** – Framing of two people.

- **Under five** – A speaking role of less than five lines.

- **Voice-over** – The actor's voice on the soundtrack. Can also be referred to as a VO or an AVO (announcer voice-over).

Appendix — Resources

Sag Branch Offices

The SAG website, www.sag.org, offers the most current information. You can call (800) SAG-0767 to be connected to your cloest branch office or dial direct:

Arizona — (602) 383-3780

Boston — (617) 262-8001

Chicago [includes Cleveland, Minneapolia, and St. Louis] — (312) 573-8081

Colorado — (720) 932-8193

Dallas [c/o Linda Dowell] — (972) 361-8185

Detroit — (248) 351-2678

Florida [Central] — (407) 788-3020

Florida [Miam] — (305) 670-7677

Georgia — (404) 239-0131

Hawaii — (808) 596-0388

Hollywood — (323) 954-1600

Houston [c/o Linda Dowell] — (972) 382-8185

Nashville [c/o Leslie L. Krensky] — (305) 670-7677

Nevada [c/o Hrair Meserlian] — (323) 549-6440

New Mexico [c/o Julie Crane] — (720) 932-8193

New York — (212) 944-1030

North Carolina [c/o Melodie Shaw] — (305) 670-7677

Philadelphia [c/o Jae Je Simmons] — (212) 944-1030

Portland [c/o Dena Beatty] — (206) 270-0493

San Diego [c/o Hrair Meserlian] — (323) 549-6440

San Francisco — (415) 391-7510

Seattle — (206) 270-0493

Utah [c/o Don Livesay] — (602) 383-3780

Washington, D.C./Baltimore — (301) 657-2560

ACTRA (Associatioon of Canadian TV & Radio Artists) Branch Offices

The ACTR website, www.actra.ca, offers the most current information.

National — (416) 489-1311

British Columbia — (604) 689-0727

Calgary — (403) 228-3123

Edmonton — (780) 43-4090

Saskatchewan — (306) 757-0885

Manitoba — (204) 339-9750

Toronto — (416) 928-2278

Ottwa — (613) 565-2168

Montreal — (514) 844-3318

Maritimes — (902) 420-1404

Newfoundland/Labrador — (709) 722-0430

Directories, Periodicals, and Books

Much has been published on acting, auditioning, modeling, getting into the business, etc.. The two best sources for purchasing this material are Samuel French, Inc (which has bookshops in three locations) and Drama Book Shop. Both of these companies will take telephone and web orders and will ship around the world:

Samuel French Bookshops (www.samuelfrench.com)

7623 Sunset Blvd.
Hollywood, CA 90046
(323) 876-0570

11963 Ventura Blvd.
Studio City, CA 91604
(818) 762-0535

45 W. 25th Street
New York, NY 10010
(212) 206-8990

The Drama Book Shop (www.dramabookshop.com)

250 W. 40th Street
New York, NY 10018
(212) 944-0595

For purchasing materials for modeling (including portfolio books) we recommend the Models Mart:

Models Mart (www.models-mart.com)

159 West 25th Street
Suite #1001
New York, NY 10001
(212) 741-6441

Following are some directories, periodicals, and books that we recommend:

Directories and Periodicals

The Agency Guide. Lists talent agents in the Southern California area. Published biannually by Breakdown Services, Ltd.

Back Stage: The Actors Resource. Publishes two weekly print editions (East and West), plus runs an online edition, www.backstage.com.

FAB (Florida Actors/Models Book). A resource directory (agents, casting, production, etc.) to the Southeastern U.S. for actors and models publsied by FAB, www.fabactor.com.

The Los Angeles C/D Directory (The Professional Casting Directory). Published quarterly and updated every two weeks by Breakdown Services, Ltd. They also publishs *The New York C/D Directory* (quarterly and updated monthly).

Model & Talent Directory. Published annually, worldwide listings. Peter Glenn Publications.

Peter Glenn Publications (www.pgdirect.com), is an online database of resources for actors, models, and everyone else working in the entertainment industry.

Ross Reports. Published monthly, contains information on agents, casting, television production, and films in development for both Los Angeles and New York.

Working Actor's Guide to Los Angeles: The Complete Resource for Performers and other Entertainment Industry Professionals. Published annually by Aaron Blake Publishers.

Books

Acting is Everything: An Actor's Guidebook for a Successful Career in Los Angeles by Judy Kerr. September Publishing.

The Actor Take a Meeting: How to Interview Successfully with Agents, Managers, Producers, and Casting Directors by Stephen Book. Silman-James Press.

The Actor's Encyclopedia of Casting Directors by Karen Kondazian. Lone Eagle.

Back To One: The Complete Movie Extra's Guidebook by Cullen Chambers. Back To One Publishers.

Book On Acting: Improvisation Technique for the Professional Actor in Film, Theater & Television by Stephen Book. Silman-James Press.

How Not to Audition: Avoid the Common Mistakes Most Actors Make by Denny Martin Flinn and Elli Kanner. Lone Eagle.

How to Become a Successful Commercial Model by Aaron Marcus. The Marcus Institute of Commercial Modeling.

How to Get The Part Without Falling Apart by Maggie Haber with Barbara Babchick. Lone Eagle.

How to Sell Yourself As An Actor: From New York to Los Angeles (and Everywhere in Between!) by K Callan. Sweden Press.

The Los Angeles Agent Book: How to Get the Agent You Need for the Career You Want by K Callan. Sweden Press.

Making Money in Voice-Overs: Winning Strategies to a Successful Career in TV, Commercials, Radio and Animation by Terri Apple. Lone Eagle.

The New York Agent Book: The: How to Get the Agent You Need for the Career You Want by K Callan. Sweden Press.

A Practical Handbook For The Actor by Melissa Bruder. Vintage.

Promoting Your Acting Career: A Step-by-Step Guide to Opening the Right Doors by Glenn Alterman. Allworth Press.

There's Money Where Your Mouth Is: An Insider's Guide to a Career in Voice-Overs by Elaine Clark. Back Stage Books.

You Can Bank On Your Voice: Your Guide to a Successful Career in Voice-Overs by Rodney Saulsberry. Tomdor Publishing.

Word of Mouth: A Guide to Commercial Voice-Over Excellence by Susan Blu, Molly Ann Mullin, and Cynthia Songé. Silman-James Press.

Index